Barnes & Noble Shakespeare

David Scott Kastan
Series Editor

BARNES & NOBLE SHAKESPEARE features newly edited texts of the plays prepared by the world's premiere Shakespeare scholars. Each edition provides new scholarship with an introduction, commentary, unusually full and informative notes, an account of the play as it would have been performed in Shakespeare's theaters, and an essay on how to read Shakespeare's language.

DAVID SCOTT KASTAN is the Old Dominion Foundation Professor in the Humanities at Columbia University and one of the world's leading authorities on Shakespeare.

Barnes & Noble Shakespeare
Published by Barnes & Noble
122 Fifth Avenue
New York, NY 10011
www.barnesandnoble.com/shakespeare

Image on p. 316:
Shakespeare, William. *Henry IV, Part One.* 1598[A2r]. This item is reproduced by permission of *The Huntington Library, San Marino, California*, RB 69310.

Library of Congress Cataloging-in-Publication Data

Shakespeare, William, 1564–1616.
  Henry IV, Part one / William Shakespeare.
    p. cm.—(Barnes & Noble Shakespeare)
  Text of Henry IV, Part one, plus an introduction, commentary, an account
of Henry IV on the early stage and significant performances, and an essay on
how to read Shakespeare's language.
  Includes bibliographical references.
  ISBN-13: 978-1-4114-9970-6
  ISBN-10: 1-4114-9970-0
  1. Henry IV, King of England, 1367–1413—Drama. 2. Great
Britain—History—Henry IV, 1399–1413—Drama. I. Title. II. Title: Henry
IV, Part 1.

PR2810.A1 2008
822.3'3—dc22
                    2007051107

Printed and bound in the United States

1 3 5 7 9 10 8 6 4 2

HENRY IV
PART ONE

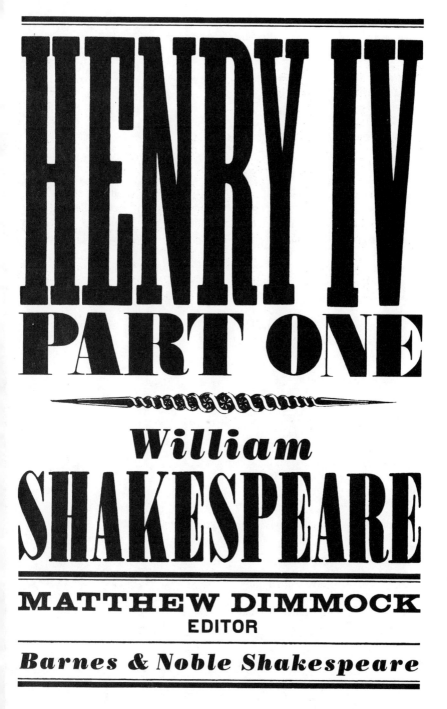

William
SHAKESPEARE

MATTHEW DIMMOCK
EDITOR

Barnes & Noble Shakespeare

Contents

Introduction to *Henry IV, Part One*
by Matthew Dimmock

 n January 14, 1559, nearly forty years before *Henry IV, Part One* was first performed, the recently enthroned Queen Elizabeth entered London in an elaborately staged procession through the streets of London. Throngs of people gathered in the streets to see their new monarch, who would be formally crowned the following day. In various locations, allegorical pageants were presented to the Queen, celebrating her rule while reminding her of her awesome responsibilities. In one of these, at the Little Conduit in West Cheapside, Elizabeth was presented with a pageant framed by two hills or mountains, one "cragged, barren and stony," featuring a single tree "all withered and dead," as an observer, Richard Mulcaster, reported. This mountain was marked the *Ruinosa Respublica*, the "decayed commonweal." The other mountain, in contrast, "was made fair, fresh, green and beautiful, the ground thereof full of flowers and beauty," with "one tree very fresh and fair." This was the *Respublica bene instituta*, the "flourishing commonweal." Inscriptions attached to each mountain explained that a ruinous commonweal was caused by "Want of the fear of God," "Disobedience to rulers," "Rebellion in subjects," "Civil disagreements," and "Bribery in magistrates." In opposition stood "Fear of God," "A wise prince," "Obedient subjects," "Virtue rewarded," and "Vice chastened."

The spectacle was no idle entertainment. The civil strife of the Wars of the Roses, ended by Elizabeth's grandfather, Henry VII, and the social as well as theological instability caused by the Reformation in England initiated by her father, Henry VIII, created a real concern for peace and stability in the nation that was coupled with the strong belief that these could be established and maintained only by a "worthy and noble prince." All of the pageants in the procession of 1559 shared this fixation on the ruler's responsibility, as well as that of her subjects, and writers across Europe, from Erasmus to Machiavelli, were similarly preoccupied with the stability of the kingdom and the role of the monarch in preserving it.

Like the coronation pageants that greeted Elizabeth, Shakespeare's *Henry IV, Part One* explores the right and wrong ways to rule. As the play dramatizes the emergence of an English national identity, it questions the relationship between rulers and their subjects and—as in the pageants—the responsibilities of both. Although this first part of the two *Henry IV* plays was and remains immensely popular—the banter between Hal and Falstaff creates some of the funniest and best-loved scenes in the Shakespearean canon—the play returns, again and again, to an exploration of the serious business of government: the nature, location, and legitimacy of authority.

As the play begins, the *Ruinosa Respublica* is a terrifyingly real possibility. Both the kingdom and the King face danger and dissolution. From the first, Henry is "shaken" and "wan with care" (1.1.1); the nation itself enjoys only a "frighted peace" (1.1.2), still threatened with "trenching war" (1.1.7) and "civil butchery" (1.1.13). Where the pageants for Elizabeth were confident about the ideal relationship between ruler and subject, *Henry IV, Part One* poses a series of questions concerning that relationship and the responsibilities it entailed, indeed about the very nature of the English nation itself.

Defining the Kingdom

This play details Henry IV's struggles to maintain his kingdom, and, as it does so, it also defines an English nation, a political entity still in the process of formation during Shakespeare's lifetime. *Henry IV, Part One* participates in the process of nation building, at once enacting and encouraging a sense of national identity that was forming around geography, language, and institutionalized forms of authority. Such a conception of nationhood, however, belongs more to the late sixteenth century than to the early fifteenth century of the play's setting. *Henry IV, Part One*, as with so many history plays and historical chronicles, is set in an earlier age but written to explore (and exploit) concerns of Shakespeare's present. This fact helps explain why, in the King's opening speech, his harrowing description of civil war refers not to his subjects but rather to the land—the very soil itself—as the ultimate source of Englishness. The land is a maternal presence endowing identity, even if what forms is immature and vulnerable. Consequently, no more shall "this soil . . . daub her lips with her own children's blood," (1.1.5–6) nor shall war "channel her fields" (1.1.7) or "bruise her flow'rets" (1.1.8).

The binding of national identity to the soil of the nation is a crucial theme in the play, and one that Shakespeare had initiated earlier in *Richard II*. In the opening speech of *Henry IV, Part One*, King Henry uses the integrity of the land to suggest the profound unnaturalness of rebellion. But the unified space of the nation is soon revealed to be more of a wish than a reality. England is less cohesive and coherent than Henry imagines. The problem is not just that rebels are a threat to the peace of England; it is also that England may not be a firm enough entity to hold together.

As if to demonstrate this, the play quickly transports us to the nation's boundaries, both geographically and socially. The trajectory of the play carries us from English battlefields to the rebellious north, and from London taverns to the savagery and sorcery of Owen Glendower's Welsh castle in the west. In doing so, the play forces us to reflect upon the nature and identity of the kingdom itself through a sustained focus on those who would threaten the unity Henry yearns for. This strategy is perhaps most apparent in the play's depiction of Wales as a place of unnaturalness and magic—the fact that the Welsh language is incomprehensible (3.1.48) is an important contributing factor—and in the Northern rebel Hotspur's absurd and misplaced obsession with valor, honor, and chivalry.

The threat of rebellion to the realm is powerfully demonstrated in Act Three, scene one, when Hotspur, Glendower, and Mortimer argue over the division of the kingdom (ironically before any military victory would allow them to divide the land in fact). The danger to the realm is evident to the audience, and is heightened through the conspicuous presence of the map, the physical embodiment of England and Wales on the stage, which is then recklessly divided amid disorder and disagreement. That this transaction is conducted explicitly in the terms of private ownership (and manipulation) of the land directly contradicts the version of England's maternal soil celebrated in Henry IV's opening speech.

Indeed, it is the very sense of order celebrated in Elizabeth's pageant and invoked in Henry's first speech that the rebels threaten. Hotspur ominously asserts that his intention is to turn the kingdom "topsy-turvy down" (4.1.81). In this way, as in the pageants performed before Elizabeth, the play celebrates the virtues of order and unity and shows them embodied in the institution of monarchy. Chaos and disruption are rendered monstrous in comparison. Hal's own self-conscious movement from rebellion and dishonor in the beginning of *Henry IV, Part One* to his near mythical status in *Henry V* exemplifies this explicitly political strategy. The rebels are thus demonized, and a nation emerges, bound to the land and to a social hierarchy capped by the monarch. Yet, however natural the nation is made to seem, troubling questions remain. What is a monarch? What renders him legitimate? These are questions made even more unsettling by the "indirect" (4.3.105) way Henry IV came to be King, not by lawful inheritance but by usurping the throne of Richard II.

Defining the King

Unsurprisingly, then, even recognizing the King in *Henry IV, Part One* is difficult. Or, to put it another way, while it's easy to identify the man wearing the crown, pinpointing the legitimate monarch among this play's many would-be kings is problematic. While Henry IV reigns, the specter of illegitimacy that hangs over him seems to generate a range of potential monarchs. Henry IV's reign is always conducted under the shadow of the legitimate monarch he has deposed. In this play, Richard II's right to the throne is personified in Mortimer, who was apparently proclaimed heir by King Richard. It is Mortimer's right that the rebels support, and it is he who consequently stands to gain Eastern and Southern England in their division of the kingdom. There are other putative kings, too. On the battlefield at Shrewsbury, the Earl of Douglas kills a man (who turns out to be Sir Walter Blunt) whom he presumes to be the King, but who only impersonates the King. We are told that many men on the field are attired like Henry IV. In response Douglas vows to "kill all his coats . . . [to] murder all his wardrobe, piece by piece" (5.3.27–28).

Henry IV is counterfeited elsewhere in a more light-hearted but no less disruptive way by both Falstaff and Hal in Eastcheap, in a scene that prefigures Hal's actual meeting with his father. Here the complex relationship between the Prince and both father figures is foregrounded. As a king, with a chair for a throne, a dagger for a scepter, and a cushion for a crown, Falstaff is transparently absurd, parodying Henry IV while taking the opportunity to ingratiate himself with the heir apparent, the Prince of Wales, of whose status Falstaff is obsessively aware.

The alternate scenario is far more darkly comic as Hal (playing his father) lambastes Falstaff: "that trunk of humors, that bolting-hutch of beastliness, that swollen parcel of dropsies, that huge bombard of sack" (2.4.437–439), and Falstaff (as Hal) attempts to defend himself. Unlike Falstaff's brief moment of kingly authority, which only confirms his position as a version of the popular Lord of Misrule, Hal's assumption of his father's role is a point at which the inevitable necessity of his rejection of Falstaff becomes starkly apparent. Here he plays his future self. Again, Falstaff pleads his case:

> No, my good lord, banish Peto, banish Bardolph, banish Poins, but for sweet Jack Falstaff, kind Jack Falstaff, true Jack Falstaff, valiant Jack Falstaff, and therefore more valiant being as he is old Jack Falstaff, banish not him thy Harry's company. . . . Banish plump Jack and banish all the world. (2.4.461–467)

Ostensibly a plea from the Prince to his father, Falstaff's repetition of his own name and erroneous list of qualities is again a bid to retain his advantageous association with Hal when he becomes King. The collapse of their theatrical artifice here is further affirmed by Hal's quick and cold response: "I do; I will" (2.4.468). While this episode indicates a great deal about the relationship between Hal and Falstaff, the impersonation of kingly authority here inevitably implies a parody and diminution of that authority. That it is the heir apparent, a king-in-waiting, who impersonates his monarch is similarly troubling, and represents a potential rebellion only resolved in *Henry IV, Part Two*.

There are many kings in this play, and their presence confirms an uncertainty enveloping Henry IV that is an inevitable consequence of his deposition of Richard II, and that is epitomized in the difficulties surrounding the new King's name. Those who remain loyal continue to refer to him as King, yet the rebels prefer to deny his authority not only by denigrating his crown but also by referring to him by his family name or ducal title. This "subtle King" (1.3.168), this "proud King" (1.3.183), has not only tainted the crown with his usurpation, but becomes in Hotspur's words merely "this thorn, this canker, Bolingbroke" (1.3.175). Later he describes how he is "whipped and scourged with rods . . . when I hear / Of this vile politician, Bolingbroke" (1.3.237–239). Glendower also avoids referring to Henry IV as King, preferring "Lancaster" (3.1.8), the name of the dukedom he inherited from his father, or simply "Henry Bolingbroke" (3.1.61). This is treason enacted in language.

Given the questions surrounding his claim to the throne, the King and his spokesmen perhaps wisely decline to debate his legitimacy, instead falling back on rhetorical invocations of cosmological order, an order in which the preeminent position of the monarch is fixed. Therefore, to undo the damage caused by the uprising, Worcester and the rebels are told they must, "move in that obedient orb again / Where you did give a fair and natural light, / And be no more an exhaled meteor, / A prodigy of fear, and a portent / Of broachèd mischief to the unborn times" (5.1.17–21). Here, as earlier, it is the profound unnaturalness of rebellion that Henry emphasizes, and, by contrast, the royalist forces, replete with a newly honorable Prince of Wales, are defined as defending a cause that is natural and right.

The [Mis]Education of a Christian Prince

Henry IV, Part One repeatedly invokes an ideal Christian warrior and a unified Christendom that he protects. Even if the imagery is tendentious, a rhetorical ploy to distract the nation from the rebellion by focusing attention on some project in which the country could "March all one way" (1.1.15), this powerful rhetoric dominates the chivalric world of the play's aristocracy and is used by the King to define his own righteous authority. The rhetoric of crusade is based upon an opposition between true Christians and pagan infidels, in which the true Christian is epitomized in the ideal Christian warrior, emulating legendary figures like Charlemagne and Godfrey of Boulogne. In this play a series of characters vie to be identified with this figure—most prominently Hotspur and Hal. Ultimately this identification culminates in the entwining of national and religious imperatives in the figure of Saint George and in Hal himself, who will, as King, in *Henry V*, exhort his soldiers with the cry, "God for Harry! England and Saint George!" (*Henry V*, 3.1.34). Such heroics are almost inconceivable at the start of this play, when Henry IV reaffirms a commitment to levy "a power of English" (1.1.22) to fight "As far as to the sepulcher of Christ" (1.1.19), a promise to wage a holy war against the infidels that he had originally made at the conclusion of *Richard I*, but which now he must admit is "twelve month old, / And bootless 'tis to tell you we will go" (1.1.28–29). The language of a crusade is of course a means (prefiguring his son's invasion of France) of externalizing internal conflict, but it further serves to define the godly English, in this case in opposition to the infidels that occupy the Holy Land.

Henry's reference to the tomb of Christ indicates an awareness of his duties as a Christian prince, duties rendered all the more urgent since he hopes this venture will wash Richard II's blood from his own "guilty hand." But while mixed motives blur the boundaries between military crusade and penitent pilgrimage, the endless deferral of crusade throughout the *Henry IV* plays and *Henry V* may also reveal an uneasiness on Shakespeare's part about the very notion of a holy war for the sepulcher of Christ. In any case, at the beginning of the play, it is clearly not the King or Prince Hal who is the epitome of the chivalrous Christian knight. Douglas and Hotspur are those "whose high deeds, / Whose hot incursions and great name in arms, / Holds from all soldiers chief majority / And military title capital / Through all the kingdoms that acknowledge Christ" (3.2.107–111). Hotspur is "the theme of Honor's tongue" (1.1.80), "sweet Fortune's minion and her pride" (1.1.82). Even as a rebel, his speech is peppered with references that indicate the certain Christian oppositions associated with crusade. A nobleman who will not join his cause becomes "a pagan rascal . . . an infidel!" (2.3.28–29), and he, in his confident masculinity, argues that "This is no world / To play with mammets and to tilt with lips" (2.3.88–89)—*mammets* derives from the medieval "Mahomet," or Muhammad, and refers to the presumption that infidels worship false idols.

That Hotspur through most of the play offers the most compelling image of the Christian prince while Hal in contrast is stained with "riot and dishonor" (1.1.84) indicates how fundamentally the time is out of joint. Even the King sees things this way, allowing himself to hope that some fairy had switched children so that Hotspur would be his son rather than Hal (1.1.88). The contrast between the two Harrys (largely Shakespeare's invention[6]) creates a series of provocative associations and inversions that are only resolved in their confrontation on the battlefield at Shrewsbury. Hal is Hotspur's opposite, and his behavior inevitably associates him with the chaotic forces of revolt his beleaguered father is straining to contain. His riotous behavior links him with the wider rebellion—a connection Henry IV later makes explicit, describing his son as "my nearest and dearest enemy" (3.2.123) and suggesting that Hal would fight against his own father at Percy's urging. The division that Henry IV's opening speech establishes between the "well-beseeming ranks" (1.1.14) of order and the "troubled Heaven" (1.1.10) of disorder initially appears to reinforce and reflect the distinction between Hotspur and his own son. Fighting for his King against the Scots, Hotspur's actions are those of a prince, defending King and kingdom and implicitly maintaining the hierarchical system. He is, at the play's opening, the champion of order.

On the other hand, the dangerous disorder of the royal heir is insisted on as we shift locales to his meeting with Falstaff and the origin of the Gadshill plot with Poins. The references to "cups of sack, . . . capons, . . . bawds," and "leaping-houses" (1.2.7–9) immediately set a chaotic tone. Here we have, as Hotspur later remarks, "The nimble-footed madcap Prince of Wales" (4.1.94), whose debauched self-indulgence threatens the stability of the realm and the very institution of monarchy. Or do we? It is certainly the case that in these exchanges Falstaff continually reminds himself, Hal, and an audience of the Prince's status: he asks, "when thou art king, as God save thy Grace—'Majesty,' I should say, for grace thou wilt have none. . . . let not us that are squires of the night's body be called thieves of the day's beauty" (1.2.16–18, 23–25). His invocation of Hal's future kingship here and elsewhere—he further mentions that Hal is the "heir apparent" (1.2.55), three times that he will be king (1.2.57, 59, and 138), and that he is a "king's son" (1.2.93), of the "blood royal" (1.2.133), and a "true prince" (1.2.146)—reminds an audience of Falstaff's ulterior motives, but also establishes a damaging disjunction between Hal's actions and the expected behavior of a Christian prince.

Falstaff's hopes, echoed later by Gadshill, that Hal's accession should usher in an amoral paradise in which the King would not "hang a thief" (1.2.59), would have seemed to an Elizabethan audience only to promise catastrophe. When considered from this perspective, the celebrated soliloquy that ends the scene may be more reassuring than is usually allowed:

> So when this loose behavior I throw off
> And pay the debt I never promisèd,
> By how much better than my word I am,
> By so much shall I falsify men's hopes;
> And, like bright metal on a sullen ground,
> My reformation, glitt'ring o'er my fault,
> Shall show more goodly and attract more eyes
> Than that which hath no foil to set it off. (1.2.197–204)

This is the side of his character he later describes as "more myself" (3.2.93), and indeed Hal actually commits no crime in the play—

the money robbed at Gadshill is returned with interest. Here he reveals himself to be the Christian prince his position requires, a force for order only masquerading as—even provoking—disorder so that he might later refute it. This is a radically different conception of virtue and authority to that exemplified and extolled by Hotspur, who publicly exhibits his honor. Hal's thinking is more akin to Machiavelli's, since it lays bare the nerves and sinews of political power. Even as it appears to offer reassurance, in doing so it perhaps raises still more troubling questions about good government as it makes effective rule depend upon manipulation.

But as Hal reveals his ability to "make offense a skill" (1.2.205), Hotspur—who had earlier upheld order on the King's behalf—quickly proves dangerously excessive, with an alarming potential to become irrational in his impatience and anger. Thus begins the process through which Hotspur's disorderly adherence to misplaced notions of honor comes to dominate the rebel cause. Simultaneously, Hal's recognition that he has "a truant been to chivalry" (5.1.94) leads finally to reconciliation and validation at Shrewsbury. As the Christian prince Hal ultimately triumphs, seemingly fortified by his miseducation in the taverns of Eastcheap. He has conspicuously learned to "seem," to "falsify men's hopes," but has also learned to "drink with any tinker in his own language" (2.4.18–19). His power is based upon a sophisticated ability to dissemble, a full awareness of the role he is expected to play, and an understanding of the languages of his subjects—he can coerce while (and by) inspiring devotion, and through him we are offered a vision of the Christian prince that is powerfully compelling and darkly complex. In her pre-coronation entrance into London, Elizabeth I had repeatedly signaled an understanding of her duties, in response to which the crowd is said to have marveled. In Harry, Prince of Wales, Shakespeare probes the impulses beneath the spectacle, and in doing so creates a sense of the Prince's self-consciousness, an inner self different from and aware of its difference from the public role he must play.

"I am no counterfeit" (5.4.114): Some Final Thoughts

In spite of the victory over the rebels and the Prince's emergence as a worthy successor to the King, at the close of the play a number of questions remain. Is Hal truly the polished prince that his conduct at Shrewsbury might suggest? Has the answer to the play's questioning of the nature of heroic action been resolved by his brave and gracious behavior on the battlefield? How much has Falstaff undercut the very terms of honor the play has celebrated? Falstaff claims that honor is only "A word" (5.1.134), nothing in itself. Only the dead have it, and Falstaff values life. As he stands over Hotspur's dead body, having just feigned death to escape Douglas and risen again, he reflects with his own impeccable logic that he is both a counterfeit and not counterfeit. He is counterfeit in playing dead to avoid being killed, but is not counterfeit since alive he is the "true and perfect image of life indeed" (5.4.117–118). Yet if Hotspur were to be simply counterfeiting death and rise up to attack Falstaff, then *he* "would prove the better counterfeit" (5.4.122–123). But here Falstaff stands triumphant, insisting on the value of life over any abstraction, however seemingly noble.

Like Feste's reflection that a "sentence is but a cheveril glove to a good wit" (*Twelfth Night*, 3.1.10–11), Falstaff's wordplay intricately undermines the aristocratic culture of honor constructed on rules and assumptions he finds absurd. When Hal again proves willing to counterfeit in order to allow Falstaff to claim the honor of Hotspur's death, an audience must surely wonder if Hal is anything but a counterfeit—and wonder how can he successfully uphold and represent a system he allows, even encourages, Falstaff to deconstruct. Earlier the Prince's power had seemed stable since it was based upon an ability to counterfeit while always retaining a secure sense of self beneath. But what if that self was itself merely a counterfeit, a manipulation in order to maintain power, to "imitate the sun" (1.2.186)? Where does the royal self end and the counterfeit begin? Is there some true self that is neither ruler nor role? As Henry IV's army divides and the play ends with the necessity of further conflict preventing resolution, it is to *Henry IV, Part Two* that we must turn to explore these themes further.

Shakespeare and His England
by David Scott Kastan

hakespeare is a household name, one of those few that don't need a first name to be instantly recognized. His first name was, of course, William, and he (and it, in its Latin form, *Gulielmus*) first came to public notice on April 26, 1564, when his baptism was recorded in the parish church of Stratford-upon-Avon, a small market town about ninety miles northwest of London. It isn't known exactly when he was born, although traditionally his birthday is taken to be April 23rd. It is a convenient date (perhaps too convenient) because that was the date of his death in 1616, as well as the date of St. George's Day, the annual feast day of England's patron saint. It is possible Shakespeare was born on the 23rd; no doubt he was born within a day or two of that date. In a time of high rates of infant mortality, parents would not wait long after a baby's birth for the baptism. Twenty percent of all children would die before their first birthday.

Life in 1564, not just for infants, was conspicuously vulnerable. If one lived to age fifteen, one was likely to live into one's fifties, but probably no more than 60 percent of those born lived past their mid-teens. Whole towns could be ravaged by epidemic disease. In 1563, the year before Shakespeare was born, an outbreak of plague claimed over one third of the population of London. Fire, too, was a constant threat; the thatched roofs of many houses were highly flammable, as well as offering handy nesting places for insects and rats. Serious crop failures in several years of the decade of the 1560s created food shortages, severe enough in many cases to lead to the starvation of the elderly and the infirm, and lowering the resistances of many others so that between 1536 and 1560 influenza claimed over 200,000 lives.

Shakespeare's own family in many ways reflected these unsettling realities. He was one of eight children, two of whom did not survive their first year, one of whom died at age eight; one lived to twenty-seven, while the four surviving siblings died at ages ranging from Edmund's thirty-nine to William's own fifty-two years. William married at an unusually early age. He was only eighteen, though his wife was twenty-six, almost exactly the norm of the day for women, though men normally married also in their mid- to late twenties. Shakespeare's wife Anne was already pregnant at the time that the marriage was formally confirmed, and a daughter, Susanna, was born six months later, in May 1583. Two years later, she gave birth to twins, Hamnet and Judith. Hamnet would die in his eleventh year.

If life was always at risk from what Shakespeare would later call "the thousand natural shocks / That flesh is heir to" (*Hamlet*, 3.1.61–62), the incessant threats to peace were no less unnerving, if usually less immediately life threatening. There were almost daily rumors of foreign invasion and civil war as the Protestant Queen Elizabeth assumed the crown in 1558 upon the death of her Catholic half-sister, Mary. Mary's reign had been marked by the public burnings of Protestant "heretics," by the seeming subordination of England to Spain, and by a commitment to a ruinous war with France, that, among its other effects, fueled inflation and encouraged a debasing of the currency. If, for many, Elizabeth represented the hopes for a peaceful and prosperous Protestant future, it seemed unlikely in the early days of her rule that the young monarch could hold her England together against the twin menace of the powerful Catholic monarchies of Europe and the significant part of her own population who were reluctant to give up their old faith. No wonder the Queen's principal secretary saw England in the early years of Elizabeth's rule as a land surrounded by "perils many, great and imminent."

In Stratford-upon-Avon, it might often have been easy to forget what threatened from without. The simple rural life, shared by about 90 percent of the English populace, had its reassuring natural rhythms and delights. Life was structured by the daily rising and setting of the sun, and by the change of seasons. Crops were planted and harvested; livestock was bred, its young delivered; sheep were sheared, some livestock slaughtered. Market days and fairs saw the produce and crafts of the town arrayed as people came to sell and shop—and be entertained by musicians, dancers, and troupes of actors. But even in Stratford, the lurking tensions and dangers could be daily sensed. A few months before Shakespeare was born, there had been a shocking "defacing" of images in the church, as workmen, not content merely to whitewash over the religious paintings decorating the interior as they were ordered, gouged large holes in those felt to be too "Catholic"; a few months after Shakespeare's birth, the register of the same church records another deadly outbreak of plague. The sleepy market town on the northern bank of the gently flowing river Avon was not immune from the menace of the world that surrounded it.

This was the world into which Shakespeare was born. England at his birth was still poor and backward, a fringe nation on the periphery of Europe. English itself was a minor language, hardly spoken outside of the country's borders. Religious tension was inescapable, as the old Catholic faith was trying determinedly to hold on, even as Protestantism was once again anxiously trying to establish itself as the national religion. The country knew itself vulnerable to serious threats both from without and from within. In 1562, the young Queen, upon whom so many people's hopes rested, almost fell victim to smallpox, and in 1569 a revolt of the Northern earls tried to remove her from power and restore Catholicism as the national religion. The following year, Pope

Pius V pronounced the excommunication of "Elizabeth, the pretended queen of England" and forbade Catholic subjects obedience to the monarch on pain of their own excommunication. "Now we are in an evil way and going to the devil," wrote one clergyman, "and have all nations in our necks."

It was a world of dearth, danger, and domestic unrest. Yet it would soon dramatically change, and Shakespeare's literary contribution would, for future generations, come to be seen as a significant measure of England's remarkable transformation. In the course of Shakespeare's life, England, hitherto an unsophisticated and underdeveloped backwater acting as a bit player in the momentous political dramas taking place on the European continent, became a confident, prosperous, global presence. But this new world was only accidentally, as it is often known today, "The Age of Shakespeare." To the degree that historical change rests in the hands of any individual, credit must be given to the Queen. This new world arguably was "The Age of Elizabeth," even if it was not the Elizabethan Golden Age, as it has often been portrayed.

The young Queen quickly imposed her personality upon the nation. She had talented councilors around her, all with strong ties to her of friendship or blood, but the direction of government was her own. She was strong willed and cautious, certain of her right to rule and convinced that stability was her greatest responsibility. The result may very well have been, as historians have often charged, that important issues facing England were never dealt with head-on and left to her successors to settle, but it meant also that she was able to keep her England unified and for the most part at peace.

Religion posed her greatest challenge, though it is important to keep in mind that in this period, as an official at Elizabeth's court said, "Religion and the commonwealth cannot be parted asunder." Faith then was not the largely voluntary commitment it is today, nor was there any idea of some separation of church and state. Religion was literally a matter of life and death, of salvation and damnation, and the Church was the Church of England. Obedience to it was not only a matter of conscience but also of law. It was the single issue on which the nation was most likely to be torn apart.

Elizabeth's great achievement was that she was successful in ensuring that the Church of England became formally a Protestant Church, but she did so without either driving most of her Catholic subjects to sedition or alienating the more radical Protestant community. The so-called "Elizabethan Settlement" forged a broad Christian community of what has been called prayer-book Protestantism, even as many of its practitioners retained, as a clergyman said, "still a smack and savor of popish principles." If there were forces on both sides who were uncomfortable with the Settlement—committed Protestants, who wanted to do away with all vestiges of the old faith, and convinced Catholics, who continued to swear their allegiance to Rome—the majority of the country, as she hoped, found ways to live comfortably both within the law and within their faith. In 1571, she wrote to the Duke of Anjou that the forms of worship she recommended would "not properly compel any man to alter his opinion in the great matters now in controversy in the Church." The official toleration of religious ambiguity, as well as the familiar experience of an official change of state religion accompanying the crowning of a new monarch, produced a world where the familiar labels of Protestant and Catholic failed to define the forms of faith that most English people practiced. But for Elizabeth, most matters of faith could be left to individuals, as long as the Church itself, and Elizabeth's position at its head, would remain unchallenged.

In international affairs, she was no less successful with her pragmatism and willingness to pursue limited goals. A complex mix of prudential concerns about religion, the economy, and national security drove her foreign policy. She did not have imperial ambitions; in the main, she wanted only to be sure there would be no invasion of England and to encourage English trade. In the event, both goals brought England into conflict with Spain, determining the increasingly anti-Catholic tendencies of English foreign policy and, almost accidentally, England's emergence as a world power. When Elizabeth came to the throne, England was in many ways a mere satellite nation to the Netherlands, which was part of the Hapsburg Empire that the Catholic Philip II (who had briefly and unhappily been married to her predecessor and half-sister, Queen Mary) ruled from Spain; by the end of her reign England was Spain's most bitter rival.

The transformation of Spain from ally to enemy came in a series of small steps (or missteps), no one of which was intended to produce what in the end came to pass. A series of posturings and provocations on both sides led to the rupture. In 1568, things moved to their breaking point, as the English confiscated a large shipment of gold that the Spanish were sending to their troops in the Netherlands. The following year saw the revolt of the Catholic earls in Northern England, followed by the papal excommunication of the Queen in 1570, both of which were by many in England assumed to be at the initiative, or at very least with the tacit support, of Philip. In fact he was not involved, but England under Elizabeth would never again think of Spain as a loyal friend or reliable ally. Indeed, Spain quickly became its mortal enemy. Protestant Dutch rebels had been opposing the Spanish domination of the Netherlands since the early 1560s, but, other than periodic financial support, Elizabeth had done little to encourage them. But in 1585, she sent troops under the command of the Earl of Leicester to support the Dutch rebels against the Spanish. Philip decided then to launch a full-scale attack on England, with the aim of deposing Elizabeth and restoring the Catholic faith. An English assault on Cadiz in 1587 destroyed a number of Spanish ships, postponing Philip's plans, but in the summer of 1588 the mightiest navy in the world, Philip's grand armada, with 132 ships and 30,493 sailors and troops, sailed for England.

By all rights, it should have been a successful invasion, but a combination of questionable Spanish tactics and a fortunate shift of wind resulted in one of England's greatest victories. The English had twice failed to intercept the armada off the coast of Portugal, and the Spanish fleet made its way to England, almost catching the English ships resupplying in Plymouth. The English navy was on its heels, when conveniently the Spanish admiral decided to anchor in the English Channel off the French port of Calais to wait for additional troops coming from the Netherlands. The English attacked with fireships, sinking four Spanish galleons, and strong winds from the south prevented an effective counterattack from the Spanish. The Spanish fleet was pushed into the North Sea, where it regrouped and decided its safest course was to attempt the difficult voyage home around Scotland and Ireland, losing almost half its ships on the way. For many in England the improbable victory was a miracle, evidence of God's favor for Elizabeth and the Protestant nation. Though war with Spain would not end for another fifteen years, the victory over the armada turned England almost overnight into a major world power, buoyed by confidence that they were chosen by God and, more tangibly, by a navy that could compete for control of the seas.

From a backward and insignificant Hapsburg satellite, Elizabeth's England had become, almost by accident, the leader of Protestant Europe. But if the victory over the armada signaled England's new place in the world, it hardly marked the end of England's travails. The economy, which initially was fueled by the military buildup, in the early 1590s fell victim to inflation, heavy taxation to support the war with Spain, the inevitable wartime disruptions of trade, as well as crop failures and a general economic downturn in Europe. Ireland, over which England had been attempting to impose its rule since 1168, continued to be a source of trouble and great expense (in some years costing the crown nearly one fifth of its total revenues). Even when the most organized of the rebellions, begun in 1594 and led by Hugh O'Neill, Earl of Tyrone, formally ended in 1603, peace and stability had not been achieved.

But perhaps the greatest instability came from the uncertainty over the succession, an uncertainty that marked Elizabeth's reign from its beginning. Her near death from smallpox in 1562 reminded the nation that an unmarried queen could not insure the succession, and Elizabeth was under constant pressure to marry and produce an heir. She was always aware of and deeply resented the pressure, announcing as early as 1559: "this shall be for me sufficient that a marble stone shall declare that a queen, having reigned such a time, lived and died a virgin." If, however, it was for her "sufficient," it was not so for her advisors and for much of the nation, who hoped she would wed. Arguably Elizabeth was the wiser, knowing that her unmarried hand was a political advantage, allowing her to diffuse threats or create alliances with the seeming possibility of a match. But as with so much in her reign, the strategy bought temporary stability at the price of longer-term solutions.

By the mid 1590s, it was clear that she would die unmarried and without an heir, and various candidates were positioning themselves to succeed her. Enough anxiety was produced that all published debate about the succession was forbidden by law. There was no direct descendant of the English crown to claim rule, and all the claimants had to reach well back into their family history to find some legitimacy. The best genealogical claim belonged to King James VI of Scotland. His mother, Mary, Queen of Scots, was the granddaughter of James IV of Scotland and Margaret Tudor, sister to Elizabeth's father, Henry VIII. Though James had right on his side, he was, it must be remembered, a foreigner. Scotland shared the island with England but was a separate nation. Great Britain, the union of England and Scotland, would not exist formally until 1707, but with Elizabeth's death early in the morning of March 24, 1603, surprisingly uneventfully the thirty-seven-year-old James succeeded to the English throne. Two nations, one king: King James VI of Scotland, King James I of England.

Most of his English subjects initially greeted the announcement of their new monarch with delight, relieved that the crown had successfully been transferred without any major disruption and reassured that the new King was married with two living sons. However, quickly many became disenchanted with a foreign King who spoke English with a heavy accent, and dismayed even further by the influx of Scots in positions of power. Nonetheless, the new King's greatest political liability may well have been less a matter of nationality than of temperament: he had none of Elizabeth's skill and ease in publicly wooing her subjects. The Venetian ambassador wrote back to the doge that the new King was unwilling to "caress the people, nor make them that good cheer the late Queen did, whereby she won their loves."

He was aloof and largely uninterested in the daily activities of governing, but he was interested in political theory and strongly committed to the cause of peace. Although a steadfast Protestant, he lacked the reflexive anti-Catholicism of many of his subjects. In England, he achieved a broadly consensual community of Protestants. The so-called King James Bible, the famous translation published first in 1611, was the result of a widespread desire to have an English Bible that spoke to all the nation, transcending the religious divisions that had placed three different translations in the hands of his subjects. Internationally, he styled himself *Rex Pacificus* (the peace-loving king). In 1604, the Treaty of London brought Elizabeth's war with Spain formally to an end, and over the next decade he worked to bring about political marriages that might cement stable alliances. In 1613, he married his daughter to the leader of the German Protestants, while the following year he began discussions with Catholic Spain to marry his son to the Infanta Maria. After some ten years of negotiations, James's hopes for what was known as the Spanish match were finally abandoned, much to the delight of the nation, whose long-felt fear and hatred for Spain outweighed the subtle political logic behind the plan.

But if James sought stability and peace, and for the most part succeeded in his aims (at least until 1618, when the bitter religio-political conflicts on the European continent swirled well out of the King's control), he never really achieved concord and cohesion. He ruled over two kingdoms that did not know, like, or even want to understand one another, and his rule did little to bring them closer together. His England remained separate from his Scotland, even as he ruled over both. And even his England remained self-divided, as in truth it always was under Elizabeth, ever more a nation of prosperity and influence but still one forged out of deep-rooted divisions of means, faiths, and allegiances that made the very nature of English identity a matter of confusion and concern. Arguably this is the very condition of great drama—sufficient peace and prosperity to support a theater industry and sufficient provocation in the troubling uncertainties about what the nation was and what fundamentally mattered to its people to inspire plays that would offer tentative solutions or at the very least make the troubling questions articulate and moving.

Nine years before James would die in 1625, Shakespeare died, having returned from London to the small market town in which he was born. If London, now a thriving modern metropolis of well over 200,000 people, had, like the nation itself, been transformed in the course of his life, the Warwickshire market town still was much the same. The house in which Shakespeare was born still stood, as did the church in which he was baptized and the school in which he learned to read and write. The river Avon still ran slowly along the town's southern limits. What had changed was that Shakespeare was now its most famous citizen, and, although it would take more than another 100 years to fully achieve this, he would in time become England's, for having turned the great ethical, social, and political issues of his own age into plays that would live forever.

William Shakespeare: A Chronology

1558	**November 17: Queen Elizabeth crowned**
1564	April 26: Shakespeare baptized, third child born to John Shakespeare and Mary Arden
1564	**May 27: Death of Jean Calvin in Geneva**
1565	John Shakespeare elected alderman in Stratford-upon-Avon
1568	**Publication of the Bishops' Bible**
1568	September 4: John Shakespeare elected Bailiff of Stratford-upon-Avon
1569	**Northern Rebellion**
1570	**Queen Elizabeth excommunicated by the Pope**
1572	**August 24: St. Bartholomew's Day Massacre in Paris**
1576	**The Theatre is built in Shoreditch**
1577–1580	**Sir Francis Drake sails around the world**
1582	November 27: Shakespeare and Anne Hathaway married (Shakespeare is 18)
1583	Queen's Men formed
1583	May 26: Shakespeare's daughter, Susanna, baptized
1584	**Failure of the Virginia Colony**

1585   February 2: Twins, Hamnet and Judith, baptized (Shakespeare is 20)

1586   Babington Plot to dethrone Elizabeth and replace her with Mary, Queen of Scots

1587   February 8: Execution of Mary, Queen of Scots

1587   Rose Theatre built

1588   August: Defeat of the Spanish armada (Shakespeare is 24)

1588   September 4: Death of Robert Dudley, Earl of Leicester

1590   First three books of Spenser's *Faerie Queene* published; Marlowe's *Tamburlaine* published

1592   March 3: *Henry VI, Part One* performed at the Rose Theatre (Shakespeare is 27)

1593   February–November: Theaters closed because of plague

1593   Publication of *Venus and Adonis*

1594   Publication of *Titus Andronicus*, first play by Shakespeare to appear in print (though anonymously)

1594   Lord Chamberlain's Men formed

1595   March 15: Payment made to Shakespeare, Will Kemp, and Richard Burbage for performances at court in December, 1594

1595   Swan Theatre built

1596   Books 4–6 of *The Faerie Queene* published

1596   August 11: Burial of Shakespeare's son, Hamnet (Shakespeare is 32)

1596–1599   Shakespeare living in St. Helen's, Bishopsgate, London

1596   October 20: Grant of Arms to John Shakespeare

1597 May 4: Shakespeare purchases New Place, one of the two largest houses in Stratford (Shakespeare is 33)

1598 Publication of *Love's Labor's Lost*, first extant play with Shakespeare's name on the title page

1598 Publication of Francis Meres's *Palladis Tamia*, citing Shakespeare as "the best for Comedy and Tragedy" among English writers

1599 Opening of the Globe Theatre

1601 February 7: Lord Chamberlain's Men paid 40 shillings to play *Richard II* by supporters of the Earl of Essex, the day before his abortive rebellion

1601 February 17: Execution of Robert Devereaux, Earl of Essex

1601 September 8: Burial of John Shakespeare

1602 May 1: Shakespeare buys 107 acres of farmland in Stratford

1603 March 24: Queen Elizabeth dies; James VI of Scotland succeeds as James I of England (Shakespeare is 39)

1603 May 19: Lord Chamberlain's Men reformed as the King's Men

1604 Shakespeare living with the Mountjoys, a French Huguenot family, in Cripplegate, London

1604 First edition of Marlowe's *Dr. Faustus* published (written c. 1589)

1604 March 15: Shakespeare named among "players" given scarlet cloth to wear at royal procession of King James

1604 Publication of authorized version of *Hamlet* (Shakespeare is 40)

1605 Gunpowder Plot

1605 June 5: Marriage of Susanna Shakespeare to John Hall

1608 Publication of *King Lear* (Shakespeare is 44)

1608–1609 Acquisition of indoor Blackfriars Theatre by King's Men

1609　　*Sonnets* published

1611　**King James Bible published** (Shakespeare is 47)

1612　**November 6: Death of Henry, eldest son of King James**

1613　**February 14: Marriage of King James's daughter Elizabeth to Frederick, the Elector Palatine**

1613　　March 10: Shakespeare, with some associates, buys gatehouse in Blackfriars, London

1613　**June 29: Fire burns the Globe Theatre**

1614　**Rebuilt Globe reopens**

1616　　February 10: Marriage of Judith Shakespeare to Thomas Quiney

1616　　March 25: Shakespeare's will signed

1616　　April 23: Shakespeare dies (age 52)

1616　**April 23: Cervantes dies in Madrid**

1616　　April 25: Shakespeare buried in Holy Trinity Church in Stratford-upon-Avon

1623　　August 6: Death of Anne Shakespeare

1623　**October: Prince Charles, King James's son, returns from Madrid, having failed to arrange his marriage to Maria Anna, Infanta of Spain**

1623　　First Folio published with 36 plays (18 never previously published)

Words, Words, Words: Understanding Shakespeare's Language
by David Scott Kastan

t is silly to pretend that it is easy to read Shakespeare. Reading Shakespeare isn't like picking up a copy of *USA Today* or *The New Yorker*, or even F. Scott Fitzgerald's *Great Gatsby* or Toni Morrison's *Beloved*. It is hard work, because the language is often unfamiliar to us and because it is more concentrated than we are used to. In the theater it is usually a bit easier. Actors can clarify meanings with gestures and actions, allowing us to get the general sense of what is going on, if not every nuance of the language that is spoken. "Action is eloquence," as Volumnia puts it in *Coriolanus*, "and the eyes of th' ignorant / More learnèd than the ears" (3.276–277). Yet the real greatness of Shakespeare rests not on "the general sense" of his plays but on the specificity and suggestiveness of the words in which they are written. It is through language that the plays' full dramatic power is realized, and it is that rich and robust language, often pushed by Shakespeare to the very limits of intelligibility, that we must learn to understand. But we can come to understand it (and enjoy it), and this essay is designed to help.

Even experienced readers and playgoers need help. They often find that his words are difficult to comprehend. Shakespeare sometimes uses words no longer current in English or with meanings that have changed. He regularly multiplies words where seemingly one might do as well or even better. He characteristically writes sentences that are syntactically complicated and imaginatively dense. And it isn't just we, removed by some 400 years from his world, who find him difficult to read; in his own time, his friends and fellow actors knew Shakespeare was hard. As two of them, John Hemings and Henry Condell, put it in their prefatory remarks to Shakespeare's First Folio in 1623, "read him, therefore, and again and again; and if then you do not like him, surely you are in some manifest danger not to understand him."

From the very beginning, then, it was obvious that the plays both deserve and demand not only careful reading but continued re-reading—and that not to read Shakespeare with all the attention a reader can bring to bear on the language is almost to guarantee that a reader will not "understand him" and remain among those who "do not like him." But Shakespeare's colleagues were nonetheless confident that the plays exerted an attraction strong enough to ensure and reward the concentration of their readers, confident, as they say, that in them "you will find enough, both to draw and hold you." The plays do exert a kind of magnetic pull, and have successfully drawn in and held readers for over 400 years.

Once we are drawn in, we confront a world of words that does not always immediately yield its delights; but it will—once we learn to see what is demanded of us. Words in Shakespeare do a lot, arguably more than anyone else has ever asked them to do. In part, it is because he needed his words to do many things at once. His stage had no sets and few props, so his words are all we have to enable us to imagine what his characters see. And they also allow us to see what the characters don't see, especially about themselves. The words are vivid and immediate, as well as complexly layered and psychologically suggestive. The difficulties they pose are not the "thee's" and "thou's" or "prithee's" and "doth's" that obviously mark the chronological distance between Shakespeare and us. When Gertrude says to Hamlet, "thou hast thy father much offended"

(3.4.8), we have no difficulty understanding her chiding, though we might miss that her use of the "thou" form of the pronoun expresses an intimacy that Hamlet pointedly refuses with his reply: "Mother, *you* have my father much offended" (3.4.9; italics mine).

Most deceptive are words that look the same as words we know but now mean something different. Words often change meanings over time. When Horatio and the soldiers try to stop Hamlet as he chases after the Ghost, Hamlet pushes past them and says, "I'll make a ghost of him that lets me" (1.4.85). It seems an odd thing to say. Why should he threaten someone who "lets" him do what he wants to do? But here "let" means "hinder," not, as it does today, "allow" (although the older meaning of the word still survives, for example, in tennis, where a "let serve" is one that is hindered by the net on its way across). There are many words that can, like this, mislead us: "his" sometimes means "its," "an" often means "if," "envy" means something more like "malice," "cousin" means more generally "kinsman," and there are others, though all are easily defined. The difficulty is that we may not stop to look thinking we already know what the word means, but in this edition a ° following the word alerts a reader that there is a gloss in the left margin, and quickly readers get used to these older meanings.

Then, of course, there is the intimidation factor—strange, polysyllabic, or Latinate words that not only are foreign to us but also must have sounded strange even to Shakespeare's audiences. When Macbeth wonders whether all the water in all the oceans of the world will be able to clean his bloody hands after the murder of Duncan, he concludes: "No; this my hand will rather / The multitudinous seas incarnadine, / Making the green one red" (2.2.64–66). Duncan's blood staining Macbeth's murderous hand is so offensive that, not merely does it resist being washed off in water, but it will "the multitudinous seas incarnadine": that is, turn the sea-green oceans blood-red. Notes will easily clarify the meaning of the two odd words, but it is worth observing that they would have been as odd to Shakespeare's readers as they are to us. The *Oxford English Dictionary* (*OED*) shows no use of "multitudinous" before this, and it records no use of "incarnadine" before 1591 (*Macbeth* was written about 1606). Both are new words, coined from the Latin, part of a process in Shakespeare's time where English adopted many Latinate words as a mark of its own emergence as an important vernacular language. Here they are used to express the magnitude of Macbeth's offense, a crime not only against the civil law but also against the cosmic order, and then the simple monosyllables of turning "the green one red" provide an immediate (and needed) paraphrase and register his own sickening awareness of the true hideousness of his deed.

As with "multitudinous" in *Macbeth*, Shakespeare is the source of a great many words in English. Sometimes he coined them himself, or, if he didn't invent them, he was the first person whose writing of them has survived. Some of these words have become part of our language, so common that it is hard to imagine they were not always part of it: for example, "assassination" (*Macbeth*, 1.7.2), "bedroom" (*A Midsummer Night's Dream*, 2.2.57), "countless" (*Titus Andronicus*, 5.3.59), "fashionable" (*Troilus and Cressida*, 3.3.165), "frugal" (*The Merry Wives of Windsor*, 2.1.28), "laughable" (*The Merchant of Venice*, 1.1.56), "lonely" (*Coriolanus*, 4.1.30), and "useful" (*King John*, 5.2.81). But other words that he originated were not as, to use yet another Shakespearean coinage, "successful" (*Titus Andronicus*, 1.1.66). Words like "crimeless" (*Henry VI, Part Two*, 2.4.63, meaning "innocent"), "facinorous" (*All's Well That Ends Well*, 2.3.30, meaning "extremely wicked"), and "recountment" (*As You Like It*, 4.3.141, meaning "narrative" or "account") have, without much resistance, slipped into oblivion. Clearly Shakespeare liked words, even unwieldy ones. His working vocabulary, about 18,000 words, is staggering, larger than almost any other English writer, and he seems to be the first person to use in print about 1,000 of these. Whether he coined the new words himself or was intrigued by the new words he heard in the streets of London doesn't really matter; the point is that he was remarkably alert to and engaged with a dynamic language that was expanding in response to England's own expanding contact with the world around it.

But it is neither new words nor old ones that are the source of the greatest difficulty of Shakespeare's language. The real difficulty (and the real delight) comes in trying to see how he uses the words, how he endows them with more than their denotative meanings. Why, for example, does Macbeth say that he hopes that the "sure and firm-set earth" (2.1.56) will not hear his steps as he goes forward to murder Duncan? Here "sure" and "firm-set" mean virtually the same thing: stable, secure, fixed. Why use two words? If this were a student paper, no doubt the teacher would circle one of them and write "redundant." But the redundancy is exactly what Shakespeare wants. One word would do if the purpose were to describe the solidity of the earth, but here the redundancy points to something different. It reveals something about Macbeth's mind, betraying through the doubling how deep is his awareness of the world of stable values that the terrible act he is about to commit must unsettle.

Shakespeare's words usually work this way: in part describing what the characters see and as often betraying what they feel. The example from *Macbeth* is a simple example of how this works. Shakespeare's words are carefully patterned. How one says something is every bit as important as what is said, and the conspicuous patterns that are created alert us to the fact that something more than the words' lexical sense has been put into play. Words can be coupled, as in the example above, or knit into even denser metaphorical constellations to reveal something about the speaker (which often the speaker does not know), as in Prince Hal's promise to his father that he will outdo the rebels' hero, Henry Percy (Hotspur):

> Percy is but my factor, good my lord,
> To engross up glorious deeds on my behalf.
> And I will call him to so strict account
> That he shall render every glory up,
> Yea, even the slightest worship of his time,
> Or I will tear the reckoning from his heart.
>
> *(Henry IV, Part One, 3.2.148–153)*

The Prince expresses his confidence that he will defeat Hotspur, but revealingly in a reiterated language of commercial exchange ("factor," "engross," "account," "render," "reckoning") that tells us something important both about the Prince and the ways in which he understands his world. In a play filled with references to coins and counterfeiting, the speech demonstrates not only that Hal has committed himself to the business at hand, repudiating his earlier, irresponsible tavern self, but also that he knows it is a business rather than a glorious world of chivalric achievement; he inhabits a world in which value (political as well as economic) is not intrinsic but determined by what people are willing to invest, and he proves himself a master of producing desire for what he has to offer.

Or sometimes it is not the network of imagery but the very syntax that speaks, as when Claudius announces his marriage to Hamlet's mother:

> Therefore our sometime sister, now our Queen,
> Th' imperial jointress to this warlike state,
> Have we—as 'twere with a defeated joy,
> With an auspicious and a dropping eye,
> With mirth in funeral and with dole in marriage,
> In equal scale weighing delight and dole—
> Taken to wife. *(Hamlet, 1.2.8–14)*

All he really wants to say here is that he has married Gertrude, his former sister-in-law: "Therefore our sometime sister . . . Have we . . . Taken to wife." But the straightforward sentence gets interrupted and complicated, revealing his own discomfort with the announcement. His elaborations and intensifications of Gertrude's role ("sometime sister," "Queen," "imperial jointress"), the self-conscious rhetorical balancing of the middle three lines (indeed "in equal scale weighing delight and dole"), all declare by the all-too obvious artifice how desperate he is to hide the awkward facts behind a veneer of normalcy and propriety. The very unnaturalness of the sentence is what alerts us that we are meant to understand more than the simple relation of fact.

Why doesn't Shakespeare just say what he means? Well, he does—exactly what he means. In the example from *Hamlet* just above, Shakespeare shows us something about Claudius that Claudius doesn't know himself. Always Shakespeare's words will offer us an immediate sense of what is happening, allowing us to follow the action, but they also offer us a counterplot, pointing us to what might be behind the action, confirming or contradicting what the characters say. It is a language that shimmers with promise and possibility, opening the characters' hearts and minds to our view—and all we have to do is learn to pay attention to what is there before us.

Shakespeare's Verse

Another distinctive feature of Shakespeare's dramatic language is that much of it is in verse. Almost all of the plays mix poetry and prose, but the poetry dominates. *The Merry Wives of Windsor* has the lowest percentage (only about 13 percent verse), while *Richard II* and *King John* are written entirely in verse (the only examples, although *Henry VI, Part One* and *Part Three* have only a very few prose lines). In most of the plays, about 70 percent of the lines are written in verse.

Shakespeare's characteristic verse line is a non-rhyming iambic pentameter ("blank verse"), ten syllables with every second one stressed. In *A Midsummer Night's Dream*, Titania comes to her senses after a magic potion has led her to fall in love with an ass-headed Bottom: "Methought I was enamored of an ass" (4.1.76). Similarly, in *Romeo and Juliet*, Romeo gazes up at Juliet's window: "But soft, what light through yonder window breaks" (2.2.2). In both these examples, the line has ten syllables organized into five regular beats (each beat consisting of the stress on the second syllable of a pair, as in "But soft," the da-dum rhythm forming an "iamb"). Still, we don't hear these lines as jingles; they seem natural enough, in large part because this dominant pattern is varied in the surrounding lines.

The play of stresses indeed becomes another key to meaning, as Shakespeare alerts us to what is important. In *Measure for Measure*, Lucio urges Isabella to plead for her brother's life: "Oh, to him, to him, wench! He will relent" (2.2.129). The iambic norm (unstressed-stressed) tells us (and an actor) that the emphasis at the beginning of the line is on "to" not "him"—it is the action not the object that is being emphasized—and at the end of the line the stress falls on "will." Alternatively, the line can play against the established norm. In *Hamlet*, Claudius corrects Polonius's idea of what is bothering the Prince: "Love? His affections do not that way tend" (3.1.161). The iambic norm forces the emphasis onto "that" ("do not *that* way tend"), while the syntax forces an unexpected stress on the opening word, "Love." In the famous line, "The course of true love never did run smooth" (*A Midsummer Night's Dream*, 1.1.134), the iambic expectation is varied in both the middle and at the end of the line. Both "love" and the first syllable of "never" are stressed, as are both syllables at the end—"run smooth"—which creates a metrical foot in which both syllables are stressed (called a "spondee"). The point to notice is that the "da-dum, da-dum, da-dum, da-dum, da-dum" line is not inevitable; it merely sets an expectation against which many variations can be heard.

In fact, even the ten-syllable norm can be varied. Shakespeare sometimes writes lines with fewer or more syllables. Often there is an extra, unstressed syllable at the end of a line (a so-called "feminine ending"); sometimes there are verse lines with only nine. In *Henry IV, Part One*, King Henry replies incredulously to the rebel Worcester's claim that he hadn't "sought" the confrontation with the King: "You have not sought it. How comes it then?" (5.1.27). There are only nine syllables here (some earlier editors, seeking to "correct" the verse, added the word "sir" after the first question to regularize the line). But the pause where one expects a stressed syllable is dramatically effective, allowing the King's anger to be powerfully present in the silence.

As even these few examples show, Shakespeare's verse is unusually flexible, allowing a range of rhythmical effects. It should not be understood as a set of strict rules but as a flexible set of practices rooted in dramatic necessity. It is designed to highlight ideas and emotions, and it is based less upon rigid syllable counts than on an arrangement of stresses within an understood temporal norm, as one might expect from a poetry written to be heard in the theater rather than read on the page.

Here Follows Prose

Although the plays are dominated by verse, prose plays a significant role. Shakespeare's prose has its own rhythms, but it lacks the formal patterning of verse, and so is printed without line breaks and without the capitals that mark the beginning of a verse line. Like many of his fellow dramatists, Shakespeare tended to use prose for comic scenes, the shift from verse serving, especially in his early plays, as a social marker. Upper-class characters speak in verse; lower-class characters speak in prose. Thus, in *A Midsummer Night's Dream*, the Athenians of the court, as well as the fairies, all speak in verse, but the "rude mechanicals," Bottom and his artisan friends, all speak in prose, except for the comic verse they speak in their performance of "Pyramis and Thisbe."

As Shakespeare grew in experience, he became more flexible about the shifts from verse to prose, letting it, among other things, mark genre rather than class and measure various kinds of intensity. Prose becomes in the main the medium of comedy. The great comedies, like *Much Ado About Nothing*, *Twelfth Night*, and *As You Like It*, are all more than 50 percent prose. But even in comedy, shifts between verse and prose may be used to measure subtle emotional changes. In Act One, scene three of *The Merchant of Venice*, Shylock and Bassanio begin the scene speaking of matters of business in prose, but when Antonio enters and the deep conflict between the Christian and the Jew becomes evident, the scene shifts to verse. But prose may itself serve in moments of emotional intensity. Shylock's famous speech at 3.1.51–64, "Hath not a Jew eyes . . ." is all in prose, as is Hamlet's expression of disgust at the world ("I have of late—but wherefore I know not—lost all my mirth . . .") at 2.2.259–260. Shakespeare comes to use prose to vary the tone of a scene, as the shift from verse subtly alerts an audience or a reader to some new emotional register.

Prose becomes, as Shakespeare's art matures, not inevitably the mark of the lower classes but the mark of a salutary daily-ness. It is appropriately the medium in which letters are written, and it is the medium of a common sense that will at least challenge the potential self-deceptions of grandiloquent speech. When Rosalind mocks the excesses and artifice of Orlando's wooing in Act Four, scene one of *As You Like It*, it is in prose that she seeks something genuine in the expression of love:

The poor world is almost six thousand years old, and in all this time there was not any man died in his own person, *videlicit* [i.e., namely], in a love cause. . . . Men have died from time to time, and worms have eaten them, but not for love.

Here the prose becomes the sound of common sense, an effective foil to the affectation of pinning poems to trees and thinking that it is real love.

It is not that prose is artless; Shakespeare's prose is no less self-conscious than his verse. The artfulness of his prose is different, of course. The seeming ordinariness of his prose is no less an effect of his artistry than is the more obvious patterning of his verse. Prose is no less serious, compressed, or indeed figurative. As with his verse, Shakespeare's prose performs numerous tasks and displays various, subtle formal qualities; and recognizing the possibilities of what it can achieve is still another way of seeing what Shakespeare puts right before us to show us what he has hidden.

Further Reading

N. F. Blake, *Shakespeare's Language: An Introduction* (New York: St. Martin's Press, 1983).

Jonathan Hope, *Shakespeare's Grammar* (London: Thomson, 2003).

Sister Miriam Joseph, *Shakespeare's Use of the Arts of Language* (New York: Columbia University Press, 1947).

M. M. Mahood, *Shakespeare's Wordplay* (London: Methuen, 1957).

Russ McDonald, *Shakespeare and the Arts of Language* (Oxford: Oxford University Press, 2001).

Brian Vickers, *The Artistry of Shakespeare's Prose* (London: Methuen, 1968).

George T. Wright, *Shakespeare's Metrical Art* (Berkeley: Univ. of California Press, 1991).

Key to the Play Text

Symbols

°	Indicates an explanation or definition in the left-hand margin.
1	Indicates a gloss on the page facing the play text.
[]	Indicates something added or changed by the editors (i.e., not in the early printed text that this edition of the play is based on).

Terms

F, *Folio*, or *First Folio*	The first collected edition of Shakespeare's plays, published in 1623.
Q, *Quarto*	The usual format in which the individual plays were first published. This edition is based on the 1598 Quartos, the fragmentary Q0 and Q1.

Henry IV, Part One

William Shakespeare

List of Roles

King Henry the Fourth — *King of England*

Prince Henry of Wales (Hal *or* Harry) — *his eldest son*

Lord John of **Lancaster** — *a younger son*

Earl of **Westmorland** } *Noblemen loyal to the King*
Sir Walter **Blunt**

Thomas Percy, Earl of **Worcester**

Henry Percy, Earl of **Northumberland** — *his older brother*

Henry Percy, known as **Hotspur** — *Northumberland's son*

Lady Percy (Kate) — *Hotspur's wife*

Lord Edmund **Mortimer** — *Lady Percy's brother*

Lady Mortimer — *his wife*

Owen **Glendower** — *Lady Mortimer's father*

Earl of **Douglas** — *a Scottish lord*

Sir Richard **Vernon** — *an English knight*

Richard Scroop, **Archbishop** of York

Sir Michael — *a member of the Archbishop's household*

Sir John **Falstaff** }
Edward (Ned) **Poins** } *the Prince's tavern friends*
Bardolph }
Peto }

Hostess (Mistress Quickly)

Francis — *a waiter*

Vintner

Gadshill — *a thief*

First Carrier

Second Carrier

Chamberlain

Ostler

Sheriff

Two **Travelers**

Messengers

Servant

Lords, soldiers, attendants, travelers

1   *So shaken as we are*

(1) so troubled as I am (using the royal plural pronoun); (2) so troubled as we all are (including both the assembled nobles and England itself). The play begins soon after the deposition and murder of Richard II, events that are depicted in Shakespeare's *Richard II*.

2   *Find we*

We hope to find

3   *for frighted peace to pant*

To allow frightened peace to catch its breath

4   *breathe short-winded accents*

Speak words while gasping for breath

5   *of new broils / To be commenced in strands afar remote*

Of new battles to be undertaken in distant countries. King Henry announces his intention to go on a crusade to regain Jerusalem for the Christians, an act intended to absolve him of the guilt of Richard II's death and to unify his war-torn country.

6   *this soil*

I.e., England

7   *armèd hoofs / Of hostile paces*

Tread of the enemy's armored horses

8   *opposèd eyes*

I.e., warring armies of soldiers (imagined here as staring at each other across a battlefield)

9   *meteors of a troubled Heaven*

I.e., bad omens. Meteors, and celestial occurrences more generally, were popularly considered to foretell disorders on Earth.

10   *All of one nature, of one substance bred*

(1) literally, meteors and other astronomical objects all made of the same substance; (2) figuratively, the soldiers on opposite sides of a civil war, who come from the same country, alike despite the differences of their allegiances

11   *intestine shock*

Internal conflict

12   *mutual well-beseeming*

Interdependent and orderly

13   *the sepulcher of Christ*

Christ's tomb in Jerusalem

14   *impressèd and engaged*

Conscripted and sworn

15   *pagans*

Anyone not of the Christian religion; here, the Muslims of Jerusalem

16   *those blessèd feet*

I.e., Christ's feet

Act 1, Scene 1

Enter the **King**, *Lord John of* **Lancaster**, *Earl of* **Westmorland**, *with others.*

King

    So shaken as we are,[1] so wan with care,
    Find we[2] a time for frighted peace to pant[3]
    And breathe short-winded accents[4] of new broils
    To be commenced in strands afar remote.[5]
i.e., mouth   No more the thirsty entrance° of this soil[6]   5
smear   Shall daub° her lips with her own children's blood.
ploughing   No more shall trenching° war channel her fields,
small flowers   Nor bruise her flow'rets° with the armèd hoofs
    Of hostile paces.[7] Those opposèd eyes,[8]
    Which, like the meteors of a troubled Heaven,[9]   10
    All of one nature, of one substance bred,[10]
    Did lately meet in the intestine shock[11]
combat   And furious close° of civil butchery,
    Shall now, in mutual well-beseeming[12] ranks,
    March all one way and be no more opposed   15
    Against acquaintance, kindred, and allies.
    The edge of war, like an ill-sheathèd knife,
its   No more shall cut his° master. Therefore, friends,
    As far as to the sepulcher of Christ[13]—
    Whose soldier now, under whose blessèd cross   20
    We are impressèd and engaged[14] to fight—
army   Forthwith a power° of English shall we levy,
    Whose arms were molded in their mothers' womb
    To chase these pagans[15] in those holy fields
    Over whose acres walked those blessèd feet,[16]   25
    Which fourteen hundred years ago were nailed
salvation   For our advantage° on the bitter cross.

1   *our purpose now is twelve month old*

King Henry stated his intention to go on a penitential pilgrimage at the end of Shakespeare's *Richard II*: "I'll make a voyage to the Holy Land / To wash this blood from off my guilty hand" (5.6.49–50). While the journey Henry has just described here is more explicitly martial, a crusade rather than a pilgrimage, the connection between pilgrimage and holy war was well established in the minds of Shakespeare's audiences. The actual Crusades took place in the 11th–13th centuries, well before Henry IV's reign, though in 1400, Henry IV did receive a call for aid against the Ottoman Turks from the Emperor of Constantinople (according to Raphael Holinshed's 1587 *Chronicle*, Shakespeare's primary historical source for this play).

2   *Therefor we meet not now.*

This (i.e., the proposed crusade) is not the purpose of our current meeting.

3   *forwarding this dear expedience*

Getting this important enterprise underway

4   *hot in question*

Fiercely debated

5   *many limits of the charge set down*

Many of the financial and military responsibilities (for the intended crusade) assigned

6   *all athwart*

Frustrating our plans

7   *Mortimer*

Edmund Mortimer, the brother of Hotspur's wife, had a nephew also named Edmund Mortimer. Richard II had intended the nephew Mortimer to succeed him as king. Shakespeare follows Holinshed in combining the two historical Mortimers into a single character.

8   *Glendower*

Owen Glendower (Owain Glyndwr) led the Welsh in their rebellion against King Henry (1400–1410).

9   *Such beastly shameless transformation, / By those Welshwomen done*

The mutilation of English bodies by Welsh women on the battlefield was attested in a number of sources, including Holinshed's *Chronicle*. Holinshed writes that, following the battle in question, the Welsh women cut off each dead English soldier's genitals and nose and placed them in, respectively, his mouth and anus.

10   *this matched with other*

I.e., this information plus other news we have received

11   *Holy-rood Day*

September 14, a church holiday in honor of Christ's cross (*rood*)

12   *Humbleton*

A town in Northumberland where a Scottish invasion was repelled in 1402

But this our purpose now is twelve month old,[1]
useless   And bootless° 'tis to tell you we will go.
Therefor we meet not now.[2] Then let me hear 30
From / kinsman   Of° you, my gentle cousin° Westmorland,
last night   What yesternight° our council did decree
In forwarding this dear expedience.[3]

Westmorland
My liege, this haste was hot in question,[4]
And many limits of the charge set down[5] 35
Just   But° yesternight, when all athwart[6] there came
messenger / laden   A post° from Wales loaden° with heavy news,
Whose worst was that the noble Mortimer,[7]
Leading the men of Herefordshire to fight
Against the irregular and wild Glendower,[8] 40
captured   Was by the rude hands of that Welshman taken,°
A thousand of his people butcherèd,
corpses   Upon whose dead corpse° there was such misuse,
mutilation   Such beastly shameless transformation,°
By those Welshwomen done,[9] as may not be 45
Without much shame retold or spoken of.

King
battle   It seems then that the tidings of this broil°
Broke   Brake° off our business for the Holy Land.

Westmorland
This matched with other[10] did, my gracious lord,
disturbing   For more uneven° and unwelcome news 50
Came from the north, and thus it did import:
On Holy-rood Day,[11] the gallant Hotspur there,
(Young Harry Percy), and brave Archibald,
battle-tested   That ever valiant and approvèd° Scot,
At Humbleton[12] met, where they did spend 55
A sad and bloody hour—
Judging by   As by° discharge of their artillery

1   *shape of likelihood*

    Likely conjecture (rather than
    certain information)

2   *take horse*

    Ride away

3   *Uncertain of the issue*

    Not knowing the outcome (of the
    battle)

4   *Here*

    None of the early texts indicate that
    Blunt enters at any point during this
    scene, nor do they assign him any
    dialogue. Blunt may have entered
    at the beginning of the scene or he
    may enter here. Alternatively,
    Henry may receive a letter at this
    point containing the news of
    Douglas's defeat, or else the King
    has been informed of the situation
    prior to the scene's commence-
    ment. *Here* in either of these latter
    cases implies that Blunt is currently
    residing in the vicinity of the
    court and is not intended as an
    announcement of his arrival.

5   *the variation of each soil*

    The various kinds of soil

6   *Balked*

    (1) piled up; (2) foiled in their
    purpose

7   *the theme of honor's tongue*

    I.e., so well-regarded that *honor*
    itself takes Hotspur as the subject
    of its speech

8   *That some night-tripping fairy had
    exchanged / In cradle-clothes our children*

    I.e., that Hotspur were my real son,
    rather than Hal. Popular belief held
    that fairies stole human children
    and left ugly fairy children, known
    as changelings, in their place.

And shape of likelihood [1] the news was told;

i.e., news of the battle For he that brought them,° in the very heat

fiercest point And pride° of their contention, did take horse,[2]   60

Uncertain of the issue [3] any way.

King

Here [4] is a dear, a true industrious friend,

Sir Walter Blunt, new lighted from his horse,

Stained with the variation of each soil [5]

dwelling Betwixt that Humbleton and this seat° of ours,   65

pleasant And he hath brought us smooth ° and welcome news.

defeated The Earl of Douglas is discomfited.°

Ten thousand bold Scots, two-and-twenty knights,

Balked [6] in their own blood, did Sir Walter see

On Humbleton's plains. Of prisoners Hotspur took   70

Murdoch, Earl of Fife and eldest son

To beaten Douglas, and the Earl of Atholl,

Of Moray, Angus, and Menteith;

And is not this an honorable spoil?

A gallant prize? Ha, cousin, is it not?   75

Westmorland

In faith, it is: a conquest for a prince to boast of.

King

with that Yea, there° thou mak'st me sad, and mak'st me sin

In envy that my Lord Northumberland

Should be the father to so blest a son,

A son who is the theme of honor's tongue,[7]   80

tree Amongst a grove the very straightest plant,°

favorite Who is sweet Fortune's minion ° and her pride;

Whilst I, by looking on the praise of him,

See riot and dishonor stain the brow

Of my young Harry. Oh, that it could be proved   85

That some night-tripping fairy had exchanged

In cradle-clothes our children [8] where they lay,

1   *"Percy," his "Plantagenet"*

    Percy, as at 1.1.53, is the family name
    of the earls of Northumberland.
    Plantagenet had been the family
    name of the English royal family
    from the time of Henry II. Hotspur's
    real name is Henry Percy, and he,
    like King Henry's son, is sometimes
    affectionately called Harry (thus
    Henry IV's wish to trade Northum-
    berland's *Harry* for his own).

2   *coz*

    I.e., kinsman. *Coz* is short for
    "cousin," a general term for a
    relative.

3   *To his own use*

    **Hotspur holds the prisoners in or-
    der to collect their ransom himself,
    rather than allowing his sovereign,
    King Henry, to collect the money,
    as the customs of chivalry normally
    required.**

4   *Malevolent to you in all aspects*

    **Having only malicious intentions
    toward you.** *Aspects* has a precise
    astrological sense of the influ-
    ence a planet might exert over an
    individual.

5   *prune*

    **Preen (like a hawk smoothing its
    feathers with its beak)**

6   *bristle up / The crest of youth against your
    dignity*

    **Set his youth against your worthi-
    ness.** A hawk raises the feathers on
    its head as a sign of aggression.

7   *for this cause*

    Because of this

And called mine "Percy," his "Plantagenet." [1]

Then would I have his Harry, and he mine.

be out of But let him from° my thoughts. What think you, coz, [2]   90

Of this young Percy's pride? The prisoners

captured Which he in this adventure hath surprised°

To his own use [3] he keeps, and sends me word

I shall have none but Murdoch, Earl of Fife.

Westmorland

This is his uncle's teaching. This is Worcester,   95

Malevolent to you in all aspects, [4]

i.e., Hotspur Which makes him° prune [5] himself and bristle up

The crest of youth against your dignity. [6]

King

But I have sent for him to answer this,

And for this cause [7] awhile we must neglect   100

Our holy purpose to Jerusalem.

Cousin, on Wednesday next our Council we

Will hold at Windsor. So inform the lords,

But come yourself with speed to us again,

For more is to be said and to be done   105

Than out of anger can be utterèd.

Westmorland

I will, my liege.   *They exit.*

1   *sack*

A Spanish white wine

2   *thee*

Yourself (i.e., your pants)

3   *to demand that truly which thou wouldst*
    truly know

To be honest and ask about things
that actually matter to you

4   *capons*

Castrated, fattened roosters (a
delicacy in Elizabethan England)

5   *in flame-colored taffeta*

I.e., dressed like a prostitute

6   *superfluous*

(1) needlessly concerned; (2) overflowing (a joke directed at Falstaff's
weight)

7   *you come near me now*

You almost have it right.

8   *go by*

(1) make our way by the light of; (2)
tell time using

9   *the seven stars*

The Pleiades (a constellation),
though also, perhaps, the name of
a tavern

10 *Phoebus*

I.e., sunlight (*Phoebus* being the sun
god in Roman mythology)

11 *that wand'ring knight so fair*

That handsome knight errant. The
line seems to come from a popular
Elizabethan ballad or chivalric
romance, but the reference has
not been identified.

12 *wag*

Mischievous fellow

13 *thy Grace—"Majesty," I should say, for*
    grace thou wilt have none

Prince Henry should be called by
the word *Majesty*, which was the
increasingly popular honorific for
a monarch, but the joke may be
that the Prince so clearly avoids
everything implied by *Grace*. Falstaff
plays on several meanings of this
word, including "virtue," "Christian
salvation," "sophistication," and
"the prayer spoken before a meal."

14 *not so much as will serve to be prologue to*
    an egg and butter

I.e., you don't even have enough
grace to say *grace* before *an egg*
and butter (a small meal that does
not require an ornate blessing
beforehand).

15 *roundly*

(1) plainly (i.e., say what you mean);
(2) with roundness (another allusion to Falstaff's weight)

Act 1, Scene 2

*Enter **Prince** of Wales and Sir John **Falstaff**.*

Falstaff

Now Hal, what time of day is it, lad?

Prince

dim-witted   Thou art so fat-witted,° with drinking of old sack,[1]
and unbuttoning thee[2] after supper, and sleeping
upon benches after noon, that thou hast forgotten to
demand that truly which thou wouldst truly know.[3]   5

the   What a° devil hast thou to do with the time of the day?
Unless hours were cups of sack, and minutes capons,[4]

prostitutes / sundials   and clocks the tongues of bawds,° and dials° the signs

brothels   of leaping-houses,° and the blessed sun himself a fair
hot wench in flame-colored taffeta,[5] I see no reason   10
why thou shouldst be so superfluous[6] to demand the
time of the day.

Falstaff

steal   Indeed, you come near me now,[7] Hal, for we that take°
purses go by[8] the moon and the seven stars,[9] and not
by Phoebus,[10] he, that wand'ring knight so fair.[11] And I   15

beg you   prithee,° sweet wag,[12] when thou art king, as God save
thy Grace—"Majesty," I should say, for grace thou wilt
have none[13]—

Prince

What, none?

Falstaff

faith   No, by my troth,° not so much as will serve to be pro-   20
logue to an egg and butter.[14]

Prince

Well, how then? Come roundly,[15] roundly.

1   *let not us that are squires of the night's body be called thieves of the day's beauty*

I.e., don't let those of us who serve the night be called lazy for sleeping during the day. Falstaff suggests that once Hal is king, those that thieve by night and sleep by day should be lauded as followers of Diana, the goddess of the moon.

2   *Diana's*

In the service of Diana, the Roman goddess of moonlight, the hunt, and chastity

3   *under whose countenance we steal*

(1) under whose face we walk softly; (2) with whose permission we thieve

4   *it holds well*

The metaphor is apt.

5   *"Lay by"*

I.e., put down your weapons (a robber's words on accosting his victims)

6   *"Bring in"*

I.e., a customer's demand for more food or wine at a tavern

7   *the ladder*

I.e., the ladder leading up to the gallows

8   *Hybla*

A town in Sicily known for its honey

9   *old lad of the castle*

A pun on Oldcastle—the original name given to Falstaff but which under pressure from some power- ful descendants of the historical Sir John Oldcastle Shakespeare changed—but also a term for a carouser.

10   *buff jerkin*

Tight leather jacket often worn by officers of the law

11   *robe of durance*

(1) durable garment; (2) prison clothing

12   *What a plague*

An expletive comparable to "What the hell"

13   *what a pox*

Another expletive (the *pox* is syphilis)

Falstaff

i.e., Truly Marry,° then, sweet wag, when thou art king, let not
us that are squires of the night's body be called thieves
of the day's beauty.[1] Let us be Diana's[2] foresters, 25
servants gentlemen of the shade, minions° of the moon, and
let men say we be men of good government, being
governed, as the sea is, by our noble and chaste mistress the moon, under whose countenance we steal.[3]

Prince

Thou sayest well, and it holds well[4] too, for the 30
fortune of us that are the moon's men doth ebb and
flow like the sea, being governed, as the sea is, by the
moon. As for proof now: a purse of gold most reso-
lutely snatched on Monday night and most dissolutely
spent on Tuesday morning, got with swearing "Lay by"[5] 35
and spent with crying "Bring in,"[6] now in as low an
ebb as the foot of the ladder,[7] and by and by in as high
crossbeam a flow as the ridge° of the gallows.

Falstaff

By the Lord, thou say'st true, lad—and is not my
hostess of the tavern a most sweet wench? 40

Prince

As the honey of Hybla,[8] my old lad of the castle.[9] And
is not a buff jerkin[10] a most sweet robe of durance?[11]

Falstaff

How now, how now, mad wag? What, in thy quips and
quibbles thy quiddities?° What a plague[12] have I to do with a
buff jerkin? 45

Prince

Why, what a pox[13] have I to do with my hostess of the
tavern?

1   *called her to a reckoning*

(1) **asked her to total up the bill; (2) had a sexual encounter with her**

2   *pay thy part*

(1) **pay your part of the bill; (2) use your *part* (i.e., penis) in the sexual encounter**

3   *so far as my coin would stretch*

(1) **as long as I could pay with my current funds; (2) as long as I could maintain my ability to father (*coin*) a child**

4   *resolution thus fubbed*

Bravery thus cheated

5   *the rusty curb of old Father Antic the law*

The law is depicted here as an old buffoon (*Father Antic*), wielding a horse's bridle (*curb*) to represent his authority.

6   *thou shalt*

(1) **you will hang thieves; (2) you will hang as a thief.**

7   *have the hanging of the thieves*

Be the one who hangs the thieves

8   *jumps with my humor*

Agrees with my disposition

9   *waiting in the court*

(1) **serving in the royal court; (2) serving as an official in a court of law**

10   *suits*

Suits of clothes. Hangmen received the clothes of the condemned as part of their pay.

Falstaff

Well, thou hast called her to a reckoning[1] many a time
and oft.

Prince

Did I ever call for thee to pay thy part?[2]   50

Falstaff

No, I'll give thee thy due; thou hast paid all there.

Prince

Yea, and elsewhere, so far as my coin would stretch,[3]
and where it would not, I have used my credit.

Falstaff

Yea, and so used it that were it not here apparent that
thou art heir apparent—but I prithee, sweet wag,   55
shall there be gallows standing in England when thou
art king? And resolution thus fubbed[4] as it is with the
rusty curb of old Father Antic the law?[5] Do not thou,
when thou art king, hang a thief.

Prince

No, thou shalt.[6]   60

Falstaff

splendid / excellent Shall I? O rare!° By the Lord, I'll be a brave° judge.

Prince

Thou judgest false already: I mean thou shalt have the
hanging of the thieves,[7] and so become a rare hangman.

Falstaff

Well, Hal, well, and in some sort it jumps with my   65
humor[8] as well as waiting in the court,[9] I can tell you.

Prince

legal petitions For obtaining of suits?°

Falstaff

Yea, for obtaining of suits,[10] whereof the hangman

1   *'Sblood*

By Christ's blood (a mild oath)

2   *a lugged bear*

A bear chained and attacked by dogs (a popular Elizabethan entertainment)

3   *hare*

Hares, like tomcats, were proverbially melancholy.

4   *Moorditch*

A remnant of the old moat around London, Moorditch had become an open sewer by Shakespeare's time.

5   *a commodity of good names*

A supply of good reputations

6   *wisdom cries out in the street and no man regards it*

An allusion to Proverbs 1:20–24: "Wisdom crieth without: she uttereth her voice in the streets . . . saying . . . 'I have called, and ye refused: I have stretched out my hand, and none would regard'" (Geneva Bible).

7   *thou hast damnable iteration*

The way you quote holy scripture for your own purposes will damn you.

8   *I'll be damned for never a king's son in Christendom.*

I.e., I won't be damned for any king's son in the whole world.

hath no lean wardrobe. 'Sblood,[1] I am as melancholy

tom   as a gib° cat or a lugged bear.[2]   70

Prince

Or an old lion or a lover's lute.

Falstaff

Yea, or the drone of a Lincolnshire bagpipe.

Prince

What sayest thou to a hare,[3] or the melancholy of

Moorditch?[4]

Falstaff

Thou hast the most unsavory similes, and art indeed   75

i.e., fond of comparisons   the most comparative,° rascaliest, sweet young

Prince. But, Hal, I prithee trouble me no more with

worldy rubbish   vanity.° I would to God thou and I knew where a

commodity of good names[5] were to be bought. An

scolded   old lord of the Council rated° me the other day in the   80

street about you, sir, but I marked him not, and yet he

talked very wisely, but I regarded him not, and yet he

talked wisely, and in the street, too.

Prince

Thou didst well, for wisdom cries out in the streets

and no man regards it.[6]   85

Falstaff

Oh, thou hast damnable iteration[7] and art indeed able

to corrupt a saint. Thou hast done much harm upon

me, Hal; God forgive thee for it. Before I knew thee,

i.e., nothing evil   Hal, I knew nothing,° and now am I, if a man should

speak truly, little better than one of the wicked. I must   90

give over this life, and I will give it over. By the Lord,

if   an° I do not, I am a villain. I'll be damned for never a

king's son in Christendom.[8]

Prince

Where shall we take a purse tomorrow, Jack?

1   *Zounds*

By Christ's wounds (a mild oath, like "'Sblood" in line 69)

2   *I'll make one.*

I'll come with you.

3   *'Tis no sin for a man to labor in his vocation.*

A further allusion to the Bible, in this case a popular Protestant citation from 1 Corinthians 7:20: "Let every man abide in the same vocation wherein he is called." The passage instructs Christians to work diligently in the vocations God has called them to.

4   *Gadshill*

The name of the thief who sets up the robbery in 2.2.49.

5   *set a match*

Planned a robbery

6   *if men were to be saved by merit*

If people earned their salvation through their good works (rather than by God's grace). Protestant doctrine held that only divine grace could ensure salvation, while Catholic doctrine placed more emphasis on a person's good deeds.

7   *"Stand!"*

I.e., stop right there (a robber's command to a victim)

8   *Monsieur Remorse*

Poins addresses Falstaff, poking fun at his declaration, in the previous lines, that he intends to repent and reform his ways.

9   *Sir John Sack-and-Sugar*

Poins mocks Falstaff's drinking habit (apparently, he likes to sweeten his white wine).

10   *Jack*

In addition to being a nickname for "John," the word means both "drinking cup" and "scoundrel."

11   *Good Friday*

The Friday before Easter, celebrated as the anniversary of Christ's crucifixion; in the Christian calendar, Good Friday was a strict fast day.

12   *for he was never yet a breaker of proverbs. He will give the devil his due.*

Falstaff will keep his word to the devil because a proverb tells him to do so. "Give the devil his due" is a proverbial phrase meaning "pay what you owe"; Prince Henry jokingly suggests that Falstaff has a greater allegiance to proverbs than to any other kind of truth.

Falstaff

If   Zounds,[1] where thou wilt, lad. I'll make one.[2] An° I do   95
disgrace   not, call me villain and baffle° me.

Prince

I see a good amendment of life in thee, from praying
to purse-taking.

Falstaff

Why, Hal, 'tis my vocation, Hal. 'Tis no sin for a man to
labor in his vocation.[3]   100

Enter **Poins**.

Poins!—Now shall we know if Gadshill[4] have set a
match.[5] Oh, if men were to be saved by merit,[6] what
hole in Hell were hot enough for him? This is the most
thorough / honest   omnipotent° villain that ever cried "Stand!"[7] to a true°
man.   105

Prince

Good morrow, Ned.

Poins

Good morrow, sweet Hal.—What says Monsieur Remorse?[8] What says Sir John Sack-and-Sugar?[9] Jack,[10]
how agrees the devil and thee about thy soul that thou
fortified white wine   soldest him on Good Friday[11] last for a cup of Madeira°   110
and a cold capon's leg?

Prince

keeps   Sir John stands° to his word. The devil shall have his
i.e., Falstaff   bargain, for he° was never yet a breaker of proverbs.
He will give the devil his due.[12]

Poins

[*to* **Falstaff**] Then art thou damned for keeping thy   115
word with the devil.

1 *Gad's Hill*

   A hill about 25 miles southeast of
   London notorious as the site
   of robberies

2 *pilgrims going to Canterbury*

   Before England became an
   officially Protestant country during
   the reign of Henry VIII (1509–1547),
   Canterbury Cathedral was a popular
   destination for pilgrims.

3 *Eastcheap*

   A market street near London Bridge
   and the location of the tavern
   scenes in the play

4 *Yedward*

   A dialectical form of Edward
   (Poins's first name; see *Ned*, another nickname, in line 106)

5 *I'll hang you*

   I'll (testify against you and) see you
   hanged.

6 *wilt thou make one*

   Will you come along?

7 *for ten shillings*

   I.e., for a *royal*, a coin worth ten
   shillings

Prince

Otherwise / cheating   Else° he had been damned for cozening° the devil.

Poins

But, my lads, my lads, tomorrow morning, by four
o'clock, early at Gad's Hill,[1] there are pilgrims going to
Canterbury[2] with rich offerings, and traders riding to   120
masks   London with fat purses. I have vizards° for you all. You
lodges   have horses for yourselves. Gadshill lies° tonight in
ordered   Rochester. I have bespoke° supper tomorrow night in
safely   Eastcheap.[3] We may do it as secure° as sleep. If you will
go, I will stuff your purses full of crowns. If you will   125
not, tarry at home and be hanged.

Falstaff

Hear ye, Yedward,[4] if I tarry at home and go not, I'll
hang you[5] for going.

Poins

fat cheeks   You will, chops?°

Falstaff

Hal, wilt thou make one?[6]   130

Prince

Who, I rob? I a thief? Not I, by my faith.

Falstaff

honor   There's neither honesty,° manhood, nor good fellowship in thee, nor thou cam'st not of the blood royal, if
thou darest not stand for ten shillings.[7]

Prince

rash person   Well then, once in my days I'll be a madcap.°   135

Falstaff

Why, that's well said.

Prince

Well, come what will, I'll tarry at home.

Falstaff

By the Lord, I'll be a traitor then when thou art king.

1   *Well, God give thee the spirit of*
    persuasion

    **Falstaff's speech parodies Puritan
    preaching, which stressed that the
    congregation should be moved by
    the spirit of God.**

2   *the poor abuses of the time want*
    countenance

    **I.e., the bad deeds committed
    nowadays are not approved (by
    those in power). Falstaff parodies
    the common sentiment that good
    deeds are not rewarded.**

3   *latter spring*

    **Late spring (an accusation that
    Falstaff does not act his age)**

4   *All-hallown summer*

    **Unseasonably warm weather on
    All-Saints' Day, November 1
    (another phrase pointing at
    Falstaff's adolescent behavior)**

5   *wherein it is at our pleasure to fail*

    **Where we will intentionally not
    show up**

6   *adventure upon the exploit*

    Attempt the robbery

Prince

I care not.

Poins

Sir John, I prithee, leave the Prince and me alone. I   140
will lay him down such reasons for this adventure that
he shall go.

Falstaff

Well, God give thee the spirit of persuasion [1] and him
the ears of profiting, that what thou speakest may
move, and what he hears may be believed, that the   145
true Prince may, for recreation sake, prove a false
thief, for the poor abuses of the time want countenance. [2] Farewell. You shall find me in Eastcheap.

Prince

Farewell, thou latter spring. [3] Farewell, All-hallown
summer. [4]   [**Falstaff** *exits.*]   150

Poins

Now, my good sweet honey lord, ride with us tomorrow. I have a jest to execute that I cannot manage
alone. Falstaff, Peto, Bardolph, and Gadshill shall rob
those men that we have already waylaid. Yourself and
I will not be there. And when they have the booty, if   155
you and I do not rob them, cut this head off from my
shoulders.

Prince

How shall we part with them in setting forth?

Poins

Why, we will set forth before or after them, and ap-
point them a place of meeting, wherein it is at our   160
pleasure to fail; [5] and then will they adventure upon
the exploit [6] themselves, which they shall have no
sooner achieved but we'll set upon them.

1   *sirrah*

     **A term of address usually used with
     social inferiors but here used as a
     sign of intimacy**

2   *cases of buckram for the nonce*

     **Overalls made of coarse linen for
     the occasion**

3   *I doubt they will be too hard for us*

     **I fear they will be too much for us
     (seemingly said sarcastically).**

4   *turned back*

     I.e., turned around and fled

5   *incomprehensible*

     (1) limitless; (2) nonsensical

6   *in the reproof of this*

     **In the denial of what actually took
     place**

7   *unyoked humor*

     Uncontrolled impulses

8   *the sun*

     Traditionally, a royal emblem

Prince

likely Yea, but 'tis like° that they will know us by our horses,

clothing / outward sign by our habits,° and by every other appointment° to be   165
ourselves.

Poins

Tut, our horses they shall not see; I'll tie them in the
wood. Our vizards we will change after we leave them.
And, sirrah,[1] I have cases of buckram for the nonce,[2]

hide / well-known to immask° our noted° outward garments.   170

Prince

Yea, but I doubt they will be too hard for us.[3]

Poins

Well, for two of them, I know them to be as true-bred
cowards as ever turned back;[4] and for the third, if he
fight longer than he sees reason, I'll forswear arms.
The virtue of this jest will be the incomprehensible[5]   175
lies that this same fat rogue will tell us when we meet
at supper: how thirty at least he fought with, what

parries wards,° what blows, what extremities he endured; and
in the reproof of this[6] lives the jest.

Prince

Well, I'll go with thee. Provide us all things necessary   180
and meet me tomorrow night in Eastcheap. There I'll
sup. Farewell.

Poins

Farewell, my lord.   **Poins** *exits.*

Prince

tolerate; encourage I know you all and will awhile uphold°
The unyoked humor[7] of your idleness.   185
Yet herein will I imitate the sun,[8]

infectious Who doth permit the base contagious° clouds
To smother up his beauty from the world,

So that That° when he please again to be himself,

1   *he may be more wondered at*

     He may seem more amazing

2   *rare accidents*

     Extraordinary events

3   *falsify men's hopes*

     Defy people's expectations

4   *on a sullen ground*

     Against a dark background

5   *foil*

     **Contrasting background (like the
     sullen ground)**

6   *I'll so offend to make offense a skill*

     **I will use my bad behavior to my
     own advantage.**

7   *Redeeming time*

     **Making up for lost time; redeeming
     my reputation**

absent; missed	Being wanted,° he may be more wondered at [1]	190
	By breaking through the foul and ugly mists	
	Of vapors that did seem to strangle him.	
	If all the year were playing holidays,	
	To sport would be as tedious as to work,	
i.e., holidays	But when they° seldom come, they wished for come,	195
	And nothing pleaseth but rare accidents. [2]	
dissolute	So when this loose° behavior I throw off	
i.e., promised to pay	And pay the debt I never promisèd,°	
	By how much better than my word I am,	
	By so much shall I falsify men's hopes; [3]	200
	And, like bright metal on a sullen ground, [4]	
	My reformation, glitt'ring o'er my fault,	
appear	Shall show° more goodly and attract more eyes	
	Than that which hath no foil [5] to set it off.	
	I'll so offend to make offense a skill, [6]	205
	Redeeming time [7] when men think least I will.	

He exits.

1   *Unapt to stir at*

       Not inclined to be provoked by

2   *found me*

       Discovered this to be true

3   *tread upon my patience*

       Test my patience; provoke me

4   *scourge of greatness*

       Punishment from the mighty

5   *moody frontier*

       Furrowed forehead

Act 1, Scene 3

Enter the **King**, **Northumberland**, **Worcester**, **Hotspur**,
Sir Walter **Blunt**, *with others.*

King

My blood hath been too cold and temperate,
Unapt to stir at[1] these indignities,
And you have found me,[2] for accordingly
You tread upon my patience.[3] But be sure

i.e., my royal self   I will from henceforth rather be myself,°   5
natural disposition   Mighty and to be feared, than my condition,°

Which hath been smooth as oil, soft as young down,
And therefore lost that title of respect

except   Which the proud soul ne'er pays but° to the proud.

Worcester

family (i.e., the Percys)   Our house,° my sovereign liege, little deserves   10
The scourge of greatness[4] to be used on it,
And that same greatness too which our own hands

helped / imposing   Have holp° to make so portly.°

Northumberland

[*to the* **King**] My lord—

King

Worcester, get thee gone, for I do see   15
Danger and disobedience in thine eye.

proud   O sir, your presence is too bold and peremptory,°
And majesty might never yet endure

i.e, servant's   The moody frontier[5] of a servant° brow.
permission   You have good leave° to leave us. When we need   20
Your use and counsel we shall send for you.

                           Worcester *exits.*

[*to* **Northumberland**] You were about to speak.

Northumberland

                          Yea, my good lord.

1 *Harry Percy*

The Earl of Northumberland's eldest son, known as Hotspur for his fiery character.

2 *with such strength*

So vehemently

3 *his chin new reaped*

His face freshly shaved

4 *a stubble land at harvest home*

I.e., the short stalks of grain that remain at the completion of the harvest

5 *milliner*

Seller of ladies' fashion accessories

6 *pouncet box*

Box with holes in the lid, filled with perfume or aromatic snuff

7 *Who therewith angry*

I.e., his nose, angry at the removing of the *pouncet box*

8 *Took it in snuff*

(1) breathed it in; (2) was offended

9 *Betwixt the wind and his nobility*

I.e., where its odor would offend his refined sensibilities

10 *holiday and lady terms*

Fancy, ladylike words (as opposed to plain-speaking soldiers' words)

11 *all smarting with my wounds being cold*

In pain because my wounds were untreated

Those prisoners in your Highness' name demanded,
Which Harry Percy[1] here at Humbleton took,
Were, as he says, not with such strength[2] denied   25
reported As is delivered° to your Majesty.
malice/mistake Either envy,° therefore, or misprision°
Is guilty of this fault, and not my son.

Hotspur
My liege, I did deny no prisoners.
But I remember, when the fight was done,   30
thirsty When I was dry° with rage and extreme toil,
Breathless and faint, leaning upon my sword,
elegantly Came there a certain lord, neat and trimly° dressed,
Fresh as a bridegroom, and his chin, new reaped,[3]
Looked Showed° like a stubble land at harvest home.[4]   35
He was perfumèd like a milliner,[5]
And 'twixt his finger and his thumb he held
A pouncet box,[6] which ever and anon
He gave his nose and took 't away again,
Who therewith angry,[7] when it next came there,   40
continually Took it in snuff;[8] and still° he smiled and talked.
And as the soldiers bore dead bodies by,
uncivilized He called them untaught° knaves, unmannerly,
To bring a slovenly unhandsome corpse
Betwixt the wind and his nobility.[9]   45
With many holiday and lady terms[10]
He questioned me; amongst the rest demanded
My prisoners in your Majesty's behalf.
I then, all smarting with my wounds being cold,[11]
parrot To be so pestered with a popinjay,°   50
pain Out of my grief° and my impatience
Answered neglectingly I know not what—
He should or he should not—for he made me mad
To see him shine so brisk and smell so sweet

1   *God save the mark*

    **God preserve us from evil (an
    expression of indignation or
    irritation).**

2   *parmacety*

    **Spermaceti (fat taken from the
    heads of whales, used in ointments
    and cosmetics)**

3   *saltpeter*

    **Potassium nitrate, a principal
    ingredient in gunpowder**

4   *Which many a good tall fellow had
    destroyed*

    **Which had killed many good, brave
    men**

5   *Come current*

    Be taken as an accurate account

6   *yet he doth deny*

    But he still refuses to give up

7   *But with proviso and exception*

    **Unless we agree to his terms and
    conditions**

8   *His brother-in-law, the foolish Mortimer*

    **Historically there were two distinct
    Edmund Mortimers whom Shake-
    speare conflates here. See 1.1.38
    and note.**

And talk so like a waiting-gentlewoman   55
Of guns, and drums, and wounds—God save the
    mark![1]—
most effective And telling me "the sovereignest° thing on earth"
Was parmacety[2] for an inward bruise,
And that it was great pity, so it was,
dug This "villanous saltpeter"[3] should be digged°   60
Out of the bowels of the harmless Earth,
Which many a good tall fellow had destroyed[4]
So cowardly, and but for these "vile guns"
He would himself have been a soldier.
trifling / pointless This bald,° unjointed° chat of his, my lord,   65
carelessly I answered indirectly,° as I said,
And I beseech you, let not his report
Come current[5] for an accusation
Betwixt my love and your high Majesty.

Blunt

The circumstance considered, good my lord,   70
may have Whate'er Lord Harry Percy then had° said
To such a person and in such a place,
At such a time, with all the rest retold,
May reasonably die and never rise
accuse To do him wrong or any way impeach°   75
deny What then he said, so he unsay° it now.

King

still Why, yet° he doth deny[6] his prisoners,
But with proviso and exception[7]
immediately That we at our own charge shall ransom straight°
His brother-in-law, the foolish Mortimer,[8]   80
Who, on my soul, hath willfully betrayed
The lives of those that he did lead to fight
Against that great magician, damned Glendower—
i.e., Mortimer Whose daughter, as we hear, that Earl of March°

1   *indent with fears*

    Make a pact with cowards

2   *fall off*

    Become disloyal

3   *mouthèd wounds*

    Open wounds, but also wounds
    that are eloquent, attesting to their
    bearer's bravery

4   *Severn's*

    The Severn River runs south-
    westerly into the Bristol Channel
    from Wales.

5   *changing hardiment*

    Exchanging blows

6   *breathed*

    I.e., had to stop to get their breath
    back

7   *crisp head*

    Wavy surface

8   *Color*

    Disguise. Hotspur claims that Mor-
    timer's wounds were too severe to
    be a deception designed to hide his
    treachery.

9   *with revolt*

    By being accused of having rebelled

Hath lately married. Shall our coffers then   85
Be emptied to redeem a traitor home?
Shall we buy treason and indent with fears[1]
When they have lost and forfeited themselves?
No, on the barren mountains let him starve,
For I shall never hold that man my friend   90
Whose tongue shall ask me for one penny cost
rebellious To ransom home revolted° Mortimer.

Hotspur

"Revolted Mortimer?"
He never did fall off,[2] my sovereign liege,
But by the chance of war. To prove that true   95
Needs no more but one tongue for all those wounds,
Those mouthèd wounds,[3] which valiantly he took
marshy When on the gentle Severn's[4] sedgy° bank
combat In single opposition,° hand to hand,
use up He did confound° the best part of an hour   100
In changing hardiment[5] with great Glendower.
Three times they breathed,[6] and three times did they
    drink,
water Upon agreement, of swift Severn's flood,°
i.e., The river Who° then, affrighted with their bloody looks,
Ran fearfully among the trembling reeds   105
And hid his crisp head[7] in the hollow bank,
Bloodstainèd with these valiant combatants.
vile / scheming Never did bare° and rotten policy°
Color[8] her working with such deadly wounds,
Nor never could the noble Mortimer   110
Receive so many, and all willingly.
Then let not him be slandered with revolt.[9]

King

misrepresent Thou dost belie° him, Percy; thou dost belie him.
He never did encounter with Glendower.

1   *An if*

     Even if

2   *I will after straight*

     I will go after the King right now.

3   *Want mercy*

     Be denied salvation

4   *But I will*

     So that I may

5   *lift the downtrod Mortimer / As high in*
     the air as this unthankful King

     Hotspur promises to dethrone King
     Henry and crown Mortimer in his
     stead.

6   *Bolingbroke*

     I.e., King Henry. By calling King
     Henry by his family name, Hotspur
     provocatively ignores the King's
     royal office and points to the
     weakness of Henry IV's claim to the
     throne.

I tell thee, he durst as well have met the devil alone   115
As Owen Glendower for an enemy.
Art thou not ashamed? But, sirrah, henceforth
Let me not hear you speak of Mortimer.
Send me your prisoners with the speediest means,
manner Or you shall hear in such a kind° from me   120
As will displease you.—My Lord Northumberland,
We license your departure with your son.
[*to* **Hotspur**] Send us your prisoners, or you will hear
         of it.   **King** *exits* [*with* **Blunt** *and attendants*].

Hotspur
An if¹ the devil come and roar for them,
I will not send them. I will after straight²   125
And tell him so, for I will ease my heart,
Although Albeit° I make a hazard of my head.

Northumberland
anger What, drunk with choler?° Stay and pause awhile.
Here comes your uncle.

                    Enter **Worcester**.

Hotspur
                                   Speak of Mortimer?
i.e., By Christ's wounds Zounds,° I will speak of him, and let my soul   130
Want mercy³ if I do not join with him.
behalf Yea, on his part° I'll empty all these veins
And shed my dear blood drop by drop in the dust,
But I will⁴ lift the downtrod Mortimer
As high in the air as this unthankful King,⁵   135
ungrateful / corrupt As this ingrate° and cankered° Bolingbroke.⁶

Northumberland
[*to* **Worcester**] Brother, the King hath made your
         nephew mad.

1   *eye of death*

     Fearful eye

2   *proclaimed / By Richard, that dead is, the*
     next of blood

     In 1398, according to Holinshed,
     Richard II had recognized as heir
     presumptive the younger of the
     two Mortimers that Shakespeare
     conflates into a single character.

3   *the unhappy King*

     The unfortunate King (i.e.,
     Richard II)

4   *Whose wrongs in us*

     The wrongs against him that we
     committed

5   *Irish expedition*

     In Shakespeare's *Richard II*, Richard
     is away fighting a war with the Irish
     when the exiled Henry Bolingbroke
     (soon to be King Henry) returns to
     England.

6   *the world's wide mouth*

     The general view of the world

7   *his cousin King*

     Referring to the King as Mortimer's
     ***cousin*, Hotspur puns on *cozen*, "to**
     cheat."

Worcester

Who struck this heat up after I was gone?

Hotspur

He will forsooth have all my prisoners,

And when I urged the ransom once again   140

Of my wife's brother, then his cheek looked pale,

And on my face he turned an eye of death,[1]

Trembling even at the name of Mortimer.

Worcester

i.e., Mortimer I cannot blame him. Was not he° proclaimed

By Richard, that dead is, the next of blood?[2]   145

Northumberland

He was; I heard the proclamation.

And then it was when the unhappy King[3]—

Whose wrongs in us[4] God pardon!—did set forth

Upon his Irish expedition,[5]

interrupted From whence he, intercepted,° did return   150

To be deposed and shortly murderèd.

Worcester

And for whose death we in the world's wide mouth[6]

disgraced Live scandalized° and foully spoken of.

Hotspur

wait But soft,° I pray you. Did King Richard then

i.e., brother-in-law Proclaim my brother° Edmund Mortimer   155

Heir to the crown?

Northumberland

                    He did; myself did hear it.

Hotspur

Nay then, I cannot blame his cousin King[7]

That wished him on the barren mountains starve;

But shall it be that you that set the crown

Upon the head of this forgetful man—   160

And for his sake wear the detested blot

1   *murderous subornation*

    Conspiring to commit murder

2   *base second means*

    Lowly instruments (of King Henry's
    ***subornation*)**

3   *line*

    (1) rank; (2) hangman's rope

4   *gage them both*

    (1) both promise their service;
    (2) commit both their *nobility* and
    power

5   *canker*

    (1) canker rose, also known as
    dog-rose (a weed); (2) cankerworm
    (a parasite that feeds on plants);
    (3) ulcer

6   *yet time serves*

    I.e., there is still time

7   *your quick-conceiving discontents*

    Unhappiness that makes you
    quickly grasp the point

8   *the unsteadfast footing of a spear*

    I.e., using a spear as a rickety bridge

Of murderous subornation[1]—shall it be
That you a world of curses undergo,
Being the agents or base second means,[2]
The cords, the ladder, or the hangman rather?   165
Oh, pardon me that I descend so low
(dangerous) situation To show the line[3] and the predicament°
are placed Wherein you range° under this subtle King.
Shall it for shame be spoken in these days,
history books Or fill up chronicles° in time to come,   170
That men of your nobility and power
Did gage them both[4] in an unjust behalf
(As both of you, God pardon it, have done)
To put down Richard, that sweet lovely rose,
And plant this thorn, this canker,[5] Bolingbroke?   175
And shall it in more shame be further spoken
That you are fooled, discarded, and shook off
By him for whom these shames ye underwent?
No, yet time serves[6] wherein you may redeem
Your banished honors and restore yourselves   180
Into the good thoughts of the world again,
disdainful Revenge the jeering and disdained° contempt
Of this proud King, who studies day and night
repay To answer° all the debt he owes to you
Even with the bloody payment of your deaths.   185
Therefore I say—

Worcester
                              Peace, cousin, say no more.
And now I will unclasp a secret book,
And to your quick-conceiving discontents[7]
I'll read you matter deep and dangerous,
As full of peril and adventurous spirit   190
walk across As to o'erwalk° a current roaring loud
On the unsteadfast footing of a spear.[8]

1   *If he fall in, good night, or sink or swim!*

    I.e., If the one who tries to cross such a bridge falls into the river, it's over, whether he sinks immediately or stays briefly afloat. Carried away by his metaphor, Hotspur misses the point of Worcester's warning.

2   *cross*

    (1) encounter; (2) oppose

3   *them*

    I.e., danger and honor

4   *fathom-line*

    Weighted line used by ships to measure ocean depth. A *fathom* is a unit of distance approximately equal to six feet.

5   *her dignities*

    I.e., the titles bestowed by honor

6   *out upon*

    Away with; forget about

7   *this half-faced fellowship*

    This unsatisfying partnership

8   *He apprehends a world of figures*

    He conceives of an entire world in his imagination.

9   *I cry you mercy.*

    I beg your pardon.

10   *scot*

    Small quantity (but obviously playing on the sense of a Scottish person)

Hotspur

If he fall in, good night, or sink or swim! [1]

Send danger from the east unto the west,

As long as So° honor cross [2] it from the north to south,   195

And let them [3] grapple. Oh, the blood more stirs

To rouse a lion than to start a hare!

Northumberland

[*to* **Worcester**] Imagination of some great exploit

self-control Drives him beyond the bounds of patience.°

Hotspur

By Heaven, methinks it were an easy leap   200

To pluck bright honor from the pale-faced moon,

Or dive into the bottom of the deep,

Where fathom-line [4] could never touch the ground,

hair And pluck up drownèd honor by the locks,°

rescue So he that doth redeem° her thence might wear   205

partner Without corrival° all her dignities. [5]

But out upon [6] this half-faced fellowship! [7]

Worcester

[*to* **Northumberland**] He apprehends a world of

        figures [8] here,

essence / focus on But not the form° of what he should attend.°

[*to* **Hotspur**] Good cousin, give me audience for a

        while.   210

Hotspur

I cry you mercy. [9]

Worcester

                    Those same noble Scots

That are your prisoners—

Hotspur

                                I'll keep them all.

By God, he shall not have a scot [10] of them.

1   *by this hand*

    A mild oath

2   *Save how to gall and pinch*

    **Besides (the study of) how to
    irritate**

3   *sword-and-buckler*

    **An insult; the rapier and dagger
    were more appropriate weapons
    for a prince than the old-fashioned
    sword and buckler, which had, by
    the time of the play's composi-
    tion, come to be associated with
    swaggering commoners. A *buckler*
    was a small shield with a sharp pike
    extending from the center.**

4   *woman's mood*

    Talkative streak

No, if a Scot would save his soul, he shall not.
I'll keep them, by this hand! [1]

Worcester

                          You start away   215
And lend no ear unto my purposes:
Those prisoners you shall keep—

Hotspur

certain   Nay, I will. That's flat!°
He said he would not ransom Mortimer,
Forbade my tongue to speak of Mortimer;
But I will find him when he lies asleep,   220
And in his ear I'll holler "Mortimer."
Nay, I'll have a starling shall be taught to speak
Nothing but "Mortimer," and give it him
continually To keep his anger still° in motion.

Worcester

Hear you, cousin, a word.   225

Hotspur

pursuits / renounce All studies° here I solemnly defy°
Save how to gall and pinch [2] this Bolingbroke,
And that same sword-and-buckler [3] Prince of Wales.
If it weren't for the fact But° that I think his father loves him not,
And would be glad he met with some mischance,   230
I would have him poisoned with a pot of ale.

Worcester

Farewell, kinsman. I'll talk to you
When you are better tempered to attend.

Northumberland

irritable [*to* **Hotspur**] Why, what a wasp-stung° and impatient
        fool
Art thou to break into this woman's mood, [4]   235
Tying thine ear to no tongue but thine own.

1   *the madcap Duke his uncle*

    **Edward Langley, the Duke of York
    and Richard II's uncle**

2   *Ravenspur*

    **The modern Spurn Head, a place on
    the promontory on the Yorkshire
    coast where the River Humber
    meets the sea**

3   *Berkeley Castle*

    **Castle (pronounced "Barkly") in
    Gloucestershire near Bristol**

4   *what a candy deal of courtesy*

    What a lot of sugary flattery

5   *"Look when his infant fortune came to
    age"*

    **I.e., wait until my newly acquired
    power is fully consolidated.
    Hotspur refers to promises that
    King Henry made when he first
    became King.**

6   *to it*

    Go to it; i.e., keep talking

7   *Deliver them up*

    Free them

8   *the Douglas' son*

    **I.e., Murdoch, the eldest son of
    the Earl of Douglas (an error that
    Shakespeare carried over from the
    historian Holinshed). When placed
    before a family name, *the* denotes
    the head of that clan or family.**

9   *mean / For powers*

    Agent for gathering an army

Hotspur

Why, look you, I am whipped and scourged with rods,

ants   Nettled and stung with pismires,° when I hear

i.e., schemer   Of this vile politician,° Bolingbroke.

In Richard's time—what do you call the place?   240

A plague upon it! It is in Gloucestershire.

lived   'Twas where the madcap Duke his uncle[1] kept°—

His uncle York—where I first bowed my knee

Unto this king of smiles, this Bolingbroke,

'Sblood, when you and he came back from Raven-

     spur.[2]   245

Northumberland

At Berkeley Castle?[3]

Hotspur

           You say true.

Why, what a candy deal of courtesy[4]

This fawning greyhound then did proffer me:

"Look when his infant fortune came to age,"[5]

And "gentle Harry Percy," and "kind cousin."   250

Oh, the devil take such cozeners!—God forgive me!

Good uncle, tell your tale. I have done.

Worcester

Nay, if you have not, to it[6] again.

wait for   We will stay° your leisure.

Hotspur

           I have done, i' faith.

Worcester

Then once more to your Scottish prisoners: 255

Deliver them up[7] without their ransom straight

And make the Douglas' son[8] your only mean

various   For powers[9] in Scotland, which, for divers° reasons

Which I shall send you written, be assured

1   *into the bosom creep*

     I.e., gain the trust

2   *bears hard*

     Is deeply affected by

3   *His brother's death at Bristol, the Lord*
     Scroop

     This is another moment in which
     Shakespeare is (perhaps intention-
     ally) loose with his history. The
     Lord Scroop who died in Bristol was
     William Scroop, Earl of Wiltshire,
     executed by Henry IV in 1399. Rich-
     ard Scroop, the Archbishop of York,
     who favors the cause of the rebels
     in the play, was in fact only distantly
     related to him.

4   *in estimation*

     Based on guesswork

5   *stays but to behold the face / Of that*
     occasion

     I.e., Only waits for an opportune
     moment

6   *Before the game is afoot thou still let'st*
     slip

     You always let your hunting dogs go
     before the quarry has been sighted
     (i.e., you're always overeager).

7   *cannot choose but be*

     Will certainly be

Will easily be granted. [*to* **Northumberland**] You, my
    lord,   260

Your son in Scotland being thus employed,

Shall secretly into the bosom creep [1]

high-ranking clergyman   Of that same noble prelate,° well beloved,

The Archbishop.

Hotspur
                       Of York, is it not?

Worcester
                               True; who bears hard [2]

His brother's death at Bristol, the Lord Scroop. [3]   265

I speak not this in estimation, [4]

As what I think might be, but what I know

Is ruminated, plotted, and set down,

And only stays but to behold the face

Of that occasion [5] that shall bring it on.   270

Hotspur

I smell it. Upon my life, it will do well.

Northumberland

Before the game is afoot thou still let'st slip. [6]

Hotspur

Why, it cannot choose but be [7] a noble plot—

army   And then the power° of Scotland and of York

To join with Mortimer, ha?

Worcester
                           And so they shall.   275

Hotspur

planned   In faith, it is exceedingly well aimed.°

Worcester

And 'tis no little reason bids us speed

army   To save our heads by raising of a head,°

correctly   For, bear ourselves as even° as we can,

himself   The King will always think him° in our debt,   280

1 *pay us home*

   **(1) fully discharge his debt to us; (2)
   administer a fatal blow upon us**

2 *To make us strangers to his looks of love*

   I.e., withhold affection from us

3 *at once*

   Together

And think we think ourselves unsatisfied,
Till he hath found a time to pay us home.[1]
And see already how he doth begin
To make us strangers to his looks of love.[2]

Hotspur

He does; he does. We'll be revenged on him.   285

Worcester

Cousin, farewell. No further go in this
Than I by letters shall direct your course.
soon When time is ripe, which will be suddenly,°
I'll steal to Glendower and Lord Mortimer,
Where you and Douglas and our powers at once,[3]   290
As I will fashion it, shall happily meet
To bear our fortunes in our own strong arms,
Which now we hold at much uncertainty.

Northumberland

Farewell, good brother. We shall thrive, I trust.

Hotspur

Uncle, adieu. Oh, let the hours be short   295
battlefields Till fields° and blows and groans applaud our sport.

They exit.

1 **Carrier**

   One who picks up and delivers
   letters and packages usually on
   regularly scheduled stops at inns

2 *four by the day*

   Four A.M.

3 *Charles's Wain*

   Charlemagne's Wagon; i.e., the
   constellation known as Ursa Major,
   or the Big Dipper

4 *beat Cut's saddle*

   The ostler beats the saddle in order
   to soften it and smooth it out. The
   horse's name, *Cut*, derives from the
   word "curtal," which could denote
   either a horse with a docked tail or
   a gelding.

5 *Put a few flocks in the point.*

   Pad the saddle's pommel with
   wool.

6 *Poor jade is wrung in the withers out of all
   cess.*

   The poor old horse is chafed on its
   shoulders beyond all measure.

7 *Peas and beans are here as dank as a dog*

   The horses' feed at the inn is wet.

8 *bots*

   Intestinal worms

9 *tench*

   Freshwater fish with dark spots

10 *first cock*

   I.e., midnight (literally, the
   rooster's first crowing)

11 *ne'er a jordan*

   Not even a chamber pot

Act 2, Scene 1

Enter a **Carrier** [1] *with a lantern in his hand.*

First Carrier

If Heigh-ho! An° it be not four by the day,[2] I'll be hanged.
Charles's Wain[3] is over the new chimney, and yet our
horses / stable boy horse° not packed.—What, ostler!°

Ostler

Coming; right away [*within*] Anon,° anon.

First Carrier

I prithee, Tom, beat Cut's saddle.[4] Put a few flocks in the   5
point.[5] Poor jade is wrung in the withers out of all cess.[6]

Enter another **Carrier**.

Second Carrier

Peas and beans are as dank here as a dog,[7] and that is
quickest the next° way to give poor jades the bots.[8] This house
is turned upside down since Robin Ostler died.

First Carrier

Poor fellow never joyed since the price of oats rose. It   10
was the death of him.

Second Carrier

I think this be the most villainous house in all London
road for fleas. I am stung like a tench.[9]

First Carrier

i.e., in Christendom Like a tench? By the mass, there is ne'er a king christen°
could be better bit than I have been since the first   15
cock.[10]

Second Carrier

Why, they will allow us ne'er a jordan,[11] and then we

1   *leak in your chimney*

    Urinate in the fireplace

2   *loach*

    **Freshwater fish commonly thought
    to harbor fleas**

3   *a gammon of bacon*

    I.e., a leg of smoked ham

4   *Charing Cross*

    **At the time, a village to the west of
    London**

5   *An 'twere not as good deed as drink*

    **A proverbial expression: "If it
    weren't a very good thing"**

6   *I know a trick worth two of that*

    I.e., I'm not that gullible.

7   *Ay, when? Canst tell?*

    **I.e., and when do you think I will do
    that? (a sarcastic way of saying, "I
    am never giving you my lantern")**

urine   leak in your chimney,[1] and your chamber-lye° breeds
fleas like a loach. [2]

First Carrier

i.e., Where are you   What,° ostler! Come away and be hanged. Come away.   20

Second Carrier

roots   I have a gammon of bacon[3] and two races° of ginger
to be delivered as far as Charing Cross.[4]

First Carrier

basket   God's body, the turkeys in my pannier° are quite
starved.—What, ostler! A plague on thee! Hast thou

If   never an eye in thy head? Canst not hear? An° 'twere   25

skull   not as good deed as drink[5] to break the pate° on thee,
I am a very villain. Come, and be hanged. Hast no faith
in thee?

Enter **Gadshill**.

Gadshill

morning   Good morrow,° carriers. What's o'clock?

First Carrier

I think it be two o'clock.   30

Gadshill

I prithee, lend me thy lantern to see my gelding in the
stable.

First Carrier

wait   Nay, by God, soft.° I know a trick worth two of that,[6] i'
faith.

Gadshill

[*to* **Second Carrier**] I pray thee, lend me thine.   35

Second Carrier

Ay, when? Canst tell?[7] "Lend me thy lantern," quoth

i.e., Truly   he. Marry,° I'll see thee hanged first.

1 *Time enough to go to bed with a candle*
   I.e., sometime tonight

2 *great charge*
   Many valuables

3 *chamberlain*
   **Servant attending the bedrooms
   at an inn, often said to be an
   accomplice to thieves**

4 *At hand, quoth pickpurse.*
   **I'm right next to you, as the pick-
   pocket said.**

5 *thou variest no more from picking of
   purses than giving direction doth from
   laboring*
   **You don't differ any more from a
   pickpocket than an overseer does
   from the laborers who work under
   him.**

6 *It holds current that I told you yesternight*
   **What I told you last night remains
   true.**

7 *Weald of Kent*
   **A wooded plain in the county of
   Kent in southeastern England**

8 *three hundred marks*
   **A mark was not a coin but a unit
   of value equal to two-thirds of a
   pound; hence 200 pounds sterling,
   a very large sum of money.**

9 *abundance of charge*
   A lot of baggage

10 *eggs and butter*
   I.e., breakfast

11 *Saint Nicholas' clerks*
   **Thieves (St. Nicholas was the patron
   saint of students, children, travelers,
   vagabonds, and thieves)**

12 *I'll give thee this neck*
   You can hang me.

Gadshill

Sirrah carrier, what time do you mean to come to
London?

Second Carrier

promise   Time enough to go to bed with a candle,[1] I warrant°   40
thee. Come, neighbor Mugs, we'll call up the gentle-
travel   men. They will along° with company, for they have
great charge.[2]   [**Carriers**] *exit.*

Gadshill

What ho, chamberlain![3]

Chamberlain

[*within*] At hand, quoth pickpurse.[4]   45

Gadshill

apt   That's even as fair° as "at hand, quoth the chamberlain," for thou variest no more from picking of purses
than giving direction doth from laboring:[5] thou layest
the plot how.

Enter **Chamberlain**.

Chamberlain

Good morrow, Master Gadshill. It holds current that I   50
small landowner   told you yesternight:[6] there's a franklin° in the Weald
of Kent[7] hath brought three hundred marks[8] with
him in gold. I heard him tell it to one of his company
last night at supper—a kind of auditor, one that hath
abundance of charge[9] too, God knows what. They   55
are up already and call for eggs and butter.[10] They will
away presently.

Gadshill

Sirrah, if they meet not with Saint Nicholas' clerks,[11]
I'll give thee this neck.[12]

1   *I'll make a fat pair of gallows*

    Two fat men will be hanged (the
    actor playing Gadshill in Shakes-
    peare's company must have been
    fat).

2   *make all whole*

    Smooth things over (with law of-
    ficials)

3   *long-staff sixpenny strikers*

    Petty thieves who carried long
    staffs with which to threaten their
    victims

4   *mad mustachio purple-hued malt-worms*

    Purple-faced drunkards with long
    mustaches

5   *hold in*

    (1) stand their ground; (2) keep
    secrets

6   *ride up and down on her*

    (1) travel throughout the country;
    (2) have sexual intercourse with her
    (i.e., take advantage of her)

7   *foul way*

    Muddy street (Chamberlain jokes
    on the more common sense of
    boots)

8   *liquored*

    Intoxicated; greased (to make her
    waterproof); bribed

9   *as in a castle*

    I.e., in complete safety

10 *receipt of fern seed*

    Recipe for invisibility. Popular
    belief held that fern seed could
    only be seen on St. John's Eve
    (June 23), and that on that night it
    could be gathered and made into a
    potion that would render the user
    invisible.

Chamberlain

No, I'll none of it. I pray thee keep that for the hang-   60
man, for I know thou worshippest Saint Nicholas as
truly as a man of falsehood may.

Gadshill

Why What° talkest thou to me of the hangman? If I hang, I'll
make a fat pair of gallows,[1] for if I hang, old Sir John

emaciated person hangs with me, and thou knowest he is no starveling.°   65

genial fellows Tut, there are other Troyans° that thou dream'st not of,

amusement's the which for sport° sake are content to do the prof-

(of thievery) ession° some grace, that would, if matters should be

i.e., credit's looked into, for their own credit° sake make all whole.[2]

vagabonds I am joined with no foot-land-rakers,° no long-staff   70
sixpenny strikers,[3] none of these mad mustachio
purple-hued malt-worms,[4] but with nobility and

aldermen / i.e., ones tranquility, burgomasters° and great oneyers,° such as
can hold in,[5] such as will strike sooner than speak, and
speak sooner than drink, and drink sooner than pray,   75
and yet, zounds, I lie, for they pray continually to their

nation saint, the commonwealth,° or rather not pray to her
but prey on her, for they ride up and down on her[6] and

source of booty make her their boots.°

Chamberlain

What, the commonwealth their boots? Will she hold   80
out water in foul way?[7]

Gadshill

She will; she will. Justice hath liquored[8] her. We steal

without a doubt as in a castle,[9] cocksure.° We have the receipt of fern
seed;[10] we walk invisible.

Chamberlain

beholden Nay, by my faith, I think you are more beholding° to   85
the night than to fern seed for your walking invisible.

1   *Go to.*

     A dismissive phrase expressing impatience or disbelief

2   Homo *is a common name to all men.*

     I.e., the Latin word for "man" (*homo*) applies to everyone. The phrase derives from a well-known Latin grammar book.

Gadshill

Give me thy hand. Thou shalt have a share in our

plunder purchase,° as I am a true man.

Chamberlain

Nay, rather let me have it as you are a false thief.

Gadshill

Go to.[1] *Homo* is a common name to all men.[2] Bid the   90

ostler bring my gelding out of the stable. Farewell, you

dull-witted muddy° knave.   [*They exit.*]

1   *frets like a gummed velvet*

Poins puns on *frets* meaning
"worries" and meaning "frays" or
"wears out." Treating velvet with
resin (*gum*) made it shiny and stiff,
but gummed velvet did not wear
well.

2   *Stand close.*

Hide.

3   *by the square*

Exactly (a *square* is a measuring tool)

4   *break my wind*

(1) be out of breath; (2) fart

5   *I doubt not but to die a fair death for*

I am sure that I will die an honorable death in spite of

Act 2, Scene 2

Enter **Prince**, **Poins**, **Peto**, *and* [**Bardolph**].

Poins

Come, shelter, shelter! I have removed Falstaff's

i.e., Falstaff horse, and he° frets like a gummed velvet.[1]

Prince

Stand close.[2]   [**Poins**, **Peto** *and* **Bardolph** *hide.*]

Enter **Falstaff**.

Falstaff

Poins! Poins, and be hanged! Poins!

Prince

Peace, ye fat-kidneyed rascal. What a brawling dost   5

make thou keep!°

Falstaff

Where's Poins, Hal?

Prince

He is walked up to the top of the hill. I'll go seek him.

[**Prince** *hides with the others.*]

Falstaff

I am accursed to rob in that thief's company. The ras-

cal hath removed my horse and tied him I know not   10

where. If I travel but four foot by the square[3] further

afoot, I shall break my wind.[4] Well, I doubt not but to

die a fair death for[5] all this, if I 'scape hanging for kill-

ing that rogue. I have forsworn his company hourly

any time this two-and-twenty years, and yet I am   15

cursed bewitched° with the rogue's company. If the rascal

potions have not given me medicines° to make me love him,

otherwise I'll be hanged. It could not be else:° I have drunk

1   *turn true man*

     (1) repent; (2) become an informant

2   *veriest varlet*

     Worst scoundrel

3   *Hang thyself in thine own heir-apparent
     garters!*

     **Falstaff plays on a familiar proverb,
     "He may hang himself in his own
     garters," but also on the fact that,
     as *heir apparent*, Prince Henry is a
     member of the highest order of
     knighthood in England, the Order
     of the Garter.**

4   *peach*

     Betray you to the authorities

medicines.—Poins! Hal! A plague upon you both.

before —Bardolph! Peto!—I'll starve ere° I'll rob a foot   20

If further. An° 'twere not as good a deed as drink to turn

true man [1] and to leave these rogues, I am the veriest

varlet [2] that ever chewed with a tooth. Eight yards of

i.e., sixty uneven ground is threescore° and ten miles afoot

with me, and the stony-hearted villains know it well   25

enough. A plague upon it when thieves cannot be true

one to another!   *They whistle.*

Whew! [**Prince**, **Poins**, **Peto**, *and* **Bardolph** *come forward.*]

A plague upon you all! Give me my horse, you rogues.

Give me my horse and be hanged!   30

Prince

Peace, ye fat guts! Lie down; lay thine ear close to

listen the ground and list° if thou canst hear the tread of

travelers.

Falstaff

Have you any levers to lift me up again being down?

'Sblood, I'll not bear my own flesh so far afoot again   35

for all the coin in thy father's exchequer. What a

trick plague mean ye to colt° me thus?

Prince

unhorsed Thou liest. Thou art not colted; thou art uncolted.°

Falstaff

I prithee, good Prince Hal, help me to my horse, good

king's son.   40

Prince

stable boy Out, ye rogue! Shall I be your ostler?°

Falstaff

Hang thyself in thine own heir-apparent garters! [3] If I

If be ta'en, I'll peach [4] for this. An° I have not ballads

1   *ballads made on you all and sung to filthy*
     tunes

     Ballads were written on various
     topical subjects and often commis-
     sioned to mock a rival or an enemy.
     They were printed on single sheets
     (broadsides) and sold cheaply in
     public places.

2   *when a jest is so forward, and afoot too*

     (1) when a robbery plot is so far
     along and is actually underway; (2)
     when you play such a presumptu-
     ous prank on me that I am left with
     no alternative but to walk

3   *setter*

     Person who lays the groundwork
     for a robbery

4   *Case ye*

     Put on your masks.

5   *make us all*

     Make us all rich

6   *lower*

     Farther down the hill

made on you all and sung to filthy tunes,[1] let a cup of
sack be my poison—when a jest is so forward, and　　45
afoot too![2] I hate it.

Enter **Gadshill**.

Gadshill

Halt　Stand!°

Falstaff

So I do, against my will.

Poins

Oh, 'tis our setter.[3] I know his voice.

Bardolph

What news?　　　　　　　　　　　　　　　50

Gadshill

masks　Case ye;[4] case ye. On with your vizards.° There's money
of the King's coming down the hill. 'Tis going to the
treasurer　King's exchequer.°

Falstaff

You lie, ye rogue. 'Tis going to the King's Tavern.

Gadshill

There's enough to make us all.[5]　　　　　　　　55

Falstaff

To be hanged.

Prince

confront　Sirs, you four shall front° them in the narrow lane;
Ned Poins and I will walk lower.[6] If they 'scape from
your encounter, then they light on us.

Peto

How many be there of them?　　　　　　　　60

Gadshill

Some eight or ten.

1   *John of Gaunt*

King Henry's father (whose name
came from his birthplace in Ghent,
a city in Flanders). Falstaff puns on
the sense of *gaunt* as "emaciated."

2   *happy man be his dole*

A proverbial expression, meaning
"Good luck to us all."

Falstaff

Zounds, will they not rob us?

Prince

What, a coward, Sir John Paunch?

Falstaff

Indeed, I am not John of Gaunt,[1] your grandfather, but

yet no coward, Hal.   65

Prince

test   Well, we leave that to the proof.°

Poins

Sirrah Jack, thy horse stands behind the hedge. When

thou need'st him, there thou shalt find him. Farewell,

and stand fast.

Falstaff

i.e., Poins   Now cannot I strike him,° if I should be hanged.   70

Prince

[*aside to* **Poins**] Ned, where are our disguises?

Poins

aside; hidden   [*aside to* **Prince**] Here, hard by. Stand close.°

[**Prince** *and* **Poins** *exit.*]

Falstaff

Now, my masters, happy man be his dole,[2] say I. Every

man to his business.

Enter the **Travelers**.

First Traveler

Come, neighbor; the boy shall lead our horses down   75

stretch   the hill. We'll walk afoot awhile and ease° our legs.

Thieves

Stand!

Travelers

Jesus bless us!

1   *whoreson caterpillars*

    Nasty parasites

2   *your store*

    All your possessions

3   *grandjurors*

    **Wealthy men. Since only men
    who owned a certain amount of
    property could sit on grand juries,
    grandjurors were necessarily rich.**

4   *We'll jure ye*

    **Mocking: "We'll show you who the
    jurors are"**

5   *no equity stirring*

    No justice anywhere

Falstaff

Strike! Down with them! Cut the villains' throats! Ah,

overfed   whoreson caterpillars,[1] bacon-fed° knaves! They hate   80

Rob   us youth. Down with them! Fleece° them!

Travelers

Oh, we are undone, both we and ours forever!

Falstaff

pot-bellied   Hang, ye gorbellied° knaves! Are ye undone? No,

misers   ye fat chuffs.° I would your store[2] were here. On,

pigs; fat men   bacons,° on! What, ye knaves? Young men must live.   85

You are grandjurors,[3] are ye? We'll jure ye,[4] faith.

Here they rob them and bind them. They exit.

Enter the **Prince** *and* **Poins**.

Prince

The thieves have bound the true men. Now could thou

and I rob the thieves and go merrily to London, it

conversation topic   would be argument° for a week, laughter for a month,

and a good jest forever.   90

Poins

Stand close; I hear them coming.

[**Prince** *and* **Poins** *hide.*]

Enter the thieves again.

Falstaff

Come, my masters; let us share, and then to horse

If / complete   before day. An° the Prince and Poins be not two arrant°

cowards, there's no equity stirring.[5] There's no more

valor in that Poins than in a wild duck.   95

As they are sharing, **Prince**

and **Poins** *set upon them.*

Prince

Your money!

Poins

Villains!

> *They all run away, and* **Falstaff**, *after a blow or two,*
> *runs away too, leaving the booty behind them.*

Prince

Got with much ease. Now merrily to horse.

The thieves are all scattered and possessed with fear

So strongly that they dare not meet each other.   100

Each takes his fellow for an officer.

Away, good Ned. Falstaff sweats to death

bastes (with fat) And lards° the lean earth as he walks along.

Were 't not for laughing, I should pity him.

Poins

How the fat rogue roared!   *They exit.*   105

1   letter

Though the identity of the letter
writer remains unspecified, the
letter clearly comes from a nobleman declining an offer to join the
rebellion against King Henry.

2   *there*

I.e., the place where the rebels have
gathered

3   *hind*

Coward (literally a female deer, a
timid animal)

4   *Douglas*

Archibald, Earl of Douglas; see
1.3.257 and note.

Act 2, Scene 3

*Enter **Hotspur** alone, reading a letter.*[1]

Hotspur

"But, for mine own part, my lord, I could be well
contented to be there,[2] in respect of the love I bear
your house."° He could be contented; why is he not,
then? In respect of the love he bears our house—he
shows in this he loves his own barn better than he   5
loves our house. Let me see some more. "The purpose
you undertake is dangerous." Why, that's certain. 'Tis
dangerous to take° a cold, to sleep, to drink; but I tell
you, my Lord Fool, out of this nettle, danger, we pluck
this flower, safety. "The purpose you undertake is   10
dangerous, the friends you have named uncertain, the
time itself unsorted,° and your whole plot too light°
for the counterpoise° of so great an opposition." Say
you so? Say you so? I say unto you again, you are a shallow, cowardly hind,[3] and you lie. What a lack-brain°   15
is this! By the Lord, our plot is a good plot as ever was
laid, our friends true and constant—a good plot,
good friends, and full of expectation;° an excellent
plot, very good friends. What a frosty-spirited rogue
is this! Why, my Lord of York° commends the plot   20
and the general course of the action. Zounds, an° I
were now by° this rascal, I could brain him with his
lady's fan. Is there not my father, my uncle, and myself, Lord Edmund Mortimer, my Lord of York, and
Owen Glendower? Is there not, besides, the Douglas?[4]   25
Have I not all their letters to meet me in arms by the
ninth of the next month, and are they not some of
them set forward already? What a pagan rascal is

family (line 3 gloss)
i.e., get (line 8 gloss)
unsuitable / weak (line 12 gloss)
counterbalance (line 13 gloss)
idiot (line 15 gloss)
promise (line 18 gloss)
i.e., Archbishop Scroop (line 20 gloss)
if (line 21 gloss)
near (line 22 gloss)

1   *What a pagan rascal is this—an infidel!*

Hotspur characterizes the letter writer using the rhetoric of a crusade or holy war—the unreliable gentleman is a *pagan* and an *infidel* as opposed to a Christian. Earlier, in 1.1., Henry had made a commitment to embark on an actual crusade to the Holy Land. Here, Hotspur brings crusading terminology inward, from the Holy Land to the realm itself, unwittingly undermining the legitimacy of his own cause through the exaggerated rhetoric.

2   *I could divide myself and go to buffets*

I could divide myself in half and fight with myself (i.e., I'm angry with myself).

3   *dish of skim milk*

I.e., worthless person

4   *my treasures and my rights*

The intimacy that is both a pleasure and a right of marriage

5   *thick-eyed*

Heavy-eyed (from care or exhaustion)

6   *terms of manage*

Horseman's terms

7   *sallies and retires*

Advances and retreats

8   *palisadoes*

Stakes driven into the ground as barriers to advancing soldiers

9   *basilisks*

Large cannon, named for a creature from classical mythology whose breath and look were fatal

10 *culverin*

An exceptionally long-ranged cannon

this—an infidel![1] Ha! You shall see now in very sincer-
go to   ity of fear and cold heart will he to° the King and lay   30
open all our proceedings. Oh, I could divide myself and
urging   go to buffets[2] for moving° such a dish of skim milk[3]
to   with° so honorable an action! Hang him; let him tell
the King. We are prepared. I will set forward tonight.

Enter his lady, [**Lady Percy**].

How now, Kate? I must leave you within these two   35
hours.
Lady Percy
O my good lord, why are you thus alone?
For what offense have I this fortnight been
A banished woman from my Harry's bed?
Tell me, sweet lord, what is 't that takes from thee   40
appetite   Thy stomach,° pleasure, and thy golden sleep?
Why dost thou bend thine eyes upon the earth
And start so often when thou sit'st alone?
Why hast thou lost the fresh blood in thy cheeks
And given my treasures and my rights[4] of thee   45
bad-tempered   To thick-eyed[5] musing and curst° melancholy?
restless / stayed awake   In thy faint° slumbers I by thee have watched°
And heard thee murmur tales of iron wars,
Speak terms of manage[6] to thy bounding steed,
Cry "Courage! To the field!" And thou hast talked   50
Of sallies and retires,[7] of trenches, tents,
fortifications   Of palisadoes,[8] frontiers,° parapets,
Of basilisks,[9] of cannon, culverin,[10]
Of prisoners' ransom and of soldiers slain,
violent   And all the currents of a heady° fight.   55
Thy spirit within thee hath been so at war,

1   *Roan*

Apparently, the horse's name,
obviously derived from the color of
its coat, dark red with white or gray
hairs mixed in.

2   *crop-ear*

Horse with the top of its ears
trimmed

3   *Oh, Esperance!*

A reference to the motto of the
Percy family (repeated at 5.2.96),
which in full was *Esperance ma
Comforte*, or "Hope is my strength."

And thus hath so bestirred thee in thy sleep,

That beads of sweat have stood upon thy brow

newly stirred up   Like bubbles in a late-disturbèd° stream,

expressions   And in thy face strange motions° have appeared,   60

Such as we see when men restrain their breath

command   On some great sudden hest.° Oh, what portents are

these?

serious   Some heavy° business hath my lord in hand,

And I must know it, else he loves me not.

Hotspur

—What, ho!

[*Enter* **Servant**.]

(of letters)   Is Gilliams with the packet° gone?   65

Servant

He is, my lord, an hour ago.

Hotspur

Hath Butler brought those horses from the sheriff?

Servant

just   One horse, my lord, he brought even° now.

Hotspur

What horse? Roan,[1] a crop-ear,[2] is it not?

Servant

It is, my lord.

Hotspur

That Roan shall be my throne.   70

mount   Well, I will back° him straight. Oh, Esperance![3]

Bid Butler lead him forth into the park.   [**Servant** *exits*.]

Lady Percy

But hear you, my lord.

Hotspur

What say'st thou, my lady?

1   *weasel*

Proverbially irritable animal

2   *stir / About his title*

Act to claim the throne

3   *So far afoot, I shall be weary, love.*

Hotspur deflects Lady Percy's attempt to keep him from leaving by mockingly completing her sentence.

4   *Love? I love thee not.*

Hotspur teasingly affirms Lady Percy's earlier accusation: since he will not tell her why he is leaving, he must not love her.

5   *mammets*

Dolls or puppets. Editors often suggest that this term refers to breasts (from the Latin word for breast, *mamma*), linking this line with the sexual double entendres of the line following. While this sense is possible, the word *mammet* (or *maumet*) often indicates a false idol, relating to the common belief that Muslims worshipped an idol by the name of *maumet* or *Mahomet*. Percy's use of the word suggests a link to his language at 2.3.28–29.

6   *cracked crowns*

(1) bloodied heads; (2) counterfeit coins (a *crown* was a coin worth five shillings)

7   *pass them current*

(1) pass them (i.e., the injuries) on to others; (2) keep them (i.e., the coins) in circulation

Lady Percy

i.e., What purpose What° is it carries you away?

Hotspur

                Why, my horse,

My love, my horse.

Lady Percy

               Out, you mad-headed ape!   75

cantankerousness A weasel[1] hath not such a deal of spleen°

As you are tossed with. In faith,

I'll know your business, Harry, that I will.

I fear my brother Mortimer doth stir

About his title,[2] and hath sent for you   80

strengthen To line° his enterprise; but if you go—

Hotspur

So far afoot, I shall be weary, love.[3]

Lady Percy

small parrot Come, come, you paraquito;° answer me

Directly unto this question that I ask.

In faith, I'll break thy little finger, Harry,   85

An if thou wilt not tell me all things true.

Hotspur

Away, away, you trifler. Love? I love thee not.[4]

I care not for thee, Kate. This is no world

joust (i.e., kiss) To play with mammets[5] and to tilt° with lips.

We must have bloody noses and cracked crowns,[6]   90

i.e., save And pass them current[7] too.—God s'° me, my horse!

—What say'st thou, Kate? What would'st thou have

    with me?

Lady Percy

Do you not love me? Do you not indeed?

Well, do not then, for since you love me not,

I will not love myself. Do you not love me?   95

Nay, tell me if you speak in jest or no.

1   *reason whereabout*

     Wonder why (I am going)

2   *Whither I must, I must*

     Where I have to go, I have to go.

3   *a woman*

     **Women were thought to be unable
     to control their talkative nature.**

4   *closer*

     Better at keeping a secret

Hotspur

Come; wilt thou see me ride?
And when I am a-horseback, I will swear
I love thee infinitely. But hark you, Kate,
I must not have you henceforth question me   100
Whither I go, nor reason whereabout.[1]
Whither I must, I must,[2] and to conclude,
This evening must I leave you, gentle Kate.
I know you wise, but yet no farther wise
Than Harry Percy's wife. Constant you are,   105
But yet a woman,[3] and for secrecy
No lady closer,[4] for I well believe
Thou wilt not utter what thou dost not know—
And so far will I trust thee, gentle Kate.

Lady Percy

How? So far?   110

Hotspur

Not an inch further. But hark you, Kate,
Whither I go, thither shall you go too.
Today will I set forth, tomorrow you.
Will this content you, Kate?

Lady Percy

necessity   It must, of force.°

They exit.

1   *three or fourscore*

     60 or 80 (a *score* is 20)

2   *I have sounded the very bass string of humility.*

     I.e., I have behaved as humbly as I possibly can.

3   *a leash of drawers*

     Three tapsters. A *leash* usually referred to a trio of hunting dogs tied together.

4   *Corinthian*

     Convivial fellow. In the Bible, St. Paul's first letter to the *Corinthians* upbraids them for their riotous and dissipated behavior.

5   *dyeing scarlet*

     Refers to the drinker's bloodshot eyes and red complexion

6   *breathe in your watering*

     Pause in your drinking

7   *they cry "Hem!"*

     They clear their throats (a sound used as a charge to encourage drinking); i.e., drink up.

8   *Play it off!*

     Drink it down!

9   *I am so good a proficient in one quarter of an hour that I can drink with any tinker in his own language during my life.*

     I am so good at this that within 15 minutes I can make friends with any sort of person for the rest of my life. (*Tinkers* were proverbially heavy drinkers.)

10   *pennyworth of sugar*

     Small amount of sugar. Taverns sold sugar to sweeten wine.

11   *bastard*

     A Spanish wine, often sweetened with sugar (and thus *bastard*, or "adulterated")

12   *the Half-moon*

     Name of one of the rooms in the tavern

Act 2, Scene 4

*Enter **Prince** and **Poins**.*

Prince

stuffy Ned, prithee, come out of that fat° room and lend me
thy hand to laugh a little.

Poins

Where hast been, Hal?

Prince

blockheads With three or four loggerheads,° amongst three or
casks (of liquor) fourscore[1] hogsheads.° I have sounded the very bass   5
string of humility.[2] Sirrah, I am sworn brother to a
leash of drawers[3] and can call them all by their Chris-
tian° names, as "Tom," "Dick," and "Francis." They take
it already, upon their salvation, that, though I be but
Prince of Wales, yet I am the king of courtesy, and   10
fellow tell me flatly I am no proud jack,° like Falstaff, but a
Corinthian,[4] a lad of mettle, a good boy—by the Lord,
so they call me—and when I am king of England, I
shall command all the good lads in Eastcheap. They
call drinking deep "dyeing scarlet,"[5] and when you   15
breathe in your watering,[6] they cry "Hem!"[7] and
bid you "Play it off!"[8] To conclude, I am so good a
proficient in one quarter of an hour that I can drink
with any tinker in his own language during my life.[9]
I tell thee, Ned, thou hast lost much honor that thou   20
wert not with me in this action; but, sweet Ned—to
sweeten which name of Ned, I give thee this pennyworth of sugar,[10] clapped even now into my hand by an
waiter underskinker,° one that never spake other English in
his life than "Eight shillings and sixpence," and "You   25
coming; right away are welcome," with this shrill addition, "Anon,° anon,
Put on the bill sir.—Score° a pint of bastard[11] in the Half-moon,"[12]

1   *puny drawer*

Inexperienced waiter

2   *the Pomgarnet, Ralph*

"The Pomegranate" is the name of
a room in the tavern, while *Ralph* is
presumably the name of another
waiter.

3   *serve*

I.e., as an apprentice. Apprentices were usually bound to their
masters when they were between
the ages of 12 and 14 and served for
seven years. In the following dia-
logue, Prince Henry tempts Francis
to leave his apprenticeship, to
which he is legally bound, in order
to test how far his new loyalty to the
Prince will go.

4   *By 'r lady*

By our Lady (i.e., the Virgin Mary)

5   *a long lease for the clinking of pewter*

A long time to spend learning to
be a tapster. *Pewter* was a common
material for cups in the Elizabethan
period.

or so. But, Ned, to drive away the time till Falstaff

side room come, I prithee, do thou stand in some by-room° while
purpose I question my puny drawer[1] to what end° he gave me   30
stop the sugar; and do thou never leave° calling "Francis,"
that his tale to me may be nothing but "Anon." Step
example aside, and I'll show thee a precedent.°   [**Poins** *exits.*]

Poins

[*within*] Francis!

Prince

[*calling to* **Poins**] Thou art perfect.   35

Poins

[*within*] Francis!

Enter [**Francis**, *a*] *drawer.*

Francis

Anon, anon, sir.—Look down into the Pomgarnet,
Ralph.[2]

Prince

Come hither, Francis.

Francis

My lord?   40

Prince

How long hast thou to serve,[3] Francis?

Francis

Forsooth, five years, and as much as to—

Poins

[*within*] Francis!

Francis

Anon, anon, sir.

Prince

Five year! By 'r lady,[4] a long lease for the clinking of   45
pewter![5] But, Francis, darest thou be so valiant as to

1   *show it a fair pair of heels*

     I.e., by departing

2   *Michaelmas*

     September 29 (a Christian holy day
     honoring the archangel Michael)

apprenticeship contract play the coward with thy indenture,° and show it a fair
pair of heels,[1] and run from it?

Francis

Bibles O Lord, sir, I'll be sworn upon all the books° in
England, I could find in my heart— 50

Poins

[*within*] Francis!

Francis

Anon, sir.

Prince

How old art thou, Francis?

Francis

Let me see: about Michaelmas[2] next, I shall be—

Poins

[*within*] Francis! 55

Francis

wait Anon, sir. [*to* **Prince**] Pray, stay° a little, my lord.

Prince

Nay, but hark you, Francis: for the sugar thou gavest
me,'twas a pennyworth, was 't not?

Francis

wish O Lord, I would° it had been two!

Prince

I will give thee for it a thousand pound. Ask me when 60
thou wilt, and thou shalt have it.

Poins

[*within*] Francis!

Francis

Anon, anon.

Prince

Anon, Francis? No, Francis, but tomorrow, Francis; or,
Francis, o' Thursday; or indeed, Francis, when thou 65
wilt. But, Francis—

1   *rob*

I.e., by abandoning your apprenticeship and *robbing* your master of
the work you owe him

2   *leathern jerkin, crystal-button, not-
pated, agate-ring, puke-stocking, caddis-
garter, smooth-tongue, Spanish-pouch*

Prince Henry describes Francis's
master as a series of possessions
that mark his pretentions to wealth
and importance: he wears a leather
jacket (*jerkin*) with *crystal buttons* and
dark (*puke*) stockings, an *agate ring*,
and garters made from *caddis*, a less
costly substitute for expensive silk.
He keeps his hair cut short (he is
not-pated), speaks obsequiously to
his customers, and carries a leather
bag that marks his trade.

3   *your brown bastard is your only drink*

The only thing to drink is *brown
bastard*, a sweet Spanish wine.

4   *Barbary*

Northern Africa, where most of
England's sugar came from

5   *come to so much*

Be worth so much. Prince Henry
seems to be trying to confuse
Francis as the Prince basically tells
the waiter to be content with his
tavern job.

Francis

My lord?

Prince

Wilt thou rob [1] this leathern jerkin, crystal-button,
not-pated, agate-ring, puke-stocking, caddis-garter,
smooth-tongue, Spanish-pouch [2]—   70

Francis

O Lord, sir, who do you mean?

Prince

Why, then, your brown bastard is your only drink, [3] for
jacket   look you, Francis, your white canvas doublet° will
become dirty / i.e., sugar   sully.° In Barbary, [4] sir, it° cannot come to so much. [5]

Francis

What, sir?   75

Poins

[*within*] Francis!

Prince

Away, you rogue! Dost thou not hear them call?
                    Here they both call him. [**Francis**] *the drawer stands*
                          amazed, not knowing which way to go.

                    Enter **Vintner**.

Vintner

What, stand'st thou still and hear'st such a calling?
Look to the guests within.   [**Francis** *exits.*]
My lord, old Sir John with half a dozen more are at the   80
door. Shall I let them in?

Prince

Let them alone awhile, and then open the door.
                                        [**Vintner** *exits.*]

Poins!

1   *I am now of all humors*

     I.e., I'm disposed to try anything.
     Renaissance physiology identified
     four bodily fluids or *humors* that
     regulated physical condition, tem-
     perament, and emotions (namely,
     choler, blood, bile, and phlegm).
     Perhaps because of his experience
     in the tavern, the Prince claims to
     be well versed in all the moods and
     temperaments that have ever been
     felt by human beings, from the
     beginnings of history (the days of
     Adam, the first man) to the *present*
     time.

2   *Goodman*

     Honorific for someone not of noble
     birth

3   *His industry is upstairs and downstairs*

     His labors consist entirely of run-
     ning up and down stairs.

4   *parcel of a reckoning*

     Entry on a bill

5   *he that kills me*

     He that kills. Here, *me* is a colloquial
     form, based on the Latin ethical
     dative, that calls attention to the
     speaker.

Enter **Poins**.

Poins

Anon, anon, sir.

Prince

Sirrah, Falstaff and the rest of the thieves are at the   85
door. Shall we be merry?

Poins

As merry as crickets, my lad. But hark ye, what
game cunning match° have you made with this jest of the
point drawer? Come; what's the issue?°

Prince

I am now of all humors¹ that have showed themselves   90
humors since the old days of Goodman² Adam to the
youthful pupil° age of this present twelve o'clock at midnight.

[*Enter* **Francis**.]

What's o'clock, Francis?

Francis

Anon, anon, sir.   [**Francis** *exits.*]

Prince

That ever this fellow should have fewer words than a   95
i.e., and still be parrot, and yet° the son of a woman! His industry is
upstairs and downstairs,³ his eloquence the parcel of a
reckoning.⁴ I am not yet of Percy's mind, the Hotspur
of the north, he that kills me⁵ some six or seven
dozen of Scots at a breakfast, washes his hands, and   100
says to his wife, "Fie upon this quiet life! I want work."
"O my sweet Harry," says she, "how many hast thou
drink killed today?" "Give my roan horse a drench,"° says he,
and answers "Some fourteen," an hour after, "A trifle,
a trifle." I prithee, call in Falstaff. I'll play Percy, and   105

1   *that damned brawn*

I.e., Falstaff. *Brawn* is meat from a boar.

2   Rivo!

A drinker's exclamation, of unknown origin and meaning

3   *Ribs*

Fatty rib meat (i.e., Falstaff)

4   *Tallow*

Fat drippings (again, an epithet for Falstaff)

5   *I'll sew netherstocks and mend them, and foot them too*

I'll sew stockings and repair them, and mend the feet on them, too. Falstaff complains of having worn his stockings out from excessive walking.

6   *Titan*

The sun. The comparison is obscure, but the sense seems to be that Falstaff resembles melting butter as he sweats at the Prince's insults.

7   *compound*

Mixture of flesh and sweat (i.e., Falstaff)

8   *lime*

Calcium oxide (often added to wines as a preservative)

9   *shotten herring*

Herring that has already spawned and is thin and weak

10 *while*

Current (bad) times

11 *weaver*

Because a significant number of weavers were also zealous Protestants from Holland, they were often said to sing Psalms from the Bible as they worked. Congregational psalm singing was a standard feature of radical Protestant worship services and home life.

that damned brawn [1] shall play Dame Mortimer his
wife. "*Rivo!*" [2] says the drunkard. Call in Ribs; [3] call in
Tallow. [4]

Enter **Falstaff**, [**Gadshill**, **Peto**, *and* **Bardolph**,
followed by **Francis** *with wine*].

Poins

Welcome, Jack. Where hast thou been?

Falstaff

A plague of all cowards, I say, and a vengeance too!   110
Marry and amen!—Give me a cup of sack, boy.—Ere
I lead this life long, I'll sew netherstocks and mend
them, and foot them too. [5] A plague of all cowards!
—Give me a cup of sack, rogue. —Is there no virtue
extant?   *He drinketh.*   115

Prince

Didst thou never see Titan [6] kiss a dish of butter—piti-
ful-hearted Titan!—that° melted at the sweet tale° of   *i.e., the butter / flattery*
the sun's? If thou didst, then behold that compound. [7]

Falstaff

[*to* **Francis**] You rogue, here's lime [8] in this sack too.
—There is nothing but roguery to be found in villain-   120
ous man, yet a coward is worse than a cup of sack with
lime in it. A villainous coward! Go thy ways, old Jack.
Die when thou wilt. If manhood, good manhood,
be not forgot upon the face of the Earth, then am I a
shotten herring. [9] There lives not three good men un-   125
hanged in England, and one of them is fat and grows
old, God help the while. [10] A bad world, I say. I would°   *wish*
I were a weaver. [11] I could sing psalms, or anything. A
plague of all cowards, I say still.

1   *dagger of lath*

     Wooden dagger. Medieval morality
     plays, which pitted allegorical
     figures against one another in a
     contest for Christian salvation,
     often featured a comic Vice, a
     figure who represented sin and
     irreverence and typically carried a
     dagger of lath.

2   *whoreson*

     A term of contempt (whose literal
     meaning is generally insignificant)

3   *who sees your back*

     Who sees you run away

4   *All is one for that.*

     That makes no difference.

Prince

How now, woolsack,° what mutter you?   130

bale of wool

Falstaff

A king's son! If I do not beat thee out of thy kingdom
with a dagger of lath[1] and drive all thy subjects afore
thee like a flock of wild geese, I'll never wear hair on
my face more. You, Prince of Wales!

Prince

Why, you whoreson[2] round man, what's the matter?   135

Falstaff

Are not you a coward? Answer me to that—and Poins
there?

Poins

Zounds, ye fat paunch, an° ye call me coward, by the
Lord, I'll stab thee.

if

Falstaff

I call thee coward? I'll see thee damned ere I call thee   140
coward, but I would give a thousand pound I could
run as fast as thou canst. You are straight enough in
the shoulders; you care not who sees your back.[3] Call
you that backing of your friends? A plague upon such
backing! Give me them that will face me.—Give me a   145
cup of sack. I am a rogue if I drunk today.

Prince

O villain, thy lips are scarce wiped since thou drunk'st
last.

Falstaff

All is one for that.[4] (*He drinketh.*) A plague of all cowards, still say I.   150

Prince

What's the matter?

1   *at half-sword*

   Fighting closely

2   Ecce signum!

   Here see the evidence! (Latin)

3   *All would not do.*

   Anything I did was inadequate.

Falstaff

What's the matter? There be four of us here have ta'en

very a thousand pound this day° morning.

Prince

Where is it, Jack? Where is it?

Falstaff

i.e., hundred men / only Where is it? Taken from us it is. A hundred° upon poor°   155
four of us.

Prince

What? A hundred, man?

Falstaff

I am a rogue if I were not at half-sword[1] with a dozen
of them two hours together. I have 'scaped by miracle.

jacket I am eight times thrust through the doublet,° four   160
trousers / shield through the hose,° my buckler° cut through and
so it looked like through, my sword hacked like° a handsaw. *Ecce signum!*[2]
i.e., fought I never dealt° better since I was a man. All would not
do.[3] A plague of all cowards! [*points to* **Gadshill**, **Peto**
and **Bardolph**] Let them speak. If they speak more   165
or less than truth, they are villains and the sons of
darkness.

Prince

Speak, sirs: how was it?

Gadshill

We four set upon some dozen.

Falstaff

Sixteen at least, my lord.   170

Bardolph

And bound them.

Peto

No, no, they were not bound.

1   *or I am a Jew else*

      **Or you should not trust me at all
      (reflecting the anti-Semitism preva-
      lent in Elizabethan England)**

2   *sharing*

      Dividing the spoils

3   *ward*

      Defensive position (in fencing)

4   *let drive at me*

      Attacked me

5   *came all afront*

      Confronted me

Falstaff

You rogue, they were bound, every man of them, or I

Hebrew (i.e., authentic)   am a Jew else,[1] an Ebrew° Jew.

Bardolph

new   As we were sharing,[2] some six or seven fresh° men set   175
upon us.

Falstaff

And unbound the rest, and then come in the other.

Prince

What? Fought you with them all?

Falstaff

All? I know not what you call "all," but if I fought not
with fifty of them I am a bunch of radish. If there were   180
not two- or three-and-fifty upon poor old Jack, then
am I no two-leggèd creature.

Prince

Pray God you have not murdered some of them.

Falstaff

trounced   Nay, that's past praying for. I have peppered° two of
killed   them. Two I am sure I have paid,° two rogues in buck-   185
ram suits. I tell thee what, Hal, if I tell thee a lie, spit in
my face, call me horse. Thou knowest my old ward.[3]
stood / sword   Here I lay,° and thus I bore my point.° Four rogues in
buckram let drive at me.[4]

Prince

What? Four? Thou said'st but two even now.   190

Falstaff

Four, Hal; I told thee four.

Poins

Ay, ay, he said four.

Falstaff

forcefully   These four came all afront[5] and mainly° thrust at

1   *these hilts*

I.e., this sword (*hilts* referring
specifically to the place where the
handle and cross guard intersect)

2   *mark thee*

Listen to what you say.

3   *points*

Falstaff uses *points* to mean
"swords," but Poins puns on a
second meaning: *points* were also
laces by which *hose* (trousers) were
held up.

4   *followed me close*

Followed close behind. (*Me* is a
colloquial use similar to the Latin
ethical dative; see 2.4.99 and note.)

5   *with a thought*

As fast as a thought

me. I made me no more ado, but took all their seven

shield   points in my target,° thus.   195

Prince

just   Seven? Why, there were but four even° now.

Falstaff

coarse linen   In buckram?°

Poins

Ay, four in buckram suits.

Falstaff

Seven, by these hilts,[1] or I am a villain else.

Prince

[*aside to* **Poins**] Prithee, let him alone. We shall have   200
more anon.

Falstaff

Dost thou hear me, Hal?

Prince

Ay, and mark thee[2] too, Jack.

Falstaff

Do so, for it is worth the listening to. These nine in
buckram that I told thee of—   205

Prince

So, two more already.

Falstaff

Their points[3] being broken—

Poins

Down fell their hose.

Falstaff

Began to give me ground, but I followed me close,[4]
came in foot and hand, and, with a thought,[5] seven of   210
the eleven I paid.

Prince

Oh, monstrous! Eleven buckram men grown out of
two!

1   *Kendal green*

Cheap green woolen cloth made in Kendal, in north west England, and often worn by forest dwellers and outlaws

2   *strappado*

Torture device upon which prisoners were suspended in the air by a rope attached to the hands, which were shackled behind their back

3   *racks*

Torture devices on which the prisoner's arms and legs were pulled in opposite directions by means of rollers at either end of a frame

4   *sanguine*

Red-faced, but also with the implication that he has a *sanguine* or hopeful temperament. In this latter sense, *sanguine coward* is something of a contradiction in terms.

5   *bed-presser*

(1) licentious man; (2) man who breaks beds (because of his weight)

6   *eelskin*

One of a series of images pointing at the Prince's thinness (in response to the Prince's images of Falstaff's fatness)

7   *bull's pizzle*

Bull's penis. When cured and stretched, a *bull's pizzle* was often used as a whip.

Falstaff

But as the devil would have it, three misbegotten
knaves in Kendal green [1] came at my back and let   215
drive at me, for it was so dark, Hal, that thou couldst
not see thy hand.

Prince

These lies are like their father that begets them: gross
as a mountain, open, palpable. Why, thou claybrained

thick-headed guts, thou knotty-pated° fool, thou whoreson,   220

lump of fat obscene, greasy tallow-catch°—

Falstaff

What, art thou mad? Art thou mad? Is not the truth
the truth?

Prince

Why, how couldst thou know these men in Kendal
green, when it was so dark thou couldst not see thy   225
hand? Come, tell us your reason. What sayest thou to
this?

Poins

Come, your reason, Jack, your reason.

Falstaff

if What, upon compulsion? Zounds, an° I were at the
strappado [2] or all the racks [3] in the world, I would not   230
tell you on compulsion. Give you a reason on compul-
sion? If reasons were as plentiful as blackberries, I
would give no man a reason upon compulsion, I.

Prince

I'll be no longer guilty of this sin. This sanguine [4]
coward, this bed-presser, [5] this horseback-breaker,   235
this huge hill of flesh—

Falstaff

emaciated person / cow's 'Sblood, you starveling,° you eelskin, [6] you dried neat's°

dried cod tongue, you bull's pizzle, [7] you stockfish!° Oh, for

1   *tailor's-yard*

      (1) tailor's yardstick; (2) tailor's
      penis (tailors were proverbially
      impotent)

2   *sheath*

      (1) knife case; (2) foreskin

3   *bowcase*

      Long, narrow sheath for an archer's
      bow

4   *vile standing tuck*

      (1) rapier that has lost its flexibility,
      hence useless; (2) erect penis

5   *Hercules*

      Hero of classical mythology

6   *The lion will not touch the true prince.*

      This commonplace, derived from
      Greek and Latin mythology, held
      that a lion would instinctively
      recognize royalty, even in disguise,
      and refuse to attack.

breath to utter what is like thee! You tailor's-yard,[1]
you sheath,[2] you bowcase,[3] you vile standing tuck [4]—   240

Prince

Well, breathe awhile and then to it again, and when
thou hast tired thyself in base comparisons, hear me
speak but this.

Poins

Mark, Jack.

Prince

We two saw you four set on four, and bound them   245
and were masters of their wealth. Mark now how a
plain tale shall put you down. Then did we two set on
frightened   you four and, with a word, outfaced° you from your
prize, and have it, yea, and can show it you here in the
house. And, Falstaff, you carried your guts away as   250
nimbly, with as quick dexterity, and roared for mercy,
kept running   and still run° and roared, as ever I heard bull-calf.
put nicks in   What a slave art thou to hack° thy sword, as thou hast
done, and then say it was in fight! What trick, what
sanctuary   device, what starting-hole° canst thou now find out to   255
hide thee from this open and apparent shame?

Poins

Come, let's hear, Jack. What trick hast thou now?

Falstaff

By the Lord, I knew ye as well as He that made ye.
appropriate for   Why, hear you, my masters, was it for° me to kill the
heir apparent? Should I turn upon the true prince?   260
Why, thou knowest I am as valiant as Hercules,[5] but
i.e., you can't escape   beware° instinct. The lion will not touch the true
prince.[6] Instinct is a great matter. I was now a coward
on instinct. I shall think the better of myself, and
thee, during my life—I for a valiant lion, and thou for   265
a true prince. But, by the Lord, lads, I am glad you have

1   *clap to*

     Close

2   *Watch tonight; pray tomorrow.*

     **Stay up (reveling) tonight; repent
     for it tomorrow.**

3   *play extempore*

     Improvised play

4   *royal man*

     **Prince Henry puns on the sense of
     noble (in *nobleman* in line 278) and
     royal as coins; a royal was worth
     more, and Prince Henry suggests
     that the *nobleman* should be given
     the difference to make him a *royal
     man* and sent away again.**

5   *Gravity*

     **Falstaff refers to the nobleman in a
     personification of his seriousness
     and respectability.**

the money. [*calls*] Hostess, clap to [1] the doors.— Watch
tonight; pray tomorrow.[2] Gallants, lads, boys, hearts
of gold, all the titles of good fellowship come to you.
What, shall we be merry? Shall we have a play extem-   270
pore?[3]

Prince

(I am) content / subject   Content,° and the argument° shall be thy running
away.

Falstaff

if   Ah, no more of that, Hal, an° thou lovest me.

Enter **Hostess**.

Hostess

O Jesu, my lord the Prince!   275

Prince

How now, my lady the hostess, what say'st thou to
me?

Hostess

Marry, my lord, there is a nobleman of the court at
door would speak with you. He says he comes from
your father.   280

Prince

Give him as much as will make him a royal man [4] and
send him back again to my mother.

Falstaff

kind   What manner° of man is he?

Hostess

An old man.

Falstaff

What doth Gravity [5] out of his bed at midnight? Shall   285
I give him his answer?

1   *swear truth out of England but*

     **Insist so passionately on his lies
     that truth would be unrecognizable
     in England unless**

2   *tickle our noses with speargrass*

     **Put the sharp leaves of the spear-
     grass plant up our noses**

3   *that I did not this seven year before*

     **What I have not done for seven
     years**

4   *monstrous devices*

     Outrageous lies

5   *taken with the manner*

     Apprehended with the stolen goods

6   *fire and sword*

     **I.e., weapons (but joking that
     the *fire* was in his face, red from
     excessive drinking, and the *sword*
     sheathed at his side)**

Prince

Prithee do, Jack.

Falstaff

Faith, and I'll send him packing.   *He exits.*

Prince

Now, sirs: [*to* **Gadshill**] by 'r lady, you fought fair.—So
did you, Peto.—So did you, Bardolph.—You are lions   290
too. You ran away upon instinct. You will not touch
the true prince. No, fie!

Bardolph

Faith, I ran when I saw others run.

Prince

Faith, tell me now in earnest, how came Falstaff's
sword so hacked?   295

Peto

Why, he hacked it with his dagger and said he would
swear truth out of England but[1] he would make you
believe it was done in fight, and persuaded us to do
the like.

Bardolph

Yea, and to tickle our noses with speargrass[2] to make   300
smear   them bleed, and then to beslubber° our garments
with it and swear it was the blood of true men. I did
that I did not this seven year before:[3] I blushed to hear
his monstrous devices.[4]

Prince

O villain, thou stolest a cup of sack eighteen years ago,   305
and wert taken with the manner,[5] and ever since thou
spontaneously   hast blushed extempore.° Thou hadst fire and sword[6]
on thy side, and yet thou ran'st away. What instinct
hadst thou for it?

1   *meteors*

Cysts or boils (on Bardoph's face)

2   *exhalations*

Like *meteors*, inflammations or abcesses on Bardolph's face

3   *Hot livers and cold purses.*

I.e., drunkness and poverty

4   *Choler*

An angry temperament was thought to be caused by an excess of *choler*, one of the four essential humors, or bodily fluids.

5   *halter*

Hangman's noose (punning on "collar" and "choler")

6   *bombast*

(1) cotton padding or stuffing (alluding to Falstaff's size and perhaps to the padded costume of the actor playing Falstaff); (2) pompous, exaggerated speech

7   *alderman's thumb-ring*

A seal ring worn by an *alderman*, a town councilor

8   *bladder*

Any bodily organ that can be filled with fluid or air; animal *bladders* were preserved and then inflated to be used as floats or windbags for instruments such as bagpipes

9   *Sir John Bracy*

Perhaps John Brace, a member of Parliament during King Henry's reign

10 *gave Amaimon the bastinado*

Beat *Amaimon* (a devil) with a cudgel

11 *made Lucifer cuckold*

Seduced the devil's wife. Men whose wives were unfaithful were said to be *cuckolds* and to acquire horns on their foreheads as a sign of their disgrace.

12 *swore the devil his true liegeman*

Made the devil swear to be his servant

13 *Welsh hook*

Weapon whose handle formed a crook rather than a cross, and was thus unsuitable for swearing oaths

Bardolph

My lord, do you see these meteors?[1] Do you behold   310
these exhalations?[2]

Prince

I do.

Bardolph

foretell What think you they portend?°

Prince

Hot livers and cold purses.[3]

Bardolph

understood Choler,[4] my lord, if rightly taken.°   315

Prince

arrested No, if rightly taken,° halter.[5]

Enter **Falstaff**.

Here comes lean Jack. Here comes bare-bone.—How
now, my sweet creature of bombast?[6] How long is 't
ago, Jack, since thou sawest thine own knee?

Falstaff

My own knee? When I was about thy years, Hal, I was   320
not an eagle's talon in the waist. I could have crept into
upon any alderman's thumb-ring.[7] A plague of° sighing and
grief! It blows a man up like a bladder.[8] There's villainous news abroad. Here was Sir John Bracy[9] from your
father. You must to the court in the morning. That   325
same mad fellow of the north, Percy, and he of Wales
that gave Amaimon the bastinado,[10] and made Lucifer
cuckold,[11] and swore the devil his true liegeman[12]
upon the cross of a Welsh hook[13]—what a plague call
you him?   330

Poins

Owen Glendower?

1   *hit it*

     Got it right

2   *So did he never the sparrow.*

     **(I may have hit your meaning), but
     Douglas never hit the sparrow.**

3   *we shall buy maidenheads as they buy*
     hobnails

     **We will obtain maidens' virgini-
     ties as cheaply as *hobnails* (small
     nails used in making shoes). Prince
     Henry suggests that hot weather
     and wartime conditions make
     women easy marks.**

Falstaff

Owen, Owen, the same, and his son-in-law Mortimer,
and old Northumberland, and that sprightly Scot
of Scots, Douglas, that runs a-horseback up a hill
perpendicular—   335

Prince

He that rides at high speed and with his pistol kills a
sparrow flying.

Falstaff

You have hit it.[1]

Prince

So did he never the sparrow.[2]

Falstaff

Well, that rascal hath good mettle in him. He will not   340
run.

Prince

Why, what a rascal art thou then to praise him so for
running?

Falstaff

A-horseback, ye cuckoo, but afoot he will not budge
a foot.   345

Prince

Yes, Jack, upon instinct.

Falstaff

I grant ye, upon instinct. Well, he is there too, and one
Scottish soldiers Murdoch, and a thousand blue-caps° more. Worcester
is stolen away tonight. Thy father's beard is turned
white with the news. You may buy land now as cheap   350
as stinking mackerel.

Prince

likely   Why, then, it is like° if there come a hot June and this
persists   civil buffeting hold,° we shall buy maidenheads as
they buy hobnails:[3] by the hundreds.

1   *stand for*

     Pretend to be

2   *joint stool*

     **Stool constructed from various
     pieces of wood joined together
     (finer than a stool made of a single
     wood block)**

3   *leaden dagger*

     **Dagger made from lead and thus
     not useful as a weapon (possibly an
     allusion to the actual stage prop-
     erty used by the actors)**

4   *bald crown*

     bald head

5   *an the fire of grace be not quite out of thee,
     now shalt thou be moved.*

     **If divine grace hasn't completely
     abandoned you, now you will be
     moved (by my performance as the
     King).**

6   *King Cambyses' vein*

     **Like the title character of the
     early Elizabethan tragedy *Cambyses*,
     whose speech is marked by a bom-
     bastic, ranting style**

Falstaff

likely By the mass, lad, thou sayest true. It is like° we shall   355
business have good trading° that way. But tell me, Hal, art not
thou horrible afeard? Thou being heir apparent, could
the world pick thee out three such enemies again as
demon that fiend Douglas, that spirit° Percy, and that devil
Glendower? Art thou not horribly afraid? Doth not thy   360
shudder blood thrill° at it?

Prince

Not a whit, i' faith; I lack some of thy instinct.

Falstaff

scolded Well, thou wilt be horribly chid° tomorrow when thou
comest to thy father. If thou love me, practice an answ   365
er.

Prince

Do thou stand for¹ my father and examine me upon
the particulars of my life.

Falstaff

All right / throne Shall I? Content.° This chair shall be my state,° this
dagger my scepter, and this cushion my crown.

Prince

Thy state is taken for a joint stool,² thy golden scepter   370
for a leaden dagger,³ and thy precious rich crown for a
pitiful bald crown.⁴

Falstaff

if Well, an° the fire of grace be not quite out of thee,
now shalt thou be moved.⁵—Give me a cup of sack to
make my eyes look red, that it may be thought I have   375
wept, for I must speak in passion, and I will do it in
King Cambyses' vein.⁶   [**Falstaff** *sits.*]

Prince

i.e., bow [*bowing*] Well, here is my leg.°

1 *Stand aside, nobility.*

   Make some space, gentlemen.

2 *Queen*

   **Falstaff brings Mistress Quickly into
   the play as Queen to his King Henry,
   but also puns on "quean" meaning
   "whore."**

3 *holds his countenance*

   Keeps a straight face

4 *harlotry players*

   Worthless actors

5 *Peace, good pint-pot. Peace, good tickle-
   brain.*

   **Falstaff addresses the Hostess with
   names that suggest her profes-
   sion as tavern keeper. Tickle-brain is
   strong liquor.**

6 *camomile*

   **The hardy herb camomile multiplies
   easily by growing runners and
   sending down new roots. Here
   and throughout his impersonation
   of King Henry, Falstaff parodies
   the elaborate, self-consciously
   patterned rhetoric made fashionable by John Lyly's prose romance
   Euphues, published in two parts in
   1578 and 1580.**

7 *foolish hanging of thy nether lip*

   **A drooping nether or lower lip was
   considered a sign of licentiousness**

8 *warrant me*

   Assure me (that you are my son)

9 *pointed at*

   Criticized; mocked

10 *This pitch, as ancient writers do report,
   doth defile*

   **An allusion to Ecclesiasticus 13:1
   in the biblical Apocrypha: "Who
   so toucheth pitch shall be defiled
   withal." Pitch is like tar, sticking to
   whomever touches it.**

Falstaff

And here is my speech.—Stand aside, nobility.[1]

Hostess

O Jesu, this is excellent sport, i' faith!   380

Falstaff

Weep not, sweet Queen,[2] for trickling tears are vain.

Hostess

O the father, how he holds his countenance![3]

Falstaff

take away / sorrowful For God's sake, lords, convey° my tristful° Queen,

fill For tears do stop° the floodgates of her eyes.

Hostess

O Jesu, he doth it as like one of these harlotry players[4]   385
as ever I see.

Falstaff

Peace, good pint-pot. Peace, good tickle-brain.[5] [*to*
Prince] Harry, I do not only marvel where thou spend-
est thy time, but also how thou art accompanied. For
though the camomile,[6] the more it is trodden on, the   390
faster it grows, so youth, the more it is wasted, the
sooner it wears. That thou art my son I have partly thy
mother's word, partly my own opinion, but chiefly a
mannerism villainous trick° of thine eye and a foolish hanging of
thy nether lip[7] that doth warrant me.[8] If, then, thou   395
be son to me, here lies the point: why, being son to
me, art thou so pointed at?[9] Shall the blessèd sun of
truant Heaven prove a micher° and eat blackberries? A ques-
i.e., prince tion not to be asked. Shall the son° of England prove a
thief and take purses? A question to be asked. There is   400
a thing, Harry, which thou hast often heard of, and it
is known to many in our land by the name of "pitch."
This pitch, as ancient writers do report, doth defile;[10]
so doth the company thou keepest. For, Harry, now I

1   *in passion*

     (1) sincerely; (2) in suffering; (3) in
     the midst of a passionate theatrical
     performance

2   *an it like*

     If it please

3   *A goodly portly man, i' faith, and a*
     corpulent

     Goodly**, **portly**,* and ***corpulent **each
     mean "fat" as well as "handsome,"
     "distinguished," and "solid,"
     respectively.**

4   *inclining to three score*

     Close to sixty

5   *lewdly given*

     Inclined to bad behavior

6   *If, then, the tree may be known by the*
     fruit, as the fruit by the tree

     **An allusion to Luke 6:44: "Every tree
     is known by its fruit."**

7   *naughty varlet*

     Ill-behaved boy

8   *Depose me?*

     Playing on the word *depose* **is pro-
     vocative and potentially dangerous
     on Falstaff's part, since Prince
     Henry's father gained the throne by
     deposing Richard II.**

9   *rabbit-sucker*

     **Baby rabbit that has not been
     weaned**

10   *poulter's hare*

     **Dead rabbit available for sale in a
     poultry shop**

do not speak to thee in drink, but in tears; not in plea-   405
sure, but in passion;[1] not in words only, but in woes
also. And yet there is a virtuous man whom I have
often noted in thy company, but I know not his name.

Prince
What manner of man, an it like[2] your Majesty?

Falstaff
A goodly portly man, i' faith, and a corpulent;[3] of   410
a cheerful look, a pleasing eye, and a most noble
bearing   carriage,° and, as I think, his age some fifty, or, by 'r
Lady, inclining to three score;[4] and, now I remember
me, his name is Falstaff. If that man should be lewdly
given,[5] he deceiveth me, for, Harry, I see virtue in his   415
looks. If, then, the tree may be known by the fruit,
certainly; decisively   as the fruit by the tree,[6] then peremptorily° I speak it:
there is virtue in that Falstaff. Him keep with; the rest
banish. And tell me now, thou naughty varlet,[7] tell
me, where hast thou been this month?   420

Prince
stand in   Dost thou speak like a king? Do thou stand° for me,
and I'll play my father.

Falstaff
Depose me?[8] If thou dost it half so gravely, so majesti-
cally, both in word and matter, hang me up by the
heels for a rabbit-sucker[9] or a poulter's hare.[10]   425

Prince
seated   [_changing places with_ **Falstaff**] Well, here I am set.°

Falstaff
And here I stand.—[_to the others_] Judge, my masters.

Prince
Now, Harry, whence come you?

Falstaff
My noble lord, from Eastcheap.

1   *'Sblood*

    By Christ's blood

2   *tickle ye for*

    Entertain you as

3   *trunk of humors*

    **Body full of *humors* (bodily fluids;
    see 2.4.90 and note). A *trunk of
    humors* represents an unhealthy
    accumulation of these fluids.**

4   *bolting-hutch*

    Receptacle for sifted flour

5   *dropsies*

    Disease that causes bloating

6   *bombard*

    Container for wine made of leather

7   *Manningtree*

    **Town in Essex on England's east
    coast, the location of a well-known
    fair and cattle market**

8   *Vice*

    **The *Vice*, *Iniquity*, *Ruffian*, and
    Vanity are all personifications
    of wickedness.**

9   *father Ruffian*

    (1) aged thug; (2) old devil

10 *Vanity in years*

    **Old man full of pride and worldly
    desires**

11 *take me with you*

    Make your meaning clear.

Prince

The complaints I hear of thee are grievous. 430

Falstaff

'Sblood,[1] my lord, they are false. [*to the others*] Nay, I'll
tickle ye for[2] a young prince, i' faith.

Prince

Swearest thou? Ungracious boy, henceforth ne'er look
on me. Thou art violently carried away from grace.
There is a devil haunts thee in the likeness of an old fat 435
man. A tun° of man is thy companion. Why dost thou
converse° with that trunk of humors,[3] that bolting-
hutch[4] of beastliness, that swollen parcel of dropsies,[5]
that huge bombard[6] of sack, that stuffed cloakbag° of
guts, that roasted Manningtree[7] ox with the pudding° 440
in his belly, that reverend Vice,[8] that gray° Iniquity,
that father Ruffian,[9] that Vanity in years?[10] Wherein°
is he good, but to taste sack and drink it? Wherein
neat and cleanly but to carve a capon and eat it?
Wherein cunning° but in craft?° Wherein crafty but in 445
villainy? Wherein villainous but in all things? Wherein
worthy but in nothing?

Falstaff

I would your Grace would take me with you.[11] Whom
means your Grace?

Prince

That villainous abominable misleader of youth, 450
Falstaff, that old white-bearded Satan.

Falstaff

My lord, the man I know.

Prince

I know thou dost.

Falstaff

But to say I know more harm in him than in myself

barrel
associate

suitcase
stuffing
gray-haired
In what way

skillful / deceit

1   *saving your reverence*

     A formulaic expression, usually
     used when speaking to a social
     superior, offering an apology for
     disagreeing or saying something
     improper

2   *Pharaoh's lean kine*

     In Genesis 41, the Egyptian Pharaoh
     dreams of seven emaciated cattle
     (*kine*). Joseph interprets the dream
     to mean that seven years of famine
     are coming.

3   *I do; I will.*

     The resolution Prince Henry makes
     here, in the character of his father,
     anticipates the eventual rejection
     of Falstaff at the end of *Henry IV,
     Part Two*.

4   *most monstrous watch*

     Unusually large group of watchmen

5   *the devil rides upon a fiddlestick*

     I.e., what a fuss about nothing

were to say more than I know. That he is old, the more   455
the pity; his white hairs do witness it. But that he is,
saving your reverence,[1] a whoremaster, that I utterly
deny. If sack and sugar be a fault, God help the wicked.

innkeeper If to be old and merry be a sin, then many an old host°
that I know is damned. If to be fat be to be hated, then   460
Pharaoh's lean kine[2] are to be loved. No, my good
lord, banish Peto, banish Bardolph, banish Poins,
but for sweet Jack Falstaff, kind Jack Falstaff, true
Jack Falstaff, valiant Jack Falstaff, and therefore more
valiant being as he is old Jack Falstaff, banish not him   465
thy Harry's company, banish not him thy Harry's company. Banish plump Jack and banish all the world.

Prince
I do; I will.[3]   [*Knocking within.* **Bardolph**, **Hostess**,
and **Francis** *exit.*]

Enter **Bardolph**, *running.*

Bardolph
O my lord, my lord, the sheriff with a most monstrous
watch[4] is at the door.   470
Falstaff
Out, ye rogue. [*to the* **Prince**] Play out the play. I have
much to say in the behalf of that Falstaff.

Enter the **Hostess**.

Hostess
O Jesu, my lord, my lord—
Prince
Heigh, heigh, the devil rides upon a fiddlestick.[5]
What's the matter?   475

1   *Never call a true piece of gold a counter-*
    feit. Thou art essentially made without
    seeming so.

    Don't call me false just because I
    seem to be so. Even you are loyal
    even though you don't always seem
    to be.

2   *deny the sheriff, so*

    Refuse to allow the sheriff to enter,
    so be it.

3   *bringing up*

    (1) upbringing; (2) being arraigned
    in court

4   *walk up above*

    Go upstairs

5   *their date is out*

    Their time has passed; they're no
    longer working.

6   *hue and cry*

    Group of people chasing a criminal
    (referring to the sounds of their
    horns and voices)

Hostess

The sheriff and all the watch are at the door. They are
come to search the house. Shall I let them in?

Falstaff

Dost thou hear, Hal? Never call a true piece of gold a
counterfeit. Thou art essentially made without seem-
ing so.[1]   480

Prince

And thou a natural coward without instinct.

Falstaff

chief premise   I deny your major.° If you will deny the sheriff, so;[2] if
suit / hangman's cart   not, let him enter. If I become° not a cart° as well as
another man, a plague on my bringing up.[3] I hope I
shall as soon be strangled with a halter as another.   485

Prince

tapestry   Go; hide thee behind the arras.° The rest walk up
above.[4]—Now, my masters, for a true face and good
conscience.

Falstaff

Both which I have had, but their date is out;[5] and
therefore I'll hide me.   [*hides behind the arras*]   490

                          [*All but the* **Prince** *and* **Peto** *exit.*]

Prince

Call in the sheriff.

                 Enter **Sheriff** *and the* **Carrier**.

Now, master sheriff, what is your will with me?

Sheriff

First pardon me, my lord. A hue and cry[6]
Hath followed certain men unto this house.

Prince

What men?   495

1   *three hundred marks*

     I.e., 200 pounds; see 2.1.52 and
     note.

2   *Paul's*

     St. Paul's Cathedral (a famous land-
     mark in London)

Sheriff

One of them is well known, my gracious lord,

A gross fat man.

Carrier

As fat as butter.

Prince

The man I do assure you is not here,

For I myself at this time have employed him.   500

pledge   And, sheriff, I will engage° my word to thee

i.e., lunch   That I will by tomorrow dinner° time

Send him to answer thee or any man

with   For anything he shall be charged withal.°

And so let me entreat you leave the house.   505

Sheriff

I will, my lord. There are two gentlemen

Have in this robbery lost three hundred marks.¹

Prince

It may be so. If he have robbed these men,

held responsible   He shall be answerable;° and so farewell.

Sheriff

Good night, my noble lord.   510

Prince

morning   I think it is good morrow,° is it not?

Sheriff

Indeed, my lord, I think it be two o'clock.

                        [**Sheriff** and **Carrier**] *exit.*

Prince

This oily rascal is known as well as Paul's.² Go call him

forth.

Peto

Falstaff! [*pulls back the arras*] Fast asleep behind the   515

snoring   arras, and snorting° like a horse.

1   *2s. 2d.*

Two shillings and two pennies (the
abbreviations are of Latin words: *s.*
is an abbreviation of *sestertius* and *d.*
of *denarius*, silver coins in classical
Rome)

2   *more advantage*

A more appropriate time

3   *a charge of foot*

The command of an infantry unit

4   *his death will be a march of twelve score*

He'll die from marching 240 (*twelve
score*) yards.

Prince

Hark how hard he fetches breath. Search his pockets.

[**Peto**] *searcheth his pockets and findeth certain papers.*

What hast thou found?

Peto

Nothing but papers, my lord.

Prince

Let's see what they be. Read them.   520

Peto

[*reads*] *Item,* a capon, . . . 2s. 2d.[1]

Item, sauce, . . . 4d.

Item, sack, two gallons, . . . 5s. 8d.

Item, anchovies and sack after supper, . . . 2s. 6d.

obulus (halfpenny) *Item,* bread, ob.°   525

Prince

in relation to O monstrous! But one halfpennyworth of bread to°

quantity this intolerable deal° of sack! What there is else, keep

secret close.° We'll read it at more advantage.[2] There let him

sleep till day. I'll to the court in the morning. We must

all to the wars, and thy place shall be honorable. I'll   530

procure this fat rogue a charge of foot,[3] and I know

his death will be a march of twelve score.[4] The money

interest shall be paid back again with advantage.° Be with me

early betimes° in the morning, and so good morrow, Peto.

Peto

Good morrow, good my lord.   535

[*The* **Prince** *closes the arras, and*] *they exit.*

1   *prosperous hope*

    Hope of success

2   *Lancaster*

    I.e., King Henry. Just as Percy re-
    ferred to the King simply as *Boling-
    broke* at 1.3.136, here Glendower
    demonstrates a similarly treason-
    ous unwillingness to acknowledge
    Henry IV as king, using instead his
    title as Duke of Lancaster, inherited
    from his father, John of Gaunt.

3   *cressets*

    I.e., meteors (literally, torches
    suspended from the ceiling or hung
    from poles in iron cages)

Act 3, Scene 1

Enter **Hotspur**, **Worcester**, *Lord* **Mortimer**, [*and*] *Owen*
Glendower.

Mortimer

reliable   These promises are fair, the parties sure,°
beginning   And our induction° full of prosperous hope.[1]

Hotspur

Lord Mortimer and cousin Glendower,
Will you sit down? And uncle Worcester—
A plague upon it, I have forgot the map.   5

Glendower

No, here it is. Sit, cousin Percy,
Sit, good cousin Hotspur, for by that name
As oft as Lancaster[2] doth speak of you
passionate   His cheek looks pale and with a rising° sigh
He wisheth you in Heaven.

Hotspur

                    And you in Hell,   10
As oft as he hears Owen Glendower spoke of.

Glendower

I cannot blame him. At my nativity
face   The front° of Heaven was full of fiery shapes,
Of burning cressets,[3] and at my birth
The frame and huge foundation of the Earth   15
Shaked like a coward.

Hotspur

                    Why, so it would have done
time   At the same season° if your mother's cat
Had but kittened, though yourself had never been
     born.

1   *clipped in with*

    Surrounded by

2   *chides the banks*

    I.e., crashes against the shores

3   *hath read to me*

    **Has instructed me (i.e., can claim to
be my teacher)**

Glendower

I say the Earth did shake when I was born.

Hotspur

And I say the Earth was not of my mind,   20

If you suppose as fearing you it shook.

Glendower

The heavens were all on fire; the Earth did tremble.

Hotspur

Oh, then the Earth shook to see the heavens on fire

And not in fear of your nativity.

Diseasèd nature often times breaks forth   25

outbreaks/fertile In strange eruptions;° oft the teeming° Earth

Is with a kind of colic pinched and vexed

By the imprisoning of unruly wind

release Within her womb, which, for enlargement° striving,

grandmother Shakes the old beldam° Earth and topples down   30

Steeples and moss-grown towers. At your birth

disorder Our grandam Earth, having this distemperature,°

suffering In passion° shook.

Glendower

from   Cousin, of° many men

insults; contradictions I do not bear these crossings.° Give me leave

To tell you once again that at my birth   35

The front of Heaven was full of fiery shapes,

The goats ran from the mountains, and the herds

Were strangely clamorous to the frighted fields.

These signs have marked me extraordinary,

And all the courses of my life do show   40

catalog; list I am not in the roll° of common men.

anyone Where is he° living, clipped in with [1] the sea

That chides the banks [2] of England, Scotland, Wales,

Who Which° calls me pupil or hath read to me? [3]

1   *And bring him out that is but woman's*
     son / Can trace me in the tedious ways
     of art / And hold me pace in deep experi-
     ments.

     And show me any mere human who
     can follow me in the demanding
     procedures of magic, or keep up
     with me in my arcane inquiries.

2   *I think there's no man speaks better*
     Welsh.

     (1) there's no one who speaks better
     Welsh; (2) there's no one who
     speaks more nonsense. Hotspur
     admits only that Glendower, a
     native Welsh speaker, speaks the
     provincial language, which few
     English speakers understood well,
     and seems to be implying that the
     language is only good for boasting.

3   *the vasty deep*

     The immense spaces of Hell

4   *"Tell truth and shame the devil."*

     A proverbial expression, meaning,
     "Tell the truth and it will embarrass
     the devil (who is the father of lies)"

5   *made head*

     Engaged in battle

6   *Wye*

     River marking the border between
     Wales and England (for the *Severn*,
     see 1.3.98 and note)

7   *weather-beaten back*

     Defeated by bad weather. Holin-
     shed reports that many believed
     that Glendower had used his magic
     to call up storms to bog down King
     Henry's army.

And bring him out that is but woman's son   45
Can trace me in the tedious ways of art
And hold me pace in deep experiments.[1]

Hotspur

I think there's no man speaks better Welsh.[2]
I'll to dinner.

Mortimer

Peace, cousin Percy; you will make him mad.   50

Glendower

I can call spirits from the vasty deep.[3]

Hotspur

Why, so can I, or so can any man,
But will they come when you do call for them?

Glendower

Why, I can teach you, cousin, to command the devil.

Hotspur

And I can teach thee, coz, to shame the devil   55
By telling truth. "Tell truth and shame the devil."[4]
If thou have power to raise him, bring him hither,
And I'll be sworn I have power to shame him hence.
Oh, while you live, tell truth and shame the devil!

Mortimer

Come, come, no more of this unprofitable chat.   60

Glendower

Three times hath Henry Bolingbroke made head[5]
army   Against my power;° thrice from the banks of Wye[6]
And sandy-bottomed Severn have I sent him
Unsuccessful   Bootless° home and weather-beaten back.[7]

Hotspur

Home without boots, and in foul weather too!   65
fevers   How 'scapes he agues,° in the devil's name?

1   *here's the map*

As in *King Lear* and in Christopher
Marlowe's *Tamburlaine*, the map
on the stage indicates poten-
tially dangerous power. The new
technologies of cartography had
enabled a new way of looking at,
and controlling, territory, and here
the rebels use the map to divide up
the territory that they have yet to
conquer, an irony that is noted in
Holinshed's account.

2   *threefold order ta'en*

Agreed upon, three-party arrangement

3   *Archdeacon*

I.e., the Archdeacon of Bangor in
Wales, who, according to Holinshed, was involved in the rebellion
and at whose home this meeting
took place

4   *Trent*

A major English river, running
northeast from the midlands until
it joins with the Ouse and empties
into the North Sea below Hull

5   *indentures tripartite*

Three-party contract (between
Mortimer, Glendower, and
Hotspur)

6   *being sealèd interchangeably*

Being marked with all our seals

7   *this night might execute*

That can be concluded tonight

8   *in my conduct*

Escorted by me

9   *world of water*

Large quantity of tears

10 *Burton*

Burton-upon-Trent, an English
town in the midlands, about 110
miles northwest of London

Glendower

Come; here's the map.[1] Shall we divide our right

According to our threefold order ta'en?[2]

Mortimer

The Archdeacon[3] hath divided it

regions Into three limits° very equally: 70

to here England, from Trent[4] and Severn hitherto,°

By south and east is to my part assigned;

All westward, Wales beyond the Severn shore,

And all the fertile land within that bound

To Owen Glendower; and, dear coz, to you   75

The remnant northward, lying off from Trent.

And our indentures tripartite[5] are drawn,

Which being sealèd interchangeably[6]—

A business that this night may execute[7]—

Tomorrow, cousin Percy, you and I   80

And my good Lord of Worcester will set forth

To meet your father and the Scottish power,

As is appointed us, at Shrewsbury.

i.e., father-in-law My father° Glendower is not ready yet,

Nor shall we need his help these fourteen days.   85

[*to* **Glendower**] Within that space you may have drawn together

Your tenants, friends, and neighboring gentlemen.

Glendower

A shorter time shall send me to you, lords,

And in my conduct[8] shall your ladies come,

From whom you now must steal and take no leave,   90

For there will be a world of water[9] shed

Upon the parting of your wives and you.

Hotspur

portion Methinks my moiety,° north from Burton[10] here,

either In quantity equals not one° of yours.

1   *comes me cranking in*

     Curves sharply inward. As in *cuts me*
     in line 96, the *me* here serves as an
     intensifier meaning "to my cost";
     the sense of Hotspur's complaint is
     that the bend of the river cuts out a
     large portion of his assigned lands.

2   *fair and evenly*

     In a straight line

3   *runs me up / With like advantage*

     Runs upward in a similar fashion

4   *Gelding the opposèd continent*

     Cutting out a significant piece from
     the opposite side. *Gelding* means
     castrating.

5   *trench him*

     Divert the river by means of a trench

See how this river comes me cranking in [1]   95
And cuts me from the best of all my land
piece   A huge half-moon, a monstrous scantle° out.
I'll have the current in this place dammed up,
smooth   And here the smug° and silver Trent shall run
In a new channel, fair and evenly. [2]   100
indentation   It shall not wind with such a deep indent°
river valley   To rob me of so rich a bottom° here.

Glendower
Not wind? It shall; it must. You see it doth.

Mortimer
it   Yea, but mark how he° bears his course and runs me up
With like advantage [3] on the other side,   105
Gelding the opposèd continent [4] as much
As on the other side it takes from you.

Worcester
expense   Yea, but a little charge° will trench him [5] here
spur   And on this north side win this cape° of land,
And then he runs straight and even.   110

Hotspur
I'll have it so. A little charge will do it.

Glendower
I'll not have it altered.

Hotspur
Will not you?

Glendower
No, nor you shall not.

Hotspur
Who shall say me nay?   115

Glendower
Why, that will I.

1   *speak it in Welsh*

    I.e., so that you'll be completely
    incomprehensible

2   *framèd to*

    Composed for

3   *English ditty*

    Song whose lyrics were in English

4   *gave the tongue a helpful ornament*

    Gave the English language (*the
    tongue*) the benefit of my musical
    accompaniment

5   *meter balladmongers*

    Peddlers of rhyming ballads

6   *brazen can'stick turned*

    Brass candlestick shaped on a lathe
    (and making a grating noise)

7   *cavil on*

    Argue about

8   *haste the writer*

    Make the scribe (drawing up the
    contract) hurry.

9   *Break with*

    Tell

Hotspur

Let me not understand you, then; speak it in Welsh.[1]

Glendower

I can speak English, lord, as well as you,

For I was trained up in the English court,

Where being but young I framèd to[2] the harp   120

Many an English ditty[3] lovely well

And gave the tongue a helpful ornament[4]—

A virtue that was never seen in you.

Hotspur

Marry, and I am glad of it with all my heart.

I had rather be a kitten and cry "mew"   125

Than one of these same meter balladmongers.[5]

I had rather hear a brazen can'stick turned,[6]

unoiled / axle Or a dry° wheel grate on the axletree,°

And that would set my teeth nothing an edge,

dainty Nothing so much as mincing° poetry.   130

hobbled 'Tis like the forced gait of a shuffling° nag.

Glendower

Come, you shall have Trent turned.

Hotspur

I do not care. I'll give thrice so much land

To any well-deserving friend,

But in the way of bargain, mark ye me,   135

I'll cavil on[7] the ninth part of a hair.

Are the indentures drawn? Shall we be gone?

Glendower

The moon shines fair. You may away by night.

at the same time I'll haste the writer,[8] and withal°

Break with[9] your wives of your departure hence.   140

I am afraid my daughter will run mad,

So much she doteth on her Mortimer.   *He exits.*

1   *moldwarp*

Mole. Holinshed reports that
Mortimer, Hotspur, and Glendower
divided the land according to a
prophecy that represented the
three conspirators as a dragon, a
lion, and a wolf, destined to take
England from King Henry, represented by a mole.

2   *Merlin*

Welsh prophet, magician, and
singer at the legendary court of
King Arthur

3   *griffin*

Mythical beast, half-eagle, half-lion

4   *A couching lion and a ramping cat*

A crouching lion and a rearing cat.
Couching and *ramping* (or couch-
ant and rampant) are terms from
heraldry used to describe figures
on coats of arms.

5   *puts me from my faith*

I.e., drives me crazy (literally,
"makes me want to give up my
religion")

6   *marked him not a word*

Paid him no attention

7   *natural scope*

Instinctive responses

8   *come cross his humor*

Frustrate his inclination; provoke
him

Mortimer

i.e., father-in-law Fie, cousin Percy, how you cross my father!°

Hotspur

help it I cannot choose.° Sometime he angers me
With telling me of the moldwarp¹ and the ant,   145
Of the dreamer Merlin² and his prophecies,
And of a dragon and a finless fish,
molted A clip-winged griffin³ and a molten° raven,
A couching lion and a ramping cat,⁴
ridiculous And such a deal of skimble-skamble° stuff   150
As puts me from my faith.⁵ I tell you what:
He held me last night at least nine hours
various In reckoning up the several° devils' names
That were his lackeys. I cried "Hum," and "Well, go to,"
But marked him not a word.⁶ Oh, he is as tedious   155
As a tired horse, a railing wife,
Worse than a smoky house. I had rather live
With cheese and garlic in a windmill, far,
delicacies Than feed on cates° and have him talk to me
country house In any summerhouse° in Christendom.   160

Mortimer

In faith, he is a worthy gentleman,
skillful Exceedingly well read and profited°
magical arts In strange concealments,° valiant as a lion,
And wondrous affable and as bountiful
As mines of India. Shall I tell you, cousin?   165
He holds your temper in a high respect
And curbs himself even of his natural scope⁷
When you come cross his humor.⁸ Faith, he does.
assure I warrant° you that man is not alive
provoked Might so have tempted° him as you have done   170
Without the taste of danger and reproof.
But do not use it oft, let me entreat you.

1   *besides his patience*

    Beyond his self-control

2   *must needs*

    Have to

3   *want of government*

    Lack of self-restraint

4   *all parts besides*

    All other qualities

5   *be your speed*

    Allow you to succeed (in battle)

6   *deadly spite*

    Horrible difficulty

7   *My wife can speak no English, I no Welsh.*

    Mortimer's lament opens a curious exchange in which the use of Welsh is only signaled in the stage directions—Shakespeare never attempts to transliterate it. This either suggests that an approximation of Welsh is attempted by these two actors that did not require any degree of verisimilitude (and thus again associating Welsh with incomprehensibility and nonsense) or that Shakespeare's playing company contained at least two passable Welsh speakers. Certainly the use of Welsh in this scene is another important signifier of the alien nature of the country and its language, since it is relatively

    rare that any language other than English was spoken on the early English stage.

8   *aunt Percy*

    I.e., Lady Percy, Hotspur's wife

9   *in your conduct*

    Along with you

Worcester

[*to* **Hotspur**] In faith, my lord, you are too willful-

obstinate   blame,°

And, since your coming hither, have done enough

To put him quite besides his patience.[1]   175

You must needs[2] learn, lord, to amend this fault.

Though sometimes it show greatness, courage,

spirit   blood°—

favor; credit And that's the dearest grace° it renders you—

indicate Yet often times it doth present° harsh rage,

Defect of manners, want of government,[3]   180

arrogance Pride, haughtiness, opinion,° and disdain,

The least of which, haunting a nobleman,

Loseth men's hearts and leaves behind a stain

Upon the beauty of all parts besides,[4]

Cheating Beguiling° them of commendation.   185

Hotspur

Well I am schooled. Good manners be your speed![5]

Here come our wives, and let us take our leave.

Enter **Glendower** *with the* **Ladies**

[**Percy** *and* **Mortimer**].

Mortimer

This is the deadly spite[6] that angers me:

My wife can speak no English, I no Welsh.[7]

Glendower

My daughter weeps; she'll not part with you.   190

She'll be a soldier too: she'll to the wars.

Mortimer

Good father, tell her that she and my aunt Percy[8]

Shall follow in your conduct[9] speedily.

1 *She is desperate here*

   This (her husband's impending departure) makes her miserable.

2 *That pretty Welsh / Which thou pourest down from these swelling heavens / I am too perfect in, and but for shame / In such a parley I should answer thee.*

   The Lady's tears, which pour from her overflowing eyes (*swelling heavens*), speak a language that Mortimer understands perfectly; if it were not unmanly, he would answer in similar language (*such a parley*), i.e., with tears of his own.

3 *feeling disputation*

   Conversation without words (based on emotional sympathy and caresses)

4 *be a truant*

   Give up trying (to learn)

5 *highly penned*

   Written in an elegant style

6 *wanton rushes*

   Floor coverings of soft reeds

7 *crown the god of sleep*

   Make sleep rule

Glendower speaks to her in Welsh, and
she answers him in the same.

Glendower

hussy   She is desperate here,[1] a peevish self-willed harlotry,°

One that no persuasion can do good upon.   195

The Lady speaks in Welsh.

Mortimer

I understand thy looks. That pretty Welsh

Which thou pourest down from these swelling heavens

I am too perfect in, and but for shame

In such a parley should I answer thee.[2]

The Lady [speaks] again in Welsh.

I understand thy kisses and thou mine,   200

And that's a feeling disputation;[3]

But I will never be a truant,[4] love,

Till I have learned thy language, for thy tongue

Makes Welsh as sweet as ditties highly penned,[5]

Sung by a fair queen in a summer's bower,   205

trills   With ravishing division,° to her lute.

Glendower

weep   Nay, if you melt,° then will she run mad.

The Lady speaks again in Welsh.

Mortimer

Oh, I am ignorance itself in this!

Glendower

She bids you on the wanton rushes[6] lay you down

And rest your gentle head upon her lap,   210

And she will sing the song that pleaseth you

And on your eyelids crown the god of sleep,[7]

sleepiness   Charming your blood with pleasing heaviness,°

Making such difference 'twixt wake and sleep

As is the difference betwixt day and night   215

1   *the heavenly harnessed team*

In Roman mythology, the sun progressed across the sky as the sun god, Phoebus, drove a team of horses through the heavens.

2   *those musicians that shall play to you / Hang in the air a thousand leagues from hence, / And straight they shall be here*

Glendower, either playfully or seriously, claims to have the power to call up spirit musicians to accompany his daughter. A *league* is a unit of distance measuring about three miles.

3   *perfect in lying down*

He jokes, playing on the phrase meaning "good at making love."

4   *lay my head in thy lap*

The intimate joking here is sexual but without any of the hostility in the similar scene in *Hamlet* 3.2.105–112.

5   *Neither; 'tis a woman's fault.*

I won't do that either (*be still*); that's a woman's characteristic.

The hour before the heavenly harnessed team[1]
Begins his golden progress in the east.

Mortimer

With all my heart I'll sit and hear her sing.

contract By that time will our book,° I think, be drawn.

Glendower

Do so, and those musicians that shall play to you   220
Hang in the air a thousand leagues from hence,
And straight they shall be here.[2] Sit and attend.

Hotspur

Come, Kate; thou art perfect in lying down.[3]
Come, quick, quick, that I may lay my head in thy lap.[4]

Lady Percy

Go, ye giddy goose.   *[They sit.]* 225
The music plays.

Hotspur

Now I perceive the devil understands Welsh,

capricious And 'tis no marvel he is so humorous.°
By 'r Lady, he is a good musician.

Lady Percy

Then should you be nothing but musical,

whims For you are altogether governed by humors.°   230
Lie still, ye thief, and hear the lady sing in Welsh.

Hotspur

female hound I had rather hear Lady, my brach,° howl in Irish.

Lady Percy

Wouldst thou have thy head broken?

Hotspur

No.

Lady Percy

Then be still.   235

Hotspur

Neither; 'tis a woman's fault.[5]

1   *in good sooth*

    Truthfully

2   *sarcenet surety*

    **Weak (*sarcenet* was a flimsy silk
    fabric) assurance**

3   *As if thou never walk'st further than
    Finsbury*

    **As if you were a simple bourgeois
    woman, as opposed to a proper
    noblewoman. *Finsbury* was a recre-
    ational ground used by middle-
    class citizens of London, located to
    the north of the city.**

4   *protest of pepper-gingerbread*

    **Mealy-mouthed oaths. *Pepper-
    gingerbread* was cheaply made
    gingerbread, which replaced the
    traditional ginger with less-
    expensive pepper.**

5   *velvet-guards and Sunday citizens*

    **People whose clothes are trimmed
    (*guarded*) with velvet, dressed in
    their Sunday best**

6   *'Tis the next way to turn tailor or be red-
    breast teacher.*

    **It's the fastest way to become a
    tailor (a profession popularly held
    to be full of singers) or a singing
    teacher for birds.**

Lady Percy

Now God help thee!

Hotspur

To the Welsh lady's bed.

Lady Percy

What's that?

Hotspur

Peace, she sings.　　　　　*(Here the lady sings a Welsh song.)*　240

Hotspur

Come, Kate, I'll have your song too.

Lady Percy

Not mine, in good sooth.[1]

Hotspur

i.e., By Christ's heart　Not yours, "in good sooth!" Heart,° you swear like a

candy maker's　comfit-maker's° wife! "Not you, in good sooth," and

"as true as I live," and "as God shall mend me," and "as　245

sure as day"—

And givest such sarcenet surety[2] for thy oaths

As if thou never walk'st further than Finsbury.[3]

for me　Swear me,° Kate, like a lady as thou art,

A good mouth-filling oath, and leave "in sooth,"　250

And such protest of pepper-gingerbread,[4]

To velvet-guards and Sunday citizens.[5]

Come, sing.

Lady Percy

I will not sing.

Hotspur

'Tis the next way to turn tailor or be red-breast　255

If / leave　teacher.[6] An° the indentures be drawn, I'll away°

within these two hours, and so come in when ye will.

He exits.

1   *our book is drawn. We'll but seal*

**The agreement is drawn up. We will
just affix our seals.**

Glendower

Come, come, Lord Mortimer; you are as slow

As hot Lord Percy is on fire to go.

this time By this° our book is drawn. We'll but seal,[1]   260

And then to horse immediately.

Mortimer

                      With all my heart.

They exit.

1	*scourge*

	Human agent of God's judgment

2	*passages of life*

	Behavior

3	*mean attempts*

	Undignified escapades

4	*matched withal*

	Known for; associated with

5	*hold their level with*

	Satisfy; be adequate to

Act 3, Scene 2

*Enter the **King**, **Prince** of Wales, and others.*

King

Lords, give us leave; the Prince of Wales and I
Must have some private conference, but be near at
    hand,
For we shall presently have need of you.   *Lords exit.*
I know not whether God will have it so
For some displeasing service I have done,   5
That, in His secret doom,° out of my blood°   *judgment / i.e., offspring*
He'll breed revengement° and a scourge[1] for me.   *retribution*
 But thou dost in thy passages of life[2]
Make me believe that thou art only marked
For° the hot vengeance and the rod° of Heaven   10   *As / instrument*
To punish my mistreadings.° Tell me else,   *transgressions*
Could such inordinate° and low desires,   *unsuitable*
Such poor, such bare,° such lewd,° such mean   *wretched / vulgar*
    attempts,[3]
Such barren pleasures, rude society
As thou art matched withal[4] and grafted° to,   15   *dedicated*
Accompany the greatness of thy blood
And hold their level with[5] thy princely heart?

Prince

So° please your Majesty, I would I could   *If it*
Quit° all offenses with as clear excuse   *Acquit myself of*
As well as I am doubtless° I can purge   20   *confident*
Myself of many I am charged withal.°   *with*
Yet such extenuation let me beg
As, in reproof° of many tales devised,   *disproof*
which oft the ear of greatness needs must hear,
By smiling pickthanks° and base newsmongers,°   25   *sycophants / gossips*

1   *I may for some things true, wherein my*
    youth / Hath faulty wandered and irregu-
    lar, / Find pardon on my true submission

    **Will allow you to pardon me if I
    make a full confession of the things
    I actually did in my impetuous and
    lawless youth**

2   *hold a wing / Quite from the flight*

    **Take a far different route than the
    paths**

3   *Thy place in Council thou hast rudely lost*

    **Prince Henry's behavior resulted in
    his removal from the Privy Council,
    the circle of the King's closest
    advisors. This line alludes to the
    popular myth, dramatized in the
    anonymous play *The Famous Victories
    of Henry V* and referred to in *Henry
    IV, Part Two* (1.2.194), in which the
    Prince's loss of position is attrib-
    uted to his having struck the Lord
    Chief Justice.**

4   *So common-hackneyed*

    **Made as cheap and ordinary as a
    hackney (hired horse). In the speech,
    King Henry claims that Hal has
    lost his royal prestige and aura of
    majesty by mingling too freely with
    common citizens.**

5   *possession*

    **The possessor of the crown (i.e.,
    Richard II)**

6   *By being seldom seen, I could not stir /
    But, like a comet, I was wondered at*

    **Since I was so rarely seen in public,
    I could not move about without
    becoming an object of amazement,
    like a comet.**

7   *I stole all courtesy from Heaven*

    I became as gracious as a god.

8   *Ne'er seen but*

    Never seen without being

I may for some things true, wherein my youth
Hath faulty wandered and irregular,
Find pardon on my true submission.[1]

King

God pardon thee. Yet let me wonder, Harry,

inclinations At thy affections,° which do hold a wing　　　　30
Quite from the flight[2] of all thy ancestors.
Thy place in Council thou hast rudely lost,[3]

filled Which by thy younger brother is supplied,°

i.e., you are And art° almost an alien to the hearts
Of all the court and princes of my blood.　　　　35

life The hope and expectation of thy time°
Is ruined, and the soul of every man
Prophetically do forethink thy fall.
Had I so lavish of my presence been,
So common-hackneyed[4] in the eyes of men,　　　　40
So stale and cheap to vulgar company,

Public opinion Opinion,° that did help me to the crown,
Had still kept loyal to possession[5]

inglorious And left me in reputeless° banishment,

distinction / promise A fellow of no mark° nor likelihood.°　　　　45
By being seldom seen, I could not stir
But, like a comet, I was wondered at,[6]
That men would tell their children "This is he."
Others would say "Where? Which is Bolingbroke?"
And then I stole all courtesy from Heaven[7]　　　　50
And dressed myself in such humility
That I did pluck allegiance from men's hearts,
Loud shouts and salutations from their mouths,

i.e., King Richard Even in the presence of the crownèd King.°
Thus did I keep my person fresh and new,　　　　55

of a bishop My presence, like a robe pontifical,°

public persona Ne'er seen but[8] wondered at; and so my state,°

1   *showed*

     Appeared; seemed

2   *rash bavin wits*

     I.e., superficial jokers; literally, a quick-burning (*rash*) bundle of firewood (*bavin*)

3   *carded*

     Contaminated; weakened (as strong liquor becomes tainted when mixed with weak liquor, or fine wool with inferior materials)

4   *scorns*

     Scornful or scorn-worthy behavior

5   *stand the push*

     Endure the impudence

6   *comparative*

     One who insults another with offensive comparisons

7   *Enfeoffed*

     Submitted (by contracting himself to *popularity* as if he were pledging fealty to a superior lord in exchange for a land grant, or *feof*)

8   *popularity*

     I.e., the affection of the people

9   *That, being daily swallowed by men's eyes, / They surfeited with honey and began / To loathe the taste of sweetness*

     King Henry compares the citizens' eyes, which took in the sight of King Richard on a daily basis, to mouths crammed with excessive amounts of honey, which as a result grow to hate it.

10   *as the cuckoo is in June*

     As ignored as is the cuckoo in June (when the bird has become commonplace)

11   *in his face*

     In front of him; in his presence

12   *vile participation*

     Association with the vulgar crowd

13   *Not an eye / But is aweary*

     There is not an eye (in England), which is not bored with

14   *common*

     (1) familiar; (2) vulgar

i.e., Seldom seen	Seldom° but sumptuous, showed[1] like a feast
dignity	And won by rareness such solemnity.°
frivolous	The skipping° King, he ambled up and down 60
	With shallow jesters and rash bavin wits,[2]
	Soon kindled and soon burnt; carded[3] his state,
prancing	Mingled his royalty with cap'ring° fools,
	Had his great name profanèd with their scorns,[4]
approval / discrediting	And gave his countenance,° against° his name, 65
mocking	To laugh at gibing° boys and stand the push[5]
	Of every beardless vain comparative;[6]
Became	Grew° a companion to the common streets,
	Enfeoffed[7] himself to popularity,[8]
So that	That,° being daily swallowed by men's eyes, 70
	They surfeited with honey and began
	To loathe the taste of sweetness,[9] whereof a little
	More than a little is by much too much.
	So, when he had occasion to be seen,
	He was but as the cuckoo is in June,[10] 75
	Heard, not regarded, seen, but with such eyes
familiarity	As, sick and blunted with community,°
Bestow	Afford° no extraordinary gaze
	Such as is bent on sunlike majesty
	When it shines seldom in admiring eyes, 80
lost interest	But rather drowsed° and hung their eyelids down,
looks	Slept in his face,[11] and rendered such aspect°
sullen	As cloudy° men use to their adversaries,
	Being with his presence glutted, gorged, and full.
category	And in that very line,° Harry, standest thou, 85
	For thou has lost thy princely privilege
	With vile participation.[12] Not an eye
	But is aweary[13] of thy common[14] sight,
	Save mine, which hath desired to see thee more,

1   *He hath more worthy interest to the state*

He (Hotspur) deserves the throne more

2   *shadow of succession*

Bad imitation of an heir

3   *color like to*

Anything resembling

4   *Turns head*

Leads armed forces

5   *no more in debt to years than thou*

The same age as you (although the historical Hotspur was 23 years older than Prince Henry)

6   *Holds from all soldiers chief majority / And military title capital*

Has, among all soldiers, the reputation as the best soldier

7   *Thrice*

Shakespeare refers to three historical battles between Hotspur's forces and the Douglas family: Otterburn (1388), Nesbit (June 1402), and Humbleton (September 1402).

8   *Mars in swaddling clothes*

I.e., infant war-god. *Mars* is the Roman god of war; *swaddling clothes* are wrappings for a baby.

9   *To fill the mouth of deep defiance up*

To add men to the already large rebel force; literally, to make defiance's *mouth* or voice louder or to satisfy its appetite

what	Which now doth that° I would not have it do, 90
i.e., tears	Make blind itself with foolish tenderness.°

Prince

I shall hereafter, my thrice gracious lord,

Be more myself.

King

For all the world

until	As thou art to° this hour was Richard then
	When I from France set foot at Ravenspur, 95
	And even as I was then is Percy now.
	Now by my scepter, and my soul to boot,
	He hath more worthy interest to the state [1]
	Than thou, the shadow of succession;[2]
having	For of° no right, nor color like to [3] right, 100
armored soldiers	He doth fill fields with harness° in the realm,
i.e., King's	Turns head [4] against the lion's° armèd jaws,
	And, being no more in debt to years than thou,[5]
	Leads ancient lords and reverend bishops on
i.e., feats of arms	To bloody battles and to bruising arms.° 105
	What never-dying honor hath he got
i.e., Hotspur's	Against renownèd Douglas, whose° high deeds,
	Whose hot incursions and great name in arms,
	Holds from all soldiers chief majority
	And military title capital [6] 110
	Through all the kingdoms that acknowledge Christ.
	Thrice [7] hath this Hotspur, Mars in swaddling clothes,[8]
	This infant warrior, in his enterprises
Defeated / captured	Discomfited° great Douglas, ta'en° him once,
Released	Enlargèd° him, and made a friend of him, 115
	To fill the mouth of deep defiance up [9]
	And shake the peace and safety of our throne.
	And what say you to this? Percy, Northumberland,
	The Archbishop's grace of York, Douglas, Mortimer,

1   *start of spleen*

    Fit of irritability

2   *To dog his heels and curtsy at his frowns*

    **To follow him subserviently and act
deferentially when he is displeased**

3   *I will redeem all this on Percy's head*

    **(1) I will prove myself by defeating
Hotspur; (2) Hotspur will pay for
this.**

4   *on my head / My shames redoubled*

    I wish my guilt was twice what it is.

5   *slightest worship of his time*

    **Smallest honor acquired during his
lifetime**

Combine / in arms Capitulate° against us and are up.°   120
why But wherefore° do I tell these news to thee?
 Why, Harry, do I tell thee of my foes,
Who Which° art my nearest and dearest enemy?
likely / ignoble Thou that art like° enough, through vassal° fear,
 Base inclination, and the start of spleen,[1]   125
 To fight against me under Percy's pay,
 To dog his heels and curtsy at his frowns,[2]
 To show how much thou art degenerate.

Prince
 Do not think so. You shall not find it so.
 And God forgive them that so much have swayed   130
 Your Majesty's good thoughts away from me.
 I will redeem all this on Percy's head,[3]
 And, in the closing of some glorious day,
 Be bold to tell you that I am your son,
 When I will wear a garment all of blood   135
facial features And stain my favors° in a bloody mask,
clean off Which, washed away, shall scour° my shame with it.
arrives And that shall be the day, whene'er it lights,°
 That this same child of honor and renown,
 This gallant Hotspur, this all-praisèd knight,   140
 And your unthought-of Harry chance to meet.
helmet For every honor sitting on his helm,°
I wish Would° they were multitudes, and on my head
 My shames redoubled![4] For the time will come
 That I shall make this northern youth exchange   145
shames His glorious deeds for my indignities.°
agent Percy is but my factor,° good my lord,
gather To engross° up glorious deeds on my behalf,
 And I will call him to so strict account
 That he shall render every glory up,   150
 Yea, even the slightest worship of his time,[5]

1   *A hundred thousand rebels die in this.*

     **An acknowledgment of the King's
     confidence in the Prince's commit-
     ment to reform**

2   *charge*

     **Command (of a company of
     soldiers)**

3   *Lord Mortimer of Scotland*

     **A Scottish nobleman, not related to
     Mortimer, the English rebel**

4   *If promises be kept on every hand*

     **If all those who promised to help
     them keep their promises**

5   *Bridgnorth*

     **A town approximately 20 miles
     southeast of Shrewsbury**

Or I will tear the reckoning from his heart.
This, in the name of God, I promise here,
may   The which if He be pleased I shall° perform,
heal   I do beseech your Majesty may salve°   155
The long-grown wounds of my intemperance.
If not, the end of life cancels all bonds,
And I will die a hundred thousand deaths
piece   Ere break the smallest parcel° of this vow.

King
A hundred thousand rebels die in this.[1]   160
Thou shalt have charge[2] and sovereign trust herein.

             Enter **Blunt**.

urgency   How now, good Blunt? Thy looks are full of speed.°

Blunt
So hath the business that I come to speak of.
Lord Mortimer of Scotland[3] hath sent word
That Douglas and the English rebels met   165
The eleventh of this month at Shrewsbury.
army   A mighty and a fearful head° they are,
If promises be kept on every hand,[4]
As ever offered foul play in a state.

King
The Earl of Westmorland set forth today,   170
With him my son, Lord John of Lancaster,
information   For this advertisement° is five days old.
     —On Wednesday next, Harry, you shall set forward.
meeting place   On Thursday we ourselves will march. Our meeting°
Is Bridgnorth.[5] And, Harry, you shall march   175
calculation   Through Gloucestershire, by which account,°

1   *Our business valuèd*

     Bearing in mind what we have to do

2   *Advantage feeds him fat*

     The opportunity is lost (grows *fat*
     through inactivity).

Our business valuèd,[1] some twelve days hence
Our general forces at Bridgnorth shall meet.
—Our hands are full of business. Let's away.
Advantage feeds him fat[2] while men delay.   *They exit.*   180

1   *action*

Battle (i.e., the Gad's Hill robbery)

2   *applejohn*

Type of apple left to shrivel and
wrinkle before being eaten

3   *in some liking*

(1) in the right mood; (2) fat

4   *out of heart*

(1) disinclined; (2) out of shape

5   *peppercorn*

Dried berry of a pepper plant (i.e.,
small and shriveled)

6   *brewer's horse*

I.e., tired old nag

7   *out of all compass*

Bardolph plays on the sense
"unable to buckle your belt."

8   *admiral*

Flagship, which led the other ships
with its *lantern*

9   *'tis in the nose of thee*

It (the lantern) is carried in your
nose. Falstaff mocks Bardolph's
red nose.

10 *Knight of the Burning Lamp*

A parody of the names taken by
wandering knights in popular
romances, e.g., Amadis, the Knight
of the Burning Sword

Act 3, Scene 3

Enter **Falstaff** *and* **Bardolph**.

Falstaff

i.e., shrunken   Bardolph, am I not fallen° away vilely since this last
become thin   action?[1] Do I not bate?° Do I not dwindle? Why, my
skin hangs about me like an old lady's loose gown. I
am withered like an old applejohn.[2] Well, I'll repent,
immediately   and that suddenly,° while I am in some liking.[3] I shall   5
be out of heart[4] shortly, and then I shall have no
If   strength to repent. An° I have not forgotten what
the inside of a church is made of, I am a peppercorn,[5]
a brewer's horse.[6] The inside of a church! Company,
villainous company, hath been the spoil of me.   10

Bardolph

anxious   Sir John, you are so fretful° you cannot live long.

Falstaff

Why, there is it. Come sing me a bawdy song; make me
inclined   merry. I was as virtuously given° as a gentleman need to
be, virtuous enough: swore little; diced not above seven
times—a week; went to a bawdy house not above once   15
in a quarter—of an hour; paid money that I borrowed—
self-control   three or four times; lived well and in good compass;°
and now I live out of all order, out of all compass.

Bardolph

Why, you are so fat, Sir John, that you must needs be
out of all compass,[7] out of all reasonable compass, Sir   20
John.

Falstaff

Do thou amend thy face, and I'll amend my life.
Thou art our admiral;[8] thou bearest the lantern in
main deck   the poop,° but 'tis in the nose of thee.[9] Thou art the
Knight of the Burning Lamp.[10]   25

1 *a death's-head or a* memento mori

A skull or a reminder of death (Latin).
Such reminders of mortality were
often engraved on rings or placed in
churches and other public places.

2 *Dives, that lived in purple*

Allusion to the biblical parable of
a rich man dressed in purple who
refuses to be charitable to a poor
man, Lazarus, and is condemned
to Hell, where he asks charity of
Lazarus but cannot receive it (Luke
16:19–23). Both the Latin Vulgate
and a host of popular ballads name
the rich man as *Dives*.

3 *burning, burning*

These references to burning in
hellfire also have connotations of
sexual disease, perhaps implying
that the red veins and boils on
Bardolph's face are due to venereal
disease, rather than excessive drink
(syphilitic sores were said to *burn*).

4 ignis fatuus

Will-o'-the-wisp or false fire (phos-
phorescent gas seen in marshes),
said to lead travelers astray at night

5 *a ball of wildfire*

Fireworks

6 *triumph*

Torch-lit triumphal procession

7 *marks*

Unit of money; three *marks* equaled
two pounds

8 *the sack that thou hast drunk me would
have bought me lights as good cheap at
the dearest chandler's in Europe*

With all the sack that you have
drunk (at my expense), I could have
bought torches at the most expensive candle shop in Europe.

9 *I have maintained that salamander of
yours with fire*

Salamanders were small lizards
thought to live in fire, but here
another reference to Bardolph's
fiery complexion.

10 *I would my face were in your belly*

Common expression of annoyance
(which Falstaff pretends to take
literally)

11 *Dame Partlet*

A traditional proper name given to
hens and, by extension, a talkative
woman

Bardolph

Why, Sir John, my face does you no harm.

Falstaff

No, I'll be sworn, I make as good use of it as many a
man doth of a death's-head or a *memento mori.*[1] I never
see thy face but I think upon hellfire and Dives, that
lived in purple,[2] for there he is in his robes, burning,   30
burning.[3] If thou wert any way given to virtue, I would
swear by thy face. My oath should be "By this fire,
that's God's angel." But thou art altogether given
(to vice)/would be   over,° and wert° indeed, but for the light in thy
face, the son of utter darkness. When thou ran'st   35
up Gads Hill in the night to catch my horse, if I did
not think thou hadst been an *ignis fatuus,*[4] or a ball of
value   wildfire,[5] there's no purchase° in money. Oh, thou art
a perpetual triumph,[6] an everlasting bonfire-light!
small torches   Thou hast saved me a thousand marks[7] in links°   40
and torches, walking with thee in the night betwixt
tavern and tavern, but the sack that thou hast drunk
i.e., at my expense   me° would have bought me lights as good cheap at
the dearest chandler's in Europe.[8] I have maintained
that salamander of yours with fire[9] any time this two   45
and thirty years, God reward me for it.

Bardolph

'Sblood, I would my face were in your belly![10]

Falstaff

God-a-mercy, so should I be sure to be heart-burned!

                          Enter **Hostess**.

How now, Dame Partlet[11] the hen? Have you enquired
yet who picked my pocket?   50

1   *was shaved and lost many a hair*

    (1) had his beard shaved; (2) had his
    head shaved because of lice; (3)
    went bald due to syphilis; (4) was
    robbed

2   *Go to*

    A dismissive phrase expressing
    impatience or disbelief

3   *you are a woman*

    A common derogatory phrase, i.e.,
    you are a liar

4   *Dowlas, filthy dowlas.*

    Dowlas was a coarse linen fabric. Fal-
    staff shrugs off the claim that she
    has bought shirts for him by saying
    they were of such cheap material
    that he gave them away to be used
    as *sieves*. The hostess in line 68 says
    they were in fact made of expensive
    holland linen.

Hostess

Why, Sir John, what do you think, Sir John? Do you
think I keep thieves in my house? I have searched, I
have enquired, so has my husband, man by man, boy

tenth part   by boy, servant by servant. The tithe° of a hair was
never lost in my house before.   55

Falstaff

Ye lie, hostess. Bardolph was shaved and lost many a
hair, [1] and I'll be sworn my pocket was picked. Go to, [2]
you are a woman; [3] go.

Hostess

i.e., By God's   Who, I? No; I defy thee! God's° light, I was never called
so in mine own house before.   60

Falstaff

Go to, I know you well enough.

Hostess

No, Sir John, you do not know me, Sir John. I know
you, Sir John. You owe me money, Sir John, and now
you pick a quarrel to beguile me of it. I bought you a
dozen of shirts to your back.   65

Falstaff

Dowlas, filthy dowlas. [4] I have given them away to
sieves   bakers' wives; they have made bolters° of them.

Hostess

fine linen fabric   Now, as I am a true woman, holland° of eight shillings
forty-five inches   an ell.° You owe money here besides, Sir John, for your
liquor between meals   diet and by-drinkings,° and money lent you, four and   70
twenty pound.

Falstaff

[*points at* **Bardolph**] He had his part of it. Let him pay.

Hostess

He? Alas, he is poor. He hath nothing.

1   *denier*

    I.e., penny (literally, a small French
    coin made of copper)

2   *Is the wind in that door*

    Is that how it is?

3   *two and two, Newgate-fashion*

    Shackled together, like prisoners
    from *Newgate* prison in London

Falstaff

How poor? Look upon his face. What call you rich?
Let them coin his nose. Let them coin his cheeks. I'll   75
dupe   not pay a denier.[1] What, will you make a younker° of
me? Shall I not take mine ease in mine inn but I shall
have my pocket picked? I have lost a seal ring of my
grandfather's worth forty mark.

Hostess

O Jesu, I have heard the Prince tell him, I know not   80
how oft, that that ring was copper!

Falstaff

rascal / devious person   How? The Prince is a jack,° a sneak-up.° 'Sblood, an he
were here, I would cudgel him like a dog if he would
say so.

> Enter the **Prince** [*and* **Peto**], *marching, and* **Falstaff**
> *meets him playing on his truncheon like a fife.*

How now, lad? Is the wind in that door,[2] i' faith? Must   85
we all march?

Bardolph

Yea, two and two, Newgate-fashion.[3]

Hostess

[*to* **Prince**] My lord, I pray you, hear me.

Prince

What say'st thou, Mistress Quickly? How doth thy
husband? I love him well; he is an honest man.   90

Hostess

Good my lord, hear me.

Falstaff

listen   Prithee, let her alone and list° to me.

Prince

What say'st thou, Jack?

1   *stewed prune*

I.e., a prostitute (in the *stews*, or
red-light district, a brothel was
often marked by a dish of stewed
prunes in the window)

2   *drawn fox*

(1) lure for a hunted fox; (2) fox
drawn out from its cover; (3) dead
fox used to create a false trail

3   *Maid Marian*

An often disreputable character
from May games and morris
dances, usually played by a boy in
women's clothing (as indeed were
women's roles on the English stage
until 1660)

4   *the deputy's wife of the ward*

The wife of the deputy of the ward
(i.e., a respectable woman)

5   *thing*

A term of contempt (implying
that she is something less than a
person, perhaps also with a sexual
insult), as *thing* was a slang term for
"vagina")

Falstaff

curtain The other night I fell asleep here behind the arras°
and had my pocket picked. This house is turned   95
brothel bawdy-house;° they pick pockets.

Prince

What didst thou lose, Jack?

Falstaff

Wilt thou believe me, Hal? Three or four bonds of forty
pound apiece and a seal ring of my grandfather's.

Prince

A trifle, some eightpenny matter.   100

Hostess

So I told him, my lord, and I said I heard your Grace say
so. And, my lord, he speaks most vilely of you, like a
beat foul-mouthed man as he is, and said he would cudgel°
you.

Prince

What? He did not!   105

Hostess

There's neither faith, truth, nor womanhood in me
otherwise else.°

Falstaff

There's no more faith in thee than in a stewed prune,[1]
nor no more truth in thee than in a drawn fox,[2] and
as for for° womanhood, Maid Marian[3] may be the deputy's   110
compared to wife of the ward[4] to° thee. Go, you thing,[5] go.

Hostess

Say, what thing, what thing?

Falstaff

What thing? Why, a thing to thank God on.

Hostess

for I am no thing to thank God on;° I would thou shouldst

1   *neither fish nor flesh*

Due to its mammalian appearance and amphibious habits, the otter's classification was subject to debate.

2   *where to have her*

(1) how to classify her; (2) where to have sex with her

know it! I am an honest man's wife, and, setting thy   115
knighthood aside, thou art a knave to call me so.

Falstaff

Setting thy womanhood aside, thou art a beast to say
otherwise.

Hostess

Say what beast, thou knave, thou?

Falstaff

What beast? Why, an otter.   120

Prince

An otter, Sir John. Why an otter?

Falstaff

Why, she's neither fish nor flesh;[1] a man knows not
where to have her.[2]

Hostess

Thou art an unjust man in saying so. Thou or any man
knows where to have me, thou knave, thou.   125

Prince

Thou say'st true, hostess, and he slanders thee most
grossly.

Hostess

So he doth you, my lord, and said this other day you
owed him a thousand pound.

Prince

Sirrah, do I owe you a thousand pound?   130

Falstaff

A thousand pound, Hal? A million. Thy love is worth a
million; thou owest me thy love.

Hostess

knave Nay, my lord, he called you "jack"° and said he would
cudgel you.

Falstaff

Did I, Bardolph?   135

1 *my girdle break*

Let my belt break (a bad omen).

2 *embossed rascal*

(1) swollen rogue; (2) hunted deer

3 *make thee long-winded*

Give you stamina

4 *injuries*

Objects whose loss would be
injurious

5 *stand to it*

Persist at it (i.e., your accusation)

6 *pocket up*

Submit to (with a pun on Falstaff's
claim to have had his *pocket* picked)

Bardolph

Indeed, Sir John, you said so.

Falstaff

Yea, if he said my ring was copper.

Prince

I say 'tis copper. Darest thou be as good as thy word
now?

Falstaff

Why, Hal, thou knowest, as thou art but man, I dare,   140
but, as thou art prince, I fear thee as I fear the roaring
cub   of a lion's whelp. °

Prince

And why not as the lion?

Falstaff

The King himself is to be feared as the lion. Dost thou
if   think I'll fear thee as I fear thy father? Nay, an ° I do, I   145
pray God my girdle break.[1]

Prince

Oh, if it should, how would thy guts fall about thy
knees! But, sirrah, there's no room for faith, truth,
nor honesty in this bosom of thine. It is all filled up
with guts and midriff. Charge an honest woman with   150
picking thy pocket? Why, thou whoreson, impudent,
embossed rascal,[2] if there were anything in thy pocket
bills   but tavern reckonings, memorandums ° of bawdy-
houses, and one poor pennyworth of sugar candy to
make thee long-winded,[3] if thy pocket were enriched   155
with any other injuries [4] but these, I am a villain.
And yet you will stand to it.[5] You will not pocket up [6]
wrong. Art thou not ashamed?

Falstaff

Dost thou hear, Hal? Thou knowest in the state of innocency Adam fell, and what should poor Jack Falstaff   160

1   *double labor*

   In taking it and then returning it

2   *with unwashed hands*

   I.e., without hesitation

3   *a charge of foot*

   Command of a company of infantry

4   *of horse*

   A cavalry unit

do in the days of villainy? Thou see'st I have more flesh
than another man and therefore more frailty. You
confess, then, you picked my pocket?

Prince

It appears so by the story.

Falstaff

Hostess, I forgive thee. Go make ready breakfast, love   165
thy husband, look to thy servants, cherish thy guests.
Thou shalt find me tractable° to any honest reason.   *agreeable*
Thou see'st I am pacified still.° Nay, prithee, be gone.   *always*

Hostess *exits.*

Now, Hal, to the news at court. For the robbery, lad,
how is that answered?°   *settled*   170

Prince

O my sweet beef, I must still° be good angel to thee.   *always*
The money is paid back again.

Falstaff

Oh, I do not like that paying back: 'tis a double labor.¹

Prince

I am good friends with my father and may do anything.

Falstaff

Rob me the exchequer° the first thing thou dost, and   175   *treasurer*
do it with unwashed hands² too.

Bardolph

Do, my lord.

Prince

I have procured thee, Jack, a charge of foot.³

Falstaff

I would it had been of horse.⁴ Where shall I find one°   *someone*
that can steal well? Oh, for a fine thief of the age of two   180
and twenty or thereabouts! I am heinously unprovided.°   *ill equipped*
Well, God be thanked for these rebels. They offend
none but the virtuous. I laud them; I praise them.

1   *in the Temple hall*

In the hall of one of the Inns of
Court (London's law schools)

2   *Oh, I could wish this tavern were my*
     drum.

I wish I could stay here in the tavern
and gather my soldiers, rather than
go around the countryside to find
them.

Prince

Bardolph!

Bardolph

My lord?   185

Prince

Go bear this letter to Lord John of Lancaster,

To my brother John; this to my Lord of Westmorland.

[**Bardolph** *exits.*]

Go, Peto, to horse, to horse, for thou and I

Have thirty miles to ride yet ere dinner time.

[**Peto** *exits.*]

Jack, meet me tomorrow in the Temple hall[1]   190

At two o'clock in the afternoon.

regiment   There shalt thou know thy charge° and there receive

equipment   Money and order for their furniture.°

The land is burning. Percy stands on high,

And either we or they must lower lie.   195

[*He exits.*]

Falstaff

splendid   Rare words! Brave° world! [*calls*] Hostess, my break-

fast; come.—Oh, I could wish this tavern were my

drum.[2]

[*He exits.*]

1   *not a soldier of this season's stamp /*
     Should go so general current through the
     world

     **Hotspur compares soldiers to
     coins, claiming that "No other sol-
     dier, minted this year, is as highly
     valued (as Douglas)." A coin *goes cur-
     rent* when it is put into circulation.**

2   *beard*

     **Challenge (literally, pull the man's
     beard in a mocking manner)**

3   *He is grievous sick.*

     **Holinshed reports Northumber-
     land's sickness, but in the chronicle
     the rebels learn the news well
     before the battle. In *Henry IV, Part
     Two*, Rumor says that Northumber-
     land "lies crafty-sick" (Induction,
     line 37).**

Act 4, Scene 1

[*Enter* **Hotspur**, **Worcester**, *and* **Douglas**.]

Hotspur

Well said, my noble Scot. If speaking truth

In this fine age were not thought flattery,

praise Such attribution° should the Douglas have

As not a soldier of this season's stamp

Should go so general current through the world.[1]   5

despise By God, I cannot flatter. I do defy°

flatterers / better The tongues of soothers.° But a braver° place

In my heart's love hath no man than yourself.

hold / test Nay, task° me to my word; approve° me, lord.

Douglas

Thou art the king of honor.   10

No man so potent breathes upon the ground

But I will beard[2] him.

Hotspur

                    Do so, and 'tis well.

Enter [*a* **Messenger**] *with letters.*

What letters hast thou there? [*to* **Douglas**] I can but

    thank you.

Messenger

These letters come from your father.

Hotspur

Letters from him. Why comes he not himself?   15

Messenger

He cannot come, my lord. He is grievous sick.[3]

Hotspur

Zounds, how has he the leisure to be sick

1   *state of time*

Current circumstances

2   *better worth*

Worth more

3   *'Tis catching hither*

The infection spreads toward this place.

4   *his friends by deputation / Could not so soon be drawn*

Messengers were unable to assemble his friends quickly enough.

5   *any soul removed but on his own*

Any person indirectly involved but only on himself

6   *is certainly possessed / Of*

Certainly knows

unquiet / army   In such a jostling° time? Who leads his power?°
command   Under whose government° come they along?

Messenger

His letters bears his mind, not I, my lord.   20

Worcester

stay in   I prithee, tell me, doth he keep° his bed?

Messenger

He did, my lord, four days ere I set forth,

And, at the time of my departure thence,

worried about   He was much feared° by his physicians.

Worcester

healthy   I would the state of time[1] had first been whole°   25

Ere he by sickness had been visited.

His health was never better worth[2] than now.

Hotspur

Sick now? Droop now? This sickness doth infect

The very lifeblood of our enterprise.

'Tis catching hither,[3] even to our camp.   30

He writes me here that inward sickness—

And that his friends by deputation

appropriate   Could not so soon be drawn,[4] nor did he think it meet°

important   To lay so dangerous and dear° a trust

On any soul removed but on his own;[5]   35

advice   Yet doth he give us bold advertisement°

joint force / go on   That with our small conjunction° we should on°

To see how fortune is disposed to us,

losing courage   For, as he writes, there is no quailing° now,

Because the King is certainly possessed   40

Of[6] all our purposes. What say you to it?

Worcester

serious injury   Your father's sickness is a maim° to us.

Hotspur

A perilous gash, a very limb lopped off!

1   *set the exact wealth of all our states / All*
    at one cast

    **Stake the precise value of all we
    have on one *cast*, or throw, of the
    dice**

2   *so rich a main*

    **(1) such high stakes; (2) such a large
    army**

3   *nice hazard*

    Uncertain chance

4   *Faith, and so we should, / Where now
    remains a sweet reversion.*

    **Yes, that's true—whereas now,
    Northumberland's army remains
    in reserve, providing us with a
    comforting backup. A *reversion* is
    literally "an inheritance": the rebels
    can fight wholeheartedly, secure in
    the knowledge that, at some point,
    they will come into possession of
    Northumberland's military rein-
    forcements.**

5   *A comfort of retirement lives in this.*

    **This gives us something to fall
    back on.**

6   *maidenhead*

    **I.e., beginning (the image is of the
    unbroken hymen of the virgin)**

7   *division*

    **Disagreement (among the leaders
    of the rebellion)**

8   *fearful faction*

    Apprehensive supporters

9   *breed a kind of question in our cause*

    **Cause doubt to arise among those
    who support us**

10 *strict arbitrament*

    Rigorous scrutiny

absence   And yet, in faith, it is not. His present want°

worse   Seems more° than we shall find it. Were it good   45

To set the exact wealth of all our states

All at one cast?[1] To set so rich a main[2]

On the nice hazard[3] of one doubtful hour?

It were not good, for therein should we read

The very bottom and the soul of hope,   50

limit   The very list,° the very utmost bound

Of all our fortunes.

Douglas

                    Faith, and so we should,

Where now remains a sweet reversion.[4]

We may boldly spend upon the hope of what is to

     come in.

A comfort of retirement lives in this.[5]   55

Hotspur

A rendezvous, a home to fly unto,

menacingly   If that the devil and mischance look big°

Upon the maidenhead[6] of our affairs.

Worcester

wish   But yet I would° your father had been here.

nature   The quality and hair° of our attempt   60

Permits   Brooks° no division.[7] It will be thought

By some that know not why he is away

absolute   That wisdom, loyalty, and mere° dislike

Of our proceedings kept the Earl from hence.

idea   And think how such an apprehension°   65

May turn the tide of fearful faction[8]

And breed a kind of question in our cause.[9]

challenging   For well you know, we of the off'ring° side

Must keep aloof from strict arbitrament[10]

opening   And stop all sight-holes, every loop° from whence   70

The eye of reason may pry in upon us.

1   *make a head*

     Gather an army

2   *joints*

     Limbs (i.e., our various forces)

3   *As heart can think.*

     As (*whole* as) one could wish for

4   *There is not such a word / Spoke of in*
     Scotland as this term of fear.

     I.e., the Scottish don't even know
     the meaning of the word "fear."

opens   This absence of your father's draws° a curtain
            That shows the ignorant a kind of fear
            Before not dreamt of.

Hotspur
                              You strain too far.
            I rather of his absence make this use: 75

prestige It lends a luster and more great opinion,°

boldness A larger dare,° to our great enterprise
            Than if the Earl were here, for men must think
            If we without his help can make a head [1]
            To push against a kingdom, with his help   80
            We shall o'erturn it topsy-turvy down.

Still   Yet° all goes well; yet all our joints [2] are whole.

Douglas
            As heart can think. [3] There is not such a word
            Spoke of in Scotland as this term of fear. [4]

                  Enter Sir Richard **Vernon**.

Hotspur
            My cousin Vernon, welcome, by my soul.   85

Vernon
            Pray God my news be worth a welcome, lord.
            The Earl of Westmorland, seven thousand strong,
            Is marching hitherwards, with him Prince John.

Hotspur
            No harm. What more?

Vernon
                              And further I have learned,
            The King himself in person is set forth,   90
            Or hitherwards intended speedily,

battle-ready troops With strong and mighty preparation.°

1   *estridges*

    Goshawks or ostriches (more likely
    the latter, since three ostrich
    feathers form the emblem of the
    Prince of Wales)

2   *Bated*

    Impatiently flapped their wings

3   *beaver on*

    Helmet visor down

4   *Mercury*

    Messenger of the gods in Roman
    mythology, often depicted with
    wings on his sandals or hat

5   *Pegasus*

    In Greek mythology, a horse with
    wings

6   *Worse than the sun in March / This praise
    doth nourish agues.*

    March was said to be a particularly
    bad time for fevers (*agues*) because
    the sun generated enough warmth
    to breed diseases without being
    hot enough to cure them.

7   *sacrifices in their trim*

    Sacrificial animals, decorated for
    the ritual killing

8   *the fire-eyed maid*

    Bellona, Roman goddess of war

9   *offer them*

    I.e., offer them up for sacrifice

10 *mailèd Mars*

    Roman war god, Mars, in his chain
    mail armor

Hotspur

He shall be welcome too. Where is his son,
The nimble-footed madcap Prince of Wales,
carelessly tossed   And his comrades, that doffed° the world aside   95
And bid it pass?

Vernon

equipped   All furnished,° all in arms,
All plumed like estridges[1] that with the wind
Bated[2] like eagles having lately bathed,
statues   Glittering in golden coats like images,°
As full of spirit as the month of May   100
And gorgeous as the sun at midsummer,
Lively   Wanton° as youthful goats, wild as young bulls.
I saw young Harry with his beaver on,[3]
armor   His cuisses° on his thighs, gallantly armed,
Rise from the ground like feathered Mercury[4]   105
And vaulted with such ease into his seat
As if an angel dropped down from the clouds
wheel around   To turn and wind° a fiery Pegasus[5]
captivate; bewitch   And witch° the world with noble horsemanship.

Hotspur

No more, no more! Worse than the sun in March   110
This praise doth nourish agues.[6] Let them come.
They come like sacrifices in their trim,[7]
And to the fire-eyed maid[8] of smoky war
All hot and bleeding will we offer them.[9]
The mailèd Mars[10] shall on his altar sit   115
Up to the ears in blood. I am on fire
prize / near   To hear this rich reprisal° is so nigh°
test   And yet not ours. Come; let me taste° my horse,
Who is to bear me like a thunderbolt
Against the bosom of the Prince of Wales.   120
Harry to Harry shall, hot horse to horse,

1   *Worcester*

    English town (pronounced Wuh-
    ster), 50 miles to the southeast of
    Shrewsbury

2   *draw his power this fourteen days*

    Assemble his army for two more
    weeks

3   *What may the King's whole battle reach
    unto?*

    What is the total number of the
    King's troops?

4   *serve*

    Be adequate for

5   *take a muster*

    Ready our troops

6   *out of*

    Free from

Meet and ne'er part till one drop down a corpse.
Oh, that Glendower were come!

Vernon

There is more news:
I learned in Worcester,[1] as I rode along,
He cannot draw his power this fourteen days.[2]   125

Douglas

That's the worst tidings that I hear of yet.

Worcester

Ay, by my faith, that bears a frosty sound.

Hotspur

What may the King's whole battle reach unto?[3]

Vernon

To thirty thousand.

Hotspur

Forty let it be.
My father and Glendower being both away,   130
armies   The powers° of us may serve[4] so great a day.
Come; let us take a muster[5] speedily.
Doomsday is near. Die all; die merrily.

Douglas

Talk not of dying. I am out of [6] fear
Of death or death's hand for this one half year.   135

They exit.

1   *Sutton Coldfield*

Town in Warwickshire, 20 miles to the northeast of Coventry

2   *Lay out*

Use your money

3   *makes an angel*

Brings what I have spent to an *angel*, a gold coin worth between six shillings and eightpence and ten shillings.

4   *An if it do*

I.e., if that bottle can (earn you money or be made into money). Falstaff deliberately misunderstands Bardolph's meaning.

5   *I'll answer the coinage.*

I'll guarantee their value.

6   *soused gurnet*

Pickled fish

7   *King's press*

Command to conscript (*press*) soldiers. Falstaff misuses the *King's press*—he first chooses wealthy men to conscript into the king's army and then encourages them to buy their way out of this service. He is left with a comically weak band of stragglers and has made himself a considerable amount of money. This was an abuse often remarked upon by Shakespeare's

contemporaries and is certainly another comic example of Falstaff's brazen flouting of his responsibilities.

8   *I press me none but good householders*

I draft no one but well-off citizens.

9   *yeomen's sons*

Sons of minor landowners

10   *such as had been asked twice on the banns*

I.e., who are just about to be married. By law, the *banns* (announcement of a marriage) had to be read publicly in church on three successive Sundays before the marriage took place.

11   *a commodity of warm slaves*

A group of well-to-do cowards

12   *caliver*

Small musket

13   *hearts*

The heart was considered the seat of courage.

14   *bought out their services*

Bribed me to release them from military service

15   *ancients*

Ensigns (who carried a military company's standard, or banner)

Act 4, Scene 2

Enter **Falstaff** *[and]* **Bardolph**.

Falstaff
Bardolph, get thee before to Coventry. Fill me a bottle
of sack. Our soldiers shall march through. We'll to
Sutton Coldfield[1] tonight.

Bardolph
Will you give me money, captain?

Falstaff
Lay out;[2] lay out.   5

Bardolph
This bottle makes an angel.[3]

Falstaff
An if it do,[4] take it for thy labor. An if it make twenty,
take them all. I'll answer the coinage.[5] Bid my lieuten-
ant Peto meet me at town's end.

Bardolph
I will, captain. Farewell.   *He exits.*   10

Falstaff
If I be not ashamed of my soldiers, I am a soused gurnet.[6] I have misused the King's press[7] damnably. I have
for got, in exchange of° a hundred and fifty soldiers, three
hundred and odd pounds. I press me none but good
householders,[8] yeomen's sons;[9] inquire me out con-   15
engaged; betrothed tracted° bachelors, such as had been asked twice on
the banns;[10] such a commodity of warm slaves[11] as
gladly had as lief° hear the devil as a drum, such as fear the
wounded report of a caliver[12] worse than a struck° fowl or a hurt
wild duck. I pressed me none but such toasts-and-   20
pampered city dwellers butter,° with hearts[13] in their bellies no bigger than
pins' heads, and they have bought out their services;[14]
and now my whole charge consists of ancients,[15]

1   *gentlemen of companies*

Gentlemen without formal military rank

2   *Lazarus in the painted cloth where the glutton's dogs licked his sores*

In the biblical story (referred to in 3.3.29–31), Lazarus is a beggar who is sent to Heaven upon his death, while the *glutton* who refused to help him is sent to Hell. A *painted cloth* was a cheap substitute for the tapestries on which stories from the Bible were often depicted.

3   *younger sons to younger brothers*

I.e., those with no chance of inheritance (which the laws of primogeniture awarded to oldest sons)

4   *revolted tapsters*

Runaway apprentices to innkeepers

5   *feazed ancient*

Tattered military banner

6   *prodigals lately come from swine-keeping, from eating draff and husks*

Allusion to the biblical parable of the prodigal son (Luke 15:11–31), in which a rich man's son wastes his inheritance and then, employed as a pigherd, is so degraded that he wishes he could eat his animals' swill (*draff*) and corn *husks*. He then returns home and is welcomed joyfully by his father.

7   *Saint Albans*

Town on the road from London to Coventry, 25 miles northwest of London

8   *Daventry*

Town in Northamptonshire, 40 miles northwest of Saint Albans

9   *they'll find linen enough on every hedge*

I.e., by stealing the linen while it dries on hedges

10   *Jack*

(1) Falstaff's informal name (properly John); (2) quilted leather *jacket* worn by soldiers over metal armor

corporals, lieutenants, gentlemen of companies[1]—
slaves as ragged as Lazarus in the painted cloth where   25
the glutton's dogs licked his sores[2]—and such as
dishonest indeed were never soldiers, but discarded, unjust°
servingmen, younger sons to younger brothers,[3] re-
unemployed / parasites volted tapsters,[4] and ostlers tradefallen,° the cankers°
of a calm world and a long peace, ten times more   30
dishonorable-ragged than an old feazed ancient.[5]
places / that And such have I to fill up the rooms° of them as° have
bought out their services that you would think that I
had a hundred and fifty tattered prodigals lately come
from swine-keeping, from eating draff and husks.[6]   35
A mad fellow met me on the way and told me I had
gallows / conscripted unloaded all the gibbets° and pressed° the dead bodies. No eye hath seen such scarecrows. I'll not march
for sure through Coventry with them, that's flat.° Nay, and the
villains march wide betwixt the legs as if they had   40
leg shackles gyves° on, for indeed I had the most of them out
of prison. There's not a shirt and a half in all my
company, and the half shirt is two napkins tacked
together and thrown over the shoulders like a herald's
coat without sleeves; and the shirt, to say the truth,   45
i.e., innkeeper stolen from my host° at Saint Albans[7] or the red-nose
innkeeper of Daventry.[8] But that's all one; they'll find
linen enough on every hedge.[9]

Enter the **Prince** *[and the] Lord of* **Westmorland**.

Prince
swollen; breathless How now, blown° Jack?[10] How now, quilt?
Falstaff
What, Hal? How now, mad wag? What a devil dost thou   50
in Warwickshire?—My good Lord of Westmorland,

1   *cry you mercy*

     Beg your pardon

2   *I think to steal cream indeed, for thy theft*
     hath already made thee butter.

     You must have been stealing cream,
     because what you've stolen has
     made you fat.

3   *food for powder*

     Cannon fodder

4   *pit*

     I.e., mass grave

5   *three fingers in the ribs*

     Fat covering the ribs, measuring
     three-fingers deep. A *finger* was
     a unit of measurement equaling
     three quarters of an inch.

I cry you mercy:[1] I thought your Honor had already
been at Shrewsbury.

Westmorland

Faith, Sir John, 'tis more than time that I were there,

troops and you too, but my powers° are there already. The   55
proceed; march King, I can tell you, looks for us all. We must away° all
night.

Falstaff

worry about Tut, never fear° me. I am as vigilant as a cat to steal
cream.

Prince

I think to steal cream indeed, for thy theft hath   60
already made thee butter.[2] But tell me, Jack, whose
fellows are these that come after?

Falstaff

Mine, Hal, mine.

Prince

I did never see such pitiful rascals.

Falstaff

impale (on pikes) Tut, tut, good enough to toss;° food for powder,[3] food   65
better men for powder. They'll fill a pit[4] as well as better.° Tush,
man, mortal men, mortal men.

Westmorland

Ay, but, Sir John, methinks they are exceeding poor

thin; bare boned and bare,° too beggarly.

Falstaff

Faith, for their poverty, I know not where they had   70
that, and for their bareness, I am sure they never
learned that of me.

Prince

No, I'll be sworn, unless you call three fingers in the
ribs[5] bare. But, sirrah, make haste. Percy is already in
the field.   *He exits.*   75

1　　*to the latter end of a fray and the begin-*
　　　ning of a feast / Fits a dull fighter and a
　　　keen guest

　　　(I wish we could wait even longer,
　　　since) the end of a battle and the
　　　start of a meal suit someone who
　　　would rather eat than fight.

Falstaff

(at the battlefield) What, is the King encamped?°

Westmorland

delay He is, Sir John. I fear we shall stay° too long.

Falstaff

Well, to the latter end of a fray and the beginning of a
    feast

Fits a dull fighter and a keen guest.[1]   [*They*] *exit.*

1   *Looks he not for supply?*

    Doesn't he expect reinforcements?

2   *If well-respected*

    Even if carefully considered

3   *hold as little counsel with*

    Am as little touched by

Act 4, Scene 3

Enter **Hotspur**, **Worcester**, **Douglas**, [*and*] **Vernon**.

Hotspur

i.e., the King We'll fight with him° tonight.

Worcester

It may not be.

Douglas

You give him then advantage.

Vernon

Not a whit.

Hotspur

Why say you so? Looks he not for supply?[1]

Vernon

So do we.

Hotspur

His is certain; ours is doubtful.

Worcester

Good cousin, be advised: stir not tonight.   5

Vernon

[*to* **Hotspur**] Do not, my lord.

Douglas

You do not counsel well.

You speak it out of fear and cold heart.

Vernon

Do me no slander, Douglas. By my life

(And I dare well maintain it with my life)

urges If well-respected[2] honor bid° me on,   10

I hold as little counsel with[3] weak fear

As you, my lord, or any Scot that this day lives.

Let it be seen tomorrow in the battle

Which of us fears.

253

1   *horse*

Cavalry; horsemen

2   *Their courage with hard labor tame and dull, / That not a horse is half the half of himself*

Their spirits have grown slow and sluggish with their travel, so that now not a single horse has even a quarter of its normal vigor.

3   The trumpet sounds a parley.

An offstage trumpet sounds, announcing a messenger from the enemy

4   *determination*

Point of view; purpose

Douglas

Yea, or tonight.

Vernon

i.e., Enough Content.°

Hotspur

Tonight, say I. 15

Vernon

Come, come, it may not be. I wonder much,

leadership Being men of such great leading° as you are,

That you foresee not what impediments

enterprise Drag back our expedition.° Certain horse [1]

Of my cousin Vernon's are not yet come up. 20

Your uncle Worcester's horse came but today,

spirit And now their pride° and mettle is asleep,

Their courage with hard labor tame and dull,

That not a horse is half the half of himself. [2]

Hotspur

So are the horses of the enemy 25

tired from traveling In general journey-bated° and brought low.

The better part of ours are full of rest.

Worcester

i.e., number of cavalry The number° of the King exceedeth ours.

wait For God's sake, cousin, stay° till all come in.

The trumpet sounds a parley. [3]

Enter Sir Walter **Blunt**.

Blunt

I come with gracious offers from the King, 30

permit If you vouchsafe° me hearing and respect.

Hotspur

Welcome, Sir Walter Blunt, and would to God

You were of our determination. [4]

1   *even those some*

Those very people

2   *out of limit*

Outside the bounds of natural order

3   *anointed majesty*

Blunt's reference to the *anointed majesty* of Henry IV is the opening salvo in the discussion that is about to take place. He immediately associates himself with the rightful king, who is sanctified by the traditional rituals of kingship, and he explicitly repudiates the naming strategies of the rebels (see 1.3.136 and 3.1.8 and notes). In doing so he also asserts that they are rebels against a lawful king and takes the moral high ground.

4   *good deserts*

Worthy deeds (deserving of respect)

5   *your desires with interest*

I.e., even more than you desire

6   *He came but to be Duke of Lancaster, / To sue his livery*

In 1399, Henry Bolingbroke (later King Henry IV) returned from France, where he had been in exile. He maintained that he only wanted to claim the dukedom and the lands attached to that title (*to sue his livery*), all of which King Richard II had appropriated after the death of John of Gaunt, Henry's father and the former Duke.

7   *beg his peace*

Be reconciled to King Richard II

Some of us love you well, and even those some [1]

Begrudge — Envy° your great deservings and good name — 35

side; party — Because you are not of our quality°

But stand against us like an enemy.

Blunt

forbid / always — And God defend° but still° I should stand so,

So long as out of limit [2] and true rule

You stand against anointed majesty. [3] — 40

But to my charge: the King hath sent to know

grievances / on what basis — The nature of your griefs° and whereupon°

call forth — You conjure° from the breast of civil peace

Such bold hostility, teaching his duteous land

Audacious cruelty. If that the King — 45

Have any way your good deserts [4] forgot,

Which he confesseth to be manifold,

He bids you name your griefs, and with all speed

You shall have your desires with interest [5]

And pardon absolute for yourself and these — 50

instigation — Herein misled by your suggestion.°

Hotspur

The King is kind, and well we know the King

Knows at what time to promise, when to pay.

My father and my uncle and myself

Did give him that same royalty he wears. — 55

And when he was not six-and-twenty strong,

Insignificant — Sick° in the world's regard, wretched and low,

unnoticed — A poor unminded° outlaw sneaking home,

My father gave him welcome to the shore;

And when he heard him swear and vow to God — 60

i.e., the King — He° came but to be Duke of Lancaster,

To sue his livery [6] and beg his peace, [7]

loyalty — With tears of innocency and terms of zeal,°

My father, in kind heart and pity moved,

1   *The more and less came in with cap and*
     knee
     Both nobles and commoners
     treated Henry Bolingbroke
     deferentially (by greeeting him
     bareheaded and kneeling)

2   *stood in lanes*
     Lined up in rows (as Henry Boling-
     broke passed by)

3   *greatness knows itself*
     I.e., as great men understand their
     own power

4   *Steps me*
     I.e., steps. The use of *me* here (see
     also line 85) is a colloquialism call-
     ing attention to the speaker. See
     2.4.99 and note.

5   *That lie too heavy on the commonwealth*
     That oppress the citizenry

6   *Cries out upon*
     Denounces; decries

7   *seeming brow*
     I.e., pretense

8   *cut me off*
     Cut off. In both Holinshed's *Chron-*
     icles and Shakespeare's *Richard II*,
     Henry Bolingbroke captures, tries,
     and executes two of King Richard's
     advisors.

9   *he deposed the King*
     A highly partisan statement: oppo-
     nents of King Henry claimed that
     he had illegally forced King Richard
     from the throne, while his supp-
     orters argued that Richard had
     in fact abdicated after naming
     Henry Bolingbroke his heir.

10   *in the neck of that, tasked*
     Right after that, taxed

11   *his kinsman March*
     I.e., Mortimer. Here the claim to
     the throne of Edmund Mortimer,
     the Earl of March, is again pressed
     by the rebels (see note to 1.3.145
     and note).

12   *if every owner were well placed*
     If all possessions (such as the
     crown) were returned to their right-
     ful owners

Swore him assistance and performed it too.   65
Now when the lords and barons of the realm
lend support Perceived Northumberland did lean° to him,
The more and less came in with cap and knee,[1]
Met him in boroughs, cities, villages,
Attended him on bridges, stood in lanes,[2]   70
Laid gifts before him, proffered him their oaths,
Gave him their heirs as pages, followed him
i.e., joyful Even at the heels in golden° multitudes.
He presently, as greatness knows itself,[3]
Steps me[4] a little higher than his vow   75
Made to my father while his blood was poor
Upon the naked shore at Ravenspur,
And now forsooth takes on him to reform
strict Some certain edicts and some strait° decrees
That lie too heavy on the commonwealth,[5]   80
Cries out upon[6] abuses, seems to weep
show (of compassion) Over his country's wrongs, and by this face,°
This seeming brow[7] of justice, did he win
The hearts of all that he did angle for;
Proceeded further: cut me off[8] the heads   85
Of all the favorites that the absent King
as deputies In deputation° left behind him here
personally engaged When he was personal° in the Irish war.

Blunt

Tut, I came not to hear this.

Hotspur

                        Then to the point:
In short time after, he deposed the King,[9]   90
Soon after that deprived him of his life
And, in the neck of that, tasked[10] the whole state.
permitted To make that worse, suffered° his kinsman March[11]—
Who is, if every owner were well placed,[12]

1   *Indeed his king*

    Rightfully Henry's king

2   *This head of safety*

    The security of our armed forces

held hostage   Indeed his king[1]—to be engaged° in Wales,   95

abandoned; unrescued   There without ransom to lie forfeited,°

Disgraced me in my happy victories,

espionage   Sought to entrap me by intelligence,°

Drove away by chiding   Rated° mine uncle from the Council board,

In rage dismissed my father from the court,   100

Broke oath on oath, committed wrong on wrong,

And, in conclusion, drove us to seek out

in addition   This head of safety,[2] and withal° to pry

Into his title, the which we find

irregular   Too indirect° for long continuance.   105

Blunt

Shall I return this answer to the King?

Hotspur

Not so, Sir Walter. We'll withdraw awhile.

pledged   Go to the King, and let there be impawned°

Some surety for a safe return again,

And in the morning early shall mine uncle   110

Bring him our purposes. And so farewell.

Blunt

I would you would accept of grace and love.

Hotspur

And maybe so we shall.

Blunt

                 Pray God you do.   [*They exit.*]

1   *the Lord Marshal*

Thomas Mowbray, an enemy of
King Henry. (At the beginning of
Richard II, Mowbray's father and
Henry Bolingbroke are exiled from
England as the result of a bitter
dispute between the two men. In
Henry IV, Part Two the son has joined
the rebellion against the King
and is one of those executed after
the rebels surrender at Gaultree
Forest.)

2   *Scroop*

It is unclear which Scroop is
meant; several are mentioned
by Holinshed, most of which are,
at one time or other, involved in
rebellions against the throne. See
1.3.265 and note.

3   *bide the touch*

Be tested

4   *was in the first proportion*

Had the greatest numbers (among
the rebel forces)

5   *rated sinew*

Anticipated source of strength

6   *o'er-ruled by prophecies*

But see 4.1.124–125. Holinshed,
however, says that Glendower in
fact "came to the aid of the Percys."

7   *instant trial*

Immediate battle

Act 4, Scene 4

Enter [the] **Archbishop** *of York [and]* **Sir Michael**.

Archbishop

Hurry / letter   Hie,° good Sir Michael; bear this sealèd brief°
With wingèd haste to the Lord Marshal,[1]
This to my cousin Scroop,[2] and all the rest
To whom they are directed. If you knew
How much they do import, you would make haste.   5

Sir Michael

content   My good lord, I guess their tenor.°

Archbishop

Likely   Like° enough you do.
Tomorrow, good Sir Michael, is a day
Wherein the fortune of ten thousand men
Must bide the touch.[3] For, sir, at Shrewsbury,

led   As I am truly given° to understand,   10
The King with mighty and quick-raisèd power

i.e., Hotspur   Meets with Lord Harry.° And I fear, Sir Michael,
What with the sickness of Northumberland,
Whose power was in the first proportion,[4]
And what with Owen Glendower's absence thence,   15
Who with them was a rated sinew[5] too
And comes not in, o'er-ruled by prophecies,[6]
I fear the power of Percy is too weak
To wage an instant trial[7] with the King.

Sir Michael

Why, my good lord, you need not fear: 20
There is Douglas and Lord Mortimer.

Archbishop

No, Mortimer is not there.

Sir Michael

But there is Murdoch, Vernon, Lord Harry Percy,

1   *special head*

Finest soldiers

2   *'tis but wisdom to make strong*

It is only prudent to raise a defense.

army And there is my Lord of Worcester and a head°
Of gallant warriors, noble gentlemen.   25

Archbishop

And so there is. But yet the King hath drawn
The special head¹ of all the land together:
The Prince of Wales, Lord John of Lancaster,
The noble Westmorland, and warlike Blunt,
partners / worthy And many more corrivals° and dear° men   30
good reputation Of estimation° and command in arms.

Sir Michael

Doubt not, my lord, they shall be well opposed.

Archbishop

I hope no less, yet needful 'tis to fear;
hurry And to prevent the worst, Sir Michael, speed.°
For if Lord Percy thrive not, ere the King   35
army Dismiss his power° he means to visit us,
alliance For he hath heard of our confederacy,°
And 'tis but wisdom to make strong² against him.
Therefore make haste. I must go write again
To other friends, and so farewell, Sir Michael.   40

They exit.

1   *his distemp'rature*

    I.e., the sun's sickly appearance

2   *Doth play the trumpet to his purposes*

    I.e., announces the sun's intentions
    (as a trumpeter might announce
    the entrance of a monarch)

3   *orb*

    Orbit. Elizabethans often compared
    the king to the Earth, which,
    according to contemporary
    cosmological theory, stood at the
    center of the universe. Worcester
    is implored to resume his former
    obedience to the King.

4   *an exhaled meteor*

    Meteors were considered bad
    omens and were thought to have
    been *exhaled* by the sun (see 1.1.10
    and note and *Romeo and Juliet*,
    3.5.13).

5   *prodigy of fear*

    Frightening omen

6   *broachèd mischief to the unborn times*

    Evil coming in the future

Act 5, Scene 1

Enter the **King**, **Prince** *of Wales, Lord John of* **Lancaster**, *Earl of* **Westmorland**, *Sir Walter* **Blunt**, *[and]* **Falstaff**.

King
How bloodily the sun begins to peer
looming Above yon bulky° hill. The day looks pale
At his distemp'rature.[1]

Prince
              The southern wind
Doth play the trumpet to his purposes,[2]
And by his hollow whistling in the leaves   5
Foretells a tempest and a blust'ring day.

King
accord; harmonize Then with the losers let it sympathize,°
For nothing can seem foul to those that win.

The trumpet sounds. Enter **Worcester** *[and* **Vernon**].

How now, my Lord of Worcester? 'Tis not well
That you and I should meet upon such terms   10
As now we meet. You have deceived our trust
take off And made us doff° our easy robes of peace
i.e., armor To crush our old limbs in ungentle steel.°
This is not well, my lord; this is not well.
What say you to it? Will you again unknit   15
ill-mannered; violent This churlish° knot of all-abhorrèd war
And move in that obedient orb[3] again
Where you did give a fair and natural light,
And be no more an exhaled meteor,[4]
A prodigy of fear[5] and a portent   20
Of broachèd mischief to the unborn times?[6]

1   *the day of this dislike*

    This time of conflict

2   *chewet*

    Jackdaw (i.e., chatterbox)

3   *your new-fall'n right*

    **The birthright you had recently in-
    herited (on the death of your father,
    John of Gaunt)**

Worcester

Hear me, my liege:

For mine own part I could be well content

latter To entertain the lag° end of my life

With quiet hours, for I do protest   25

I have not sought the day of this dislike.[1]

King

You have not sought it? How comes it then?

Falstaff

i.e., stumbled upon Rebellion lay in his way, and he found° it.

Prince

[*to* **Falstaff**] Peace, chewet,[2] peace.

Worcester

[*to the* **King**] It pleased your Majesty to turn your looks   30

Of favor from myself and all our house,

remind And yet I must remember° you, my lord,

We were the first and dearest of your friends.

For you my staff of office did I break

rode In Richard's time, and posted° day and night   35

To meet you on the way and kiss your hand

status / reputation When yet you were in place° and in account°

Nothing so strong and fortunate as I.

It was myself, my brother, and his son

escorted That brought° you home and boldly did outdare   40

The dangers of the time. You swore to us,

And you did swear that oath at Doncaster,

plan That you did nothing purpose° 'gainst the state,

Nor claim no further than your new-fall'n right,[3]

estates The seat° of Gaunt, dukedom of Lancaster.   45

To this we swore our aid. But in short space

It rained down fortune show'ring on your head,

And such a flood of greatness fell on you—

What with our help, what with the absent King,

1   *grip the general sway*

   I.e., seize control

2   *As that ungentle gull, the cuckoo's bird, /*
   Useth the sparrow

   **As that discourteous bird, the
   cuckoo chick, exploits the sparrow.
   (Adult cuckoos lay their eggs in the
   nests of other, smaller birds; the
   young cuckoos then use their larger
   size to monopolize the nest.)**

3   *our love*

   We who loved you

4   *opposèd*

   Ready to fight you

5   *rub the elbow*

   I.e., hug themselves (in delight)

6   *hurlyburly innovation*

   Turbulent changes

7   *water colors*

   **I.e., thin excuses (the image comes
   from the translucency of *water colors*
   compared with oil paints)**

What with the injuries° of a wanton° time,   50

The seeming sufferances° that you had borne,

And the contrarious° winds that held the King

So long in his unlucky Irish wars

That all in England did repute him dead—

And from this swarm of fair advantages   55

You took occasion° to be quickly wooed

To grip the general sway¹ into your hand,

Forgot your oath to us at Doncaster;

And, being fed by us, you used us so

As that ungentle gull, the cuckoo's bird,   60

Useth the sparrow:² did oppress our nest,

Grew by our feeding to so great a bulk

That even our love³ durst not come near your sight

For fear of swallowing.° But with nimble wing

We were enforced for safety° sake to fly   65

Out of your sight and raise this present head°

Whereby we stand opposèd⁴ by such means

As you yourself have forged against° yourself

By unkind usage, dangerous° countenance,

And violation of all faith and troth°   70

Sworn to us in your younger° enterprise.

King

These things indeed you have articulate,°

Proclaimed at market crosses, read in churches,

To face° the garment of rebellion

With some fine color° that may please the eye   75

Of fickle changelings° and poor discontents,

Which gape and rub the elbow⁵ at the news

Of hurlyburly innovation.⁶

And never yet did insurrection want°

Such water colors⁷ to impaint his cause,   80

(marginal glosses, left column)

abuses / ungovernable

injustices

unfavorable

the opportunity

being swallowed

i.e., our safety's

army

to be turned against

threatening

vows

earlier

publicly stated

adorn

hue; excuse

turncoats

lack

1   *set off his head*

     Notwithstanding

2   *take the odds*

     Have the benefit

3   *so dare we venture thee, / Albeit consider-*
     ations infinite / Do make against it

     We would support you in that
     attempt, although innumerable
     considerations argue against it.

4   *Rebuke and dread correction wait on us*

     (The power of) admonishment
     and severe punishment are at my
     command.

sullen / eager	Nor moody° beggars starving° for a time
chaotic	Of pellmell° havoc and confusion.

Prince

In both your armies there is many a soul
Shall pay full dearly for this encounter

| combat | If once they join in trial.° Tell your nephew | 85 |

The Prince of Wales doth join with all the world
In praise of Henry Percy. By my hopes,
This present enterprise set off his head,[1]
I do not think a braver gentleman,
More active-valiant or more valiant-young,   90
More daring or more bold, is now alive

| i.e., present | To grace this latter° age with noble deeds. |

For my part, I may speak it to my shame,
I have a truant been to chivalry,
And so I hear he doth account me too.   95
Yet this before my father's majesty:
I am content that he shall take the odds[2]

reputation	Of his great name and estimation,°
(of soldiers)	And will, to save the blood° on either side,
my luck	Try fortune° with him in a single fight. 100

King

And, Prince of Wales, so dare we venture thee,
Albeit considerations infinite
Do make against it.[3]—No, good Worcester, no.
We love our people well, even those we love

| kinsman's | That are misled upon your cousin's° part;   105 |
| i.e., if they will / mercy | And, will° they take the offer of our grace,° |

Both he and they and you, yea, every man
Shall be my friend again, and I'll be his.

| This | So° tell your cousin, and bring me word |

What he will do. But if he will not yield,   110
Rebuke and dread correction wait on us,[4]

1   *bestride me, so*

**Stand over me (to shield me from
further attacks), so be it**

2   *colossus*

**One of the seven wonders of the
ancient world, the Colossus of
Rhodes was a massive statue of
the Roman god Apollo. It was
mistakenly believed that the statue
straddled the entrance to the
harbor at Rhodes, so that incoming
ships sailed between its legs.**

3   *Why, thou owest God a death.*

**A proverbial expression of the
inevitability of death (with a pun on
"debt," which Falstaff plays on in
the next line)**

4   *prick me off*

**Cross me off (the list of living
people)**

5   *set to a leg*

Set a broken leg

6   *A trim reckoning.*

**A fine sense of honor's value
(ironic).**

And they shall do their office. So be gone.

We will not now be troubled with reply.

under advisement   We offer fair. Take it advisedly.°

                    Worcester [*and* **Vernon**] *exit.*

Prince

It will not be accepted, on my life.   115

The Douglas and the Hotspur both together

Are confident against the world in arms.

King

regiment   Hence, therefore; every leader to his charge,°

For on their answer will we set on them,

And God befriend us as our cause is just.   120

                    All but the **Prince** *and* **Falstaff** *exit.*

Falstaff

Hal, if thou see me down in the battle and bestride

me, so.[1] 'Tis a point of friendship.

Prince

Nothing but a colossus[2] can do thee that friendship.

Say thy prayers, and farewell.

Falstaff

I would 'twere bedtime, Hal, and all well.   125

Prince

Why, thou owest God a death.[3]   [*He exits.*]

Falstaff

'Tis not due yet. I would be loath to pay him before his

eager   day. What need I be so forward° with him that calls

spurs   not on me? Well, 'tis no matter. Honor pricks° me on.

Yea, but how if honor prick me off[4] when I come on?   130

How then? Can honor set to a leg?[5] No. Or an arm?

pain   No. Or take away the grief° of a wound? No. Honor

hath no skill in surgery, then? No. What is honor?

A word. What is in that word "honor"? What is that

"honor"? Air. A trim reckoning.[6] Who hath it? He that   135

1   *insensible*

Unable to be experienced by the
senses

2   *scutcheon*

Shield or canvas painted with a
coat of arms, often displayed as a
memorial to a dead man

3   *catechism*

An instructional technique based
on set questions and answers (used
regularly in Catholic religious
teaching)

died o' Wednesday. Doth he feel it? No. Doth he
hear it? No. 'Tis insensible,[1] then? Yea, to the dead.
But will it not live with the living? No. Why? Detrac-

Slander / permit tion° will not suffer° it. Therefore, I'll none of it. Hon-
or is a mere scutcheon.[2] And so ends my catechism.[3]   140

                                              He exits.

1   *Suspicion all our lives shall be stuck full of*
    eyes

I.e., because he suspects us (of
treachery), the King will set spies
to watch us for as long as we live.
Worcester imagines suspicion as
a creature with many eyes, like the
legendary monster, Argus, with 100
eyes, some of which never closed.

2   *never so tame, so cherished and locked up*

However tame he might seem, however well cared for and caged

3   *The better cherished still the nearer death*

Who are always (*still*) treated better when they're close to being
slaughtered

4   *an adopted name of privilege*

A nickname (i.e., "Hotspur") that
explains his reckless behavior

5   *his corruption being ta'en from us*

Since his disobedience to the King
derived from us

Act 5, Scene 2

Enter **Worcester** *[and] Sir Richard* **Vernon**.

Worcester
Oh no, my nephew must not know, Sir Richard,
generous The liberal° and kind offer of the King.

Vernon
'Twere best he did.

Worcester
ruined   Then are we all undone.°
It is not possible; it cannot be
The King should keep his word in loving us.   5
continually He will suspect us still° and find a time
To punish this offense in other faults.
Suspicion all our lives shall be stuck full of eyes,[1]
For treason is but trusted like the fox,
Who, never so tame, so cherished and locked up,[2]   10
quality Will have a wild trick° of his ancestors.
either Look how we can, or° sad or merrily,
misunderstand Interpretation will misquote° our looks,
And we shall feed like oxen at a stall,
The better cherished still the nearer death.[3]   15
My nephew's trespass may be well forgot.
It hath the excuse of youth and heat of blood,
And an adopted name of privilege:[4]
hot-tempered disposition A hairbrained Hotspur governed by a spleen.°
All his offenses live upon my head   20
lead And on his father's. We did train° him on,
And, his corruption being ta'en from us,[5]
source We as the spring° of all shall pay for all.
Therefore, good cousin, let not Harry know
In any case the offer of the King.   25

1   *Deliver up*

    Release (Westmorland has been
    held hostage for the safe return
    of Worcester and Vernon; see
    4.3.108–109 and 5.2.43.)

2   *forswearing that he is forsworn*

    Falsely swearing that he has been
    falsely accused (by Worcester)

Vernon

Report Deliver° what you will; I'll say 'tis so.

Enter **Hotspur** [*and* **Douglas**].

Here comes your cousin.

Hotspur

                              My uncle is returned.

Deliver up [1] my Lord of Westmorland.

—Uncle, what news?

Worcester

The King will bid you battle presently.   30

Douglas

Defy him by the Lord of Westmorland.

Hotspur

Lord Douglas, go you and tell him so.

Douglas

Marry, and shall, and very willingly.   **Douglas** *exits.*

Worcester

indication of There is no seeming° mercy in the King.

Hotspur

Did you beg any? God forbid!   35

Worcester

I told him gently of our grievances,

amended Of his oath-breaking, which he mended° thus

By now forswearing that he is forsworn. [2]

He calls us "rebels," "traitors," and will scourge

With haughty arms this hateful name in us.   40

Enter **Douglas**.

Douglas

Arm, gentlemen! To arms, for I have thrown

1   *Which cannot choose but bring him*
    quickly on

    Which (i.e., the *defiance*) must insure
    the King will soon attack

2   *draw short breath*

    I.e., exert himself

3   *Harry Monmouth*

    I.e., Prince Henry, who was born in
    Monmouth, Wales

4   *proof of arms*

    A test of his skills in armed combat

5   *duties of*

    Respect owed to

6   *Trimmed up your praises*

    Ornamented his praise for you

7   *still dispraising praise valued with you*

    Constantly saying that his praise did
    not match your real worth

8   *blushing cital*

    Embarrassed mention

A brave° defiance in King Henry's teeth,°   *proud / i.e., face*
And Westmorland, that was engaged,° did bear° it,   *held hostage / carry*
Which cannot choose but bring him quickly on.[1]

Worcester
The Prince of Wales stepped forth before the King,   45
And, nephew, challenged you to single fight.

Hotspur
Oh, would° the quarrel lay upon our heads,   *I wish*
And that no man might draw short breath[2] today
But I and Harry Monmouth![3] Tell me, tell me,
How showed his tasking?° Seemed it in contempt?   *challenge*   50

Vernon
No, by my soul. I never in my life
Did hear a challenge urged more modestly,
Unless a brother should a brother dare
To gentle° exercise and proof of arms.[4]   *noble*
He gave you all the duties of[5] a man,   55
Trimmed up your praises[6] with a princely tongue,
Spoke your deservings like a chronicle,
Making you ever better than his praise
By still dispraising praise valued with you,[7]
And, which became him like a prince indeed,   60
He made a blushing cital[8] of himself,
And chid° his truant youth with such a grace   *rebuked*
As if he mastered there a double spirit
Of teaching and of learning instantly.°   *simultaneously*
There did he pause, but let me tell the world: 65
If he outlive the envy° of this day,   *malice*
England did never owe° so sweet a hope,   *own*
So much misconstrued in his wantonness.°   *wild behavior*

Hotspur
Cousin, I think thou art enamorèd
On° his follies. Never did I hear   *Of*   70

1   *so wild a liberty*

     So irresponsibly free

2   *shrink under my courtesy*

     **Cower at my own show of courtesy
     (i.e., my attack)**

3   *Than I that have not well the gift of
     tongue / Can lift your blood up with
     persuasion*

     **Than (listen to) me, who lacks the
     eloquence to rouse you with my
     rhetoric**

4   *To spend that shortness basely were too
     long / If life did ride upon a dial's point, /
     Still ending at the arrival of an hour.*

     **A life spent in wasteful pursuits
     would be too long, even if it only
     lasted as long as takes a clock's
     hand (*dial's point*) to travel around
     the clock face, always ending upon
     the hour.**

5   *An if*

     If

6   *profess not*

     Have no skill in

Of any prince so wild a liberty.[1]
But be he as he will, yet once ere night
I will embrace him with a soldier's arm,
That he shall shrink under my courtesy.[2]
—Arm, arm, with speed! And fellows, soldiers, friends,   75
Better consider what you have to do
Than I that have not well the gift of tongue
Can lift your blood up with persuasion.[3]

Enter a **Messenger**.

Messenger
My lord, here are letters for you.
Hotspur
I cannot read them now.   80
—O gentlemen, the time of life is short.
To spend that shortness basely were too long

Even if If° life did ride upon a dial's point,
Still ending at the arrival of an hour.[4]
An if[5] we live, we live to tread on kings;   85

glorious If die, brave° death, when princes die with us.
as for Now, for° our consciences, the arms are fair
When the intent of bearing them is just.

Enter another [**Messenger**].

Second Messenger
quickly My lord, prepare. The King comes on apace.°
Hotspur
I thank him that he cuts me from my tale,   90
For I profess not[6] talking. Only this:
Let each man do his best. And here draw I a sword,
tempered steel Whose temper° I intend to stain

1   Esperance!

     **Hope! (family motto of the Percys;
     see 2.3.71 and note)**

2   *Heaven to Earth*

     **It is most likely (literally, "I would
     bet Heaven against Earth")**

3   *A second time*

     Again

With the best blood that I can meet withal
In the adventure of this perilous day.   95
Now, *Esperance!*[1] Percy! And set on!
Sound all the lofty instruments of war,
And by that music let us all embrace,
For, Heaven to Earth,[2] some of us never shall
A second time[3] do such a courtesy.   100

Here they embrace. The trumpets sound.

[They exit.]

1   Alarum

     Call to arms on trumpet or drums

2   *crossest me*

     Fight with me

3   *upon my head*

     I.e., by fighting me

4   *dear today hath bought / Thy likeness*

     **Has paid heavily today for pretend-
ing to be you**

5   *Humbleton*

     See 1.1.55 and note.

Act 5, Scene 3

*The **King** enters with his power [and they cross the stage]. Alarum* [1]
*to the battle. Then enter **Douglas** and Sir Walter **Blunt**,*
*[disguised as the **King**].*

Blunt

What is thy name that in the battle thus
Thou crossest me? [2]
What honor dost thou seek upon my head? [3]

Douglas

Know then, my name is Douglas,

follow   And I do haunt° thee in the battle thus   5
Because some tell me that thou art a king.

Blunt

They tell thee true.

Douglas

The Lord of Stafford dear today hath bought
Thy likeness, [4] for instead of thee, King Harry,
This sword hath ended him. So shall it thee,   10

yourself   Unless thou yield thee° as my prisoner.

Blunt

I was not born a yielder, thou proud Scot,
And thou shalt find a king that will revenge
Lord Stafford's death.   *They fight.* **Douglas** *kills* **Blunt**.

         *Then enter **Hotspur**.*

Hotspur

O Douglas, hadst thou fought at Humbleton [5] thus,   15
I never had triumphed upon a Scot.

Douglas

All's done; all's won. Here breathless lies the King.

1   *Semblably furnished like*

Dressed identically to. The battlefield seems to have many fighting
in the King's *coats*—the surcoat
worn over armor featuring the
royal coat of arms—to divert and
confuse the enemy.

2   *A fool*

I.e., the name "fool"

3   *The King hath many marching in his
coats.*

I.e., there are many decoy kings
on the field. For *coats*, see note 1
above.

4   *stand full fairly for the day*

Seem likely to gain the victory

5   *'scape shot-free*

(1) i.e., leave without settling the
tavern bill; (2) escape the battle
with no *shot* (bullets) in me

6   *scoring*

(1) marking a tab (as in a tavern)
by *scoring* notches in a board; (2)
wounding

7   *Here's no vanity.*

Sir Walter Blunt has no more concern about worldly things (since he
is dead), an allusion to Ecclesiastes
12:8 in the Bible: "Vanity of vanities,
says the Teacher; all is vanity."

8   *where they are peppered*

I.e., into the heat of the battle. Corrupt officers were known to lead
their men into the thick of the fighting, where many were certain to
be killed, and then to collect their
fallen men's pay after the battle.

Hotspur

Where?

Douglas

Here.

Hotspur

This, Douglas? No, I know this face full well.   20

A gallant knight he was. His name was Blunt,

Semblably furnished like [1] the King himself.

Douglas

wherever   [*to* **Blunt**] A fool [2] go with thy soul whither° it goes!

A borrowed title hast thou bought too dear.

Why didst thou tell me that thou wert a king?   25

Hotspur

The King hath many marching in his coats. [3]

Douglas

Now, by my sword, I will kill all his coats.

I'll murder all his wardrobe, piece by piece,

Until I meet the King.

Hotspur

                    Up and away!

Our soldiers stand full fairly for the day. [4]   [*They exit.*]   30

Alarum. Enter **Falstaff** *alone.*

Falstaff

Though I could 'scape shot-free [5] at London, I fear the

head   shot here. Here's no scoring [6] but upon the pate.°

Soft, who are you? Sir Walter Blunt. There's honor for

you. Here's no vanity. [7] I am as hot as molten lead and

as heavy too. God keep lead out of me; I need no more   35

weight than mine own bowels. I have led my ragamuf-

fins where they are peppered. [8] There's not three of my

1   *for the town's end*

    Fit only for the town gates, a com-
    mon gathering place for beggars.
    Falstaff's surviving men will have to
    beg because they are permanently
    disabled.

2   *Turk Gregory*

    The figure of *Turk Gregory* is a fasci-
    nating combination. Falstaff con-
    flates the Turk, commonly associ-
    ated with martial valor, cruelty, and
    impiety, with either Pope Gregory
    VII or Gregory XIII, both character-
    ized as tyrannical and violent by
    English Protestants. The very office
    of the pope was associated with the
    antichrist, as indeed was the *Turk*.
    So common was this connection
    that John Foxe, author of the monu-
    mental *Actes and Monumentes* (1563),
    cannot determine who is the actual
    antichrist, the pope or the Turk. In
    connecting the two so explicitly
    here, Falstaff plays on their shared
    negative connotations, demoniz-
    ing both in a provocative conflation
    common to English Protestant
    polemicists.

3   *paid*

    Settled accounts with (i.e., killed)

4   *made him sure*

    Killed him. The Prince, however,
    takes the line to mean, "found him
    reliable."

5   *sack*

    Plunder (but with a play on the
    name of Falstaff's favorite drink)

6   *Well, if Percy be alive, I'll pierce him.*

    A play on the similarity between
    Percy and *pierce* (pronounced, at the
    time, like the word "purse")

hundred and fifty left alive, and they are for the
town's end[1] to beg during life. But who comes here?

Enter the **Prince**.

Prince

What, stand'st thou idle here? Lend me thy sword.   40
Many a nobleman lies stark and stiff
gloating   Under the hoofs of vaunting° enemies,
Whose deaths are yet unrevenged. I prithee,
Lend me thy sword.

Falstaff

O Hal, I prithee, give me leave to breathe awhile. Turk   45
Gregory[2] never did such deeds in arms as I have done
this day. I have paid[3] Percy; I have made him sure.[4]

Prince

He is indeed, and living to kill thee.
I prithee, lend me thy sword.

Falstaff

Nay, before God, Hal, if Percy be alive, thou gets not   50
my sword; but take my pistol, if thou wilt.

Prince

holster   Give it me. What, is it in the case?°

Falstaff

Ay, Hal, 'tis hot; 'tis hot. There's that will sack[5] a city.
          The **Prince** *draws it out and finds it to be a bottle of sack.*

Prince

What, is it a time to jest and dally now?
                              He throws the bottle at him; he exits.

Falstaff

Well, if Percy be alive, I'll pierce him.[6] If he do come in   55

1   *carbonado*

     Meat slashed with a knife in
     preparation for grilling

so be it my way, so;° if he do not, if I come in his willingly, let
him make a carbonado ¹ of me. I like not such grin-
ning honor as Sir Walter hath. Give me life, which if
I can save, so. If not, honor comes unlooked for, and
there's an end.   [*He exits, with* **Blunt**'s *body.*]   60

1   Excursions

     The term indicates various sword
     fights on the stage used to indicate
     the continuing battle.

2   *stained*

     Blood-stained (and perhaps also
     "shamed")

Act 5, Scene 4

Alarum. Excursions.[1] *Enter the* **King**, *the* **Prince**, *Lord John of*
Lancaster, *[and the] Earl of* **Westmorland**.

King

I prithee, Harry, withdraw thyself. Thou bleedest too
    much.
—Lord John of Lancaster, go you with him.

Lancaster

Not I, my lord, unless I did bleed too.

Prince

advances   I beseech your Majesty, make up,°
retreat / alarm   Lest your retirement° do amaze° your friends.   5

King

I will do so.—My Lord of Westmorland,
Lead him to his tent.

Westmorland

Come, my lord, I'll lead you to your tent.

Prince

Lead me, my lord? I do not need your help,
And God forbid a shallow scratch should drive   10
The Prince of Wales from such a field as this,
Where stained[2] nobility lies trodden on
and rebels' arms triumph in massacres.

Lancaster

pause   We breathe° too long. Come, cousin Westmorland;
Our duty this way lies. For God's sake, come.   15

                    [He and **Westmorland** *exit.]*

Prince

By God, thou hast deceived me, Lancaster.
possessor   I did not think thee lord° of such a spirit.
Before, I loved thee as a brother, John,
But now, I do respect thee as my soul.

1   *lustier maintenance*

     More enthusiastic conduct

2   *Hydra's heads*

     The mythical Hydra was a beast with
     many heads; whenever one head
     was cut off, two would grow in its
     place. The monster was eventu-
     ally killed by the legendary hero
     Hercules.

3   *those colors*

     I.e., uniforms that mark the wearer
     as a supporter of the King

4   *shadows*

     Substitutes; images (though
     shadows was also used as a slang
     term for actors)

King

(of his sword) I saw him hold Lord Percy at the point° 20
With lustier maintenance¹ than I did look for
youthful Of such an ungrown° warrior.

Prince

Oh, this boy lends mettle to us all. *He exits.*

[*Enter* **Douglas**.]

Douglas

Another king! They grow like Hydra's heads.²
—I am the Douglas, fatal to all those 25
That wear those colors³ on them. What art thou
That counterfeit'st the person of a king?

King

The King himself, who, Douglas, grieves at heart,
So many of his shadows⁴ thou hast met
actual And not the very° King. I have two boys 30
Who seek Seek° Percy and thyself about the field,
But, seeing thou fall'st on me so luckily,
challenge; test I will assay° thee. And defend thyself.

Douglas

I fear thou art another counterfeit,
And yet, in faith, thou bearest thee like a king. 35
i.e., my prize But mine° I am sure thou art, whoe'er thou be;
And thus I win thee. *They fight.*

*The **King** being in danger, enter **Prince** of Wales.*

Prince

likely Hold up thy head, vile Scot, or thou art like°
Never to hold it up again. The spirits

1   *valiant Shirley, Stafford, Blunt*

    Noblemen (like *Sir Nicholas Gawsey*
    and *Clifton* mentioned in lines 44
    and 45) taking part in the battle

2   *Cheerly*

    An exclamation of encouragement
    (which the Prince speaks before
    realizing that the soldier he is ad-
    dressing is the King and that there
    is a lull in the fighting)

3   *mak'st some tender of*

    Care something for

4   *Make up*

    I.e., take your troops

Of valiant Shirley, Stafford, Blunt[1] are in my arms. 40
It is the Prince of Wales that threatens thee,

except when Who never promiseth but° he means to pay.

They fight. **Douglas** *flieth.*

Cheerly,[2] my lord. How fares your Grace?

aid Sir Nicholas Gawsey hath for succor° sent,
And so hath Clifton. I'll to Clifton straight. 45

King

Stay and breathe awhile.

reputation Thou hast redeemed thy lost opinion°
And showed thou mak'st some tender of[3] my life
In this fair rescue thou hast brought to me.

Prince

O God, they did me too much injury 50

yearned That ever said I hearkened° for your death.
If it were so, I might have let alone

disdainful The insulting° hand of Douglas over you,
Which would have been as speedy in your end
As all the poisonous potions in the world, 55
And saved the treacherous labor of your son.

King

Make up[4] to Clifton. I'll to Sir Nicholas Gawsey.

King *exits.*

Enter **Hotspur**.

Hotspur

If I mistake not, thou art Harry Monmouth.

Prince

Thou speak'st as if I would deny my name.

Hotspur

My name is Harry Percy.

1   *Two stars keep not their motion in one*
     sphere

     I.e., there is only room for one
     Harry in England. Prince Henry
     refers to the idea in Renaissance
     cosmology that each star orbitted
     (*kept . . . their motion*) in a discrete,
     concentric sphere

2   *crest*

     (1) i.e., head; (2) heraldic crest or
     coat of arms

3   The **Prince** killeth **Hotspur**.

     In Holinshed's account of the
     battle, Hotspur's killer remains
     unidentified, though earlier in
     the history he says that "the king
     got the victory and slew the Lord
     Percy."

Prince

                                        Why, then I see   60
A very valiant rebel of the name.
I am the Prince of Wales; and think not, Percy,
To share with me in glory any more.
Two stars keep not their motion in one sphere,¹
endure   Nor can one England brook° a double reign   65
Of Harry Percy and the Prince of Wales.

Hotspur

Nor shall it, Harry, for the hour is come
I wish   To end the one of us, and would° to God
Thy name in arms were now as great as mine.

Prince

I'll make it greater ere I part from thee,   70
And all the budding honors on thy crest²
cut   I'll crop° to make a garland for my head.

Hotspur

boasts   I can no longer brook thy vanities.°   *They fight.*

                        Enter **Falstaff**.

Falstaff

Well said, Hal! To it, Hal! Nay, you shall find no boys'
play here, I can tell you.   75

                    Enter **Douglas**. *He fighteth with* **Falstaff**,
                    [*who*] *falls down as if he were dead.* [**Douglas** *exits.*]
                    The **Prince** *killeth* **Hotspur**.³

Hotspur

O Harry, thou hast robbed me of my youth.
I better brook the loss of brittle life
Than those proud titles thou hast won of me.

1   *But thoughts, the slave of life, and life,*
    time's fool, / And time, that takes survey
    of all the world, / Must have a stop.

    **Not only thoughts, which end when
    life does, nor life itself, which is
    finite for all, but even time, which
    controls the whole world, will come
    to an end.**

2   *two paces*

    I.e., enough room for a grave

3   *wert sensible of*

    Could feel

4   *favors*

    **Scarves or plumes worn on the
    helmet (often as a sign of a lady's
    favor)**

5   *Have a heavy miss of thee*

    **Keenly miss you (with an obvious
    pun on *heavy*)**

6   *Emboweled*

    **Disemboweled (in preparation for
    embalming)**

They wound my thoughts worse than thy sword my
    flesh.
But thoughts, the slaves of life, and life, time's fool,   80
And time, that takes survey of all the world,
Must have a stop.[1] Oh, I could prophesy,
But that the earthy and cold hand of death
Lies on my tongue. No, Percy, thou art dust,
And food for—   [*He dies.*]   85

Prince

For worms, brave Percy. Fare thee well, great heart.
Ill-weaved ambition, how much art thou shrunk!
When that this body did contain a spirit,
enclosure A kingdom for it was too small a bound,°
But now two paces[2] of the vilest earth   90
Is room enough. This earth that bears thee dead
valiant Bears not alive so stout° a gentleman.
If thou wert sensible of[3] courtesy,
heartfelt / affection I should not make so dear° a show of zeal.°
But let my favors[4] hide thy mangled face,   95
And even in thy behalf I'll thank myself
deserved For doing these fair° rites of tenderness.
Adieu, and take thy praise with thee to Heaven.
Thy ignominy sleep with thee in the grave,
But not remembered in thy epitaph.   100

                 He spieth **Falstaff** *on the ground.*

What, old acquaintance, could not all this flesh
Keep in a little life? Poor Jack, farewell.
I could have better spared a better man.
Oh, I should have a heavy miss of thee[5]
If I were much in love with vanity.   105
Death hath not struck so fat a deer today,
Though many dearer in this bloody fray.
Emboweled[6] will I see thee by and by;

1 *powder*

   (1) embalm; (2) salt (in order to
   preserve me as food)

2 *termagant*

   Blustering and savage. *Termagant*
   was a fabricated deity supposedly
   worshipped by Muslims as part
   of an unholy trinity (along with
   Mahomet and Apollo). He was proverbially furious and cruel, and he
   is invoked here in association with
   the unruly Scot, Douglas.

3 *scot and lot*

   Completely (with the obvious play
   on *scot*)

4 *to counterfeit dying when a man thereby*
   liveth

   To fake your own death in order to
   stay alive

5 *Nothing confutes me but eyes*

   Only someone who sees what I'm
   doing could refute my story later.

6 *fleshed / Thy maiden sword*

   Initiated your sword in bloodshed;
   participated in your first battle

Till then in blood by noble Percy lie.   *He exits.*
                                              Falstaff *riseth up.*

Falstaff

"Emboweled"? If thou embowel me today, I'll give   110
you leave to powder[1] me and eat me too tomorrow.
'Sblood, 'twas time to counterfeit, or that hot termagant[2] Scot had paid° me scot and lot[3] too. Counterfeit?
I lie; I am no counterfeit. To die is to be a counterfeit,
for he° is but the counterfeit of a man who hath not   115
the life of a man; but to counterfeit dying when a man
thereby liveth[4] is to be no counterfeit, but the true
and perfect image of life indeed. The better part of
valor is discretion, in the which better part° I have
saved my life. Zounds, I am afraid of this gunpowder°   120
Percy, though he be dead. How if he should counterfeit too and rise? By my faith, I am afraid he would
prove the better counterfeit. Therefore I'll make him
sure, yea, and I'll swear I killed him. Why may not he
rise as well as I? Nothing confutes me but eyes,[5] and   125
nobody sees me. Therefore, sirrah, [*stabs the body*] with
a new wound in your thigh, come you along with me.
                          He takes up **Hotspur** *on his back.*

                  Enter **Prince** [*and*] *John of* **Lancaster**.

Prince

Come, brother John. Full bravely hast thou fleshed
Thy maiden sword.[6]

Lancaster

But soft, whom have we here?   130
Did you not tell me this fat man was dead?

Prince

I did. I saw him dead,

(marginal glosses, left column:)
i.e., killed
i.e., a dead man
share; role
hot-headed

1   *a double man*

     (1) an apparition (a dead man who
     appears again to the living and thus
     leads a *double* existence); (2) two
     men (since he is carrying Hotspur
     on his back, and presumably drops
     him here)

2   *at an instant*

     Simultaneously

3   *long hour*

     I.e., for a long time

4   *do thee grace*

     Bring you honor

Breathless and bleeding on the ground.—Art thou
    alive?
Or is it fantasy that plays upon our eyesight?
I prithee, speak. We will not trust our eyes   135
Without our ears. Thou art not what thou seem'st.

Falstaff

No, that's certain. I am not a double man.[1] But if I be
knave   not Jack Falstaff, then am I a jack.° There is Percy. If
so be it   your father will do me any honor, so;° if not, let him
kill the next Percy himself. I look to be either earl or   140
duke, I can assure you.

Prince

Why, Percy I killed myself, and saw thee dead.

Falstaff

Didst thou? Lord, Lord, how this world is given to
lying. I grant you, I was down and out of breath, and
so was he, but we rose both at an instant[2] and fought   145
a long hour[3] by Shrewsbury clock. If I may be believed,
so; if not, let them that should reward valor bear the
swear   sin upon their own heads. I'll take° it upon my death,
I gave him this wound in the thigh. If the man were
alive and would deny it, zounds, I would make him eat   150
a piece of my sword.

Lancaster

This is the strangest tale that ever I heard.

Prince

This is the strangest fellow, brother John.
[*to* **Falstaff**] Come, bring your luggage nobly on your
    back.
For my part, if a lie may do thee grace,[4]   155
most complimentary   I'll gild it with the happiest° terms I have.

                       A retreat is sounded.

The trumpet sounds retreat. The day is ours.

1   *grow great*

     Become a nobleman

2   *purge*

     (1) take purgatives so I vomit and
     thus lose weight; (2) be penitent
     and reform

i.e., highest point   Come, brother, let us to the highest° of the field
                         To see what friends are living, who are dead.

                                                 [*He and **Lancaster**] exit.*

                         Falstaff
                         I'll follow, as they say, for reward. He that rewards me,   160
                         God reward him. If I do grow great,[1] I'll grow less, for
                         I'll purge[2] and leave sack and live cleanly as a noble-
                         man should do.   *He exits [carrying the body].*

1   *grace*

     Promise of forgiveness

2   *turn our offers contrary*

     Reverse the intention of our offer

3   *upon our party*

     Fighting on our side

4   *pause upon*

     Think about later

5   *Upon the foot of fear*

     Running in fear

Act 5, Scene 5

The trumpets sound. Enter the **King**, **Prince** *of Wales, Lord John of* **Lancaster**, *Earl of* **Westmorland**, *with* **Worcester** *and* **Vernon** *prisoners [with soldiers].*

King

i.e., defeat   Thus ever did rebellion find rebuke.°

Malicious   —Ill-spirited° Worcester, did not we send grace,[1]

Pardon, and terms of love to all of you?

And wouldst thou turn our offers contrary,[2]

quality   Misuse the tenor° of thy kinsman's trust?   5

Three knights upon our party[3] slain today,

A noble earl and many a creature else

Had been alive this hour,

If like a Christian thou hadst truly borne

information   Betwixt our armies true intelligence.°   10

Worcester

What I have done my safety urged me to,

And I embrace this fortune patiently,

Since not to be avoided it falls on me.

King

Bear Worcester to the death and Vernon too.

Other offenders we will pause upon.[4]   15

               [**Worcester** *and* **Vernon** *exit under guard.*]

battle   How goes the field?°

Prince

The noble Scot, Lord Douglas, when he saw

The fortune of the day quite turned from him,

The noble Percy slain, and all his men

Upon the foot of fear,[5] fled with the rest,   20

And, falling from a hill, he was so bruised

That the pursuers took him. At my tent

1   *This honorable bounty*

     **The honor of performing this
     generous deed**

2   *give away*

     Confer on (Douglas)

3   *bend you*

     Direct yourselves

4   *so fair is done*

     Is so successfully completed

5   *till all our own be won*

     **Until everything that is rightfully
     ours be brought back under control**

The Douglas is, and I beseech your Grace
I may dispose of him.

King

                    With all my heart.

Prince

Then, brother John of Lancaster, to you   25
This honorable bounty[1] shall belong.
Go to the Douglas and deliver him
Up to his pleasure, ransomless and free.

helmets His valors shown upon our crests° today
Have taught us how to cherish such high deeds   30
Even in the bosom of our adversaries.

Lancaster

I thank your Grace for this high courtesy,
Which I shall give away[2] immediately.

King

forces Then this remains, that we divide our power.°
You, son John, and my cousin Westmorland,   35

greatest Towards York shall bend you[3] with your dearest° speed
To meet Northumberland and the prelate Scroop,
Who, as we hear, are busily in arms.
Myself and you, son Harry, will towards Wales
To fight with Glendower and the Earl of March.   40

its Rebellion in this land shall lose his° sway,
Meeting the check of such another day;

i.e., battle And since this business° so fair is done,[4]

stop Let us not leave° till all our own be won.[5]   *They exit.*

THE HISTORIE OF
Henry the fourth.

Enter the King, Lord Iohn of Lancaster, Earle of Westmerland, with others.

King.

O shaken as we are, so wan with care,
Find we a time for frighted peace to pant,
And breath short winded accents of new broiles
To be commenc̃te in stronds a far remote?
No more the thirsty entrance of this soile
Shal dawbe her lips with her own childrens bloud,
No more shall trenching war channel her fields,
Nor bruise her flourets with the armed hoofes
Of hostile paces: those opposed eies,
Which like the meteors of a troubled heauen,
Al of one nature, of one substance bred,
Did lately meete in the intestine shocke
And furious close of ciuill butcherie,
Shall now in mutuall welbeseeming rankes,
March all one way, and be no more oppos'd
Against acquaintance, kindred and allyes.
The edge of war, like an ill sheathed knife,
No more shall cut his maister: therefore friends,
As far as to the sepulcher of Christ,
Whose soldiour now, vnder whose blessed crosse
We are impressed and ingag'd to fight,
Forthwith a power of English shall we leauy,
Whose armes were moulded in their mothers wombe,
To chase these pagans in those holy fields,
Ouer whose acres walkt those blessed feet,

A 2   Which

A reproduction of the first page of *Henry IV, Part One* in the Quarto (1598).

Editing *Henry IV, Part One*
by David Scott Kastan

The earliest surviving complete text of *Henry IV, Part One* is found in the Quarto published in 1598 (Q1), though the play had been published earlier that year in an edition of which only a single fragment survives (Q0). Of all the plays published in England before 1640, only twelve had a second edition published in the same year as the first, so this reissuing is a sign of the play's remarkable popularity. In fact, the play is Shakespeare's best-selling play text, with further editions in 1599, 1604, 1608, 1613, and 1622, before it was published among the plays in the Folio of 1623. (A "quarto" refers to a book made from sheets of paper each folded twice to provide four leaves or eight pages; a folio is a larger book made from sheets of paper folded once to provide two leaves or four pages.)

Although the 1599 Quarto (Q2) claims on its title page to be "Newly corrected by W. Shakespeare," the claim is merely a publisher's puff. In fact, the edition is based completely on Q1, and indeed every edition of this play after the first seems to have been printed from the one before it. What minor differences exist between them are merely the result of the usual printing house procedures in which obvious errors would be corrected even as new ones accidentally crept in. No manuscript of any of Shakespeare's plays has survived, so in the case of *Henry IV, Part One* we can get only as close to Shakespeare's hand as the earliest printed text from which the others derive. Therefore, a modern edition of the play must be based on Q1, with the exception of 1.3.200 to 2.2.105, which is all that exists of Q0, the text from which Q1 was printed.

In general, the editorial work of this present edition is conservative, preserving and clarifying the text that appears in the 1598 Quartos, emending only when a reading seems to be manifestly in error, as at 2.2.11, where the reading (of both Q0 and Q1) is "squire" but "square" is obviously the intended word, or in 3.2.59, where the Quarto prints "wan" but clearly "won" is what is required. All such changes are recorded in the Textual Notes below. All other changes to the Quarto texts are in accord with modern practices of editing Shakespeare: normalizing spelling, capitalization, and punctuation, removing superfluous italics and capitalization, regularizing the names of characters, and rationalizing entrances and exits. Place names are given in their modern form, and the names of historical figures are spelled as they are in the *Dictionary of National Biography*. Editorial stage directions are kept to a minimum and added always in brackets.

A comparison of the edited text of Act 1, scene 1, lines 1–25 with the facsimile page of Q1 (on p. 316) reveals some of the issues in this process of editing. Most of the changes are simple matters of modernization. Spelling is regularized to reflect modern spelling practices. As spelling in Shakespeare's time had not yet been standardized, words were spelled in various ways that indicated their proximate pronunciation, and compositors, in any case, were under no obligation to follow the spelling of their copy. Little, then, is to be gained in an edition such as this by following the spelling of the original printed text. Therefore in line 4 "commencte" unproblematically becomes "commenced, while in the line 14 "mutuall" becomes "mutual" and "rankes" "ranks." As these examples indicate, old spellings are consistently modernized, but old *forms* of words (e.g., "thou

mak'st" later in the scene at line 77, where we would say "you make")
are retained. Punctuation, too, is adjusted to reflect modern practice
(which is designed to clarify the logical relations between grammatical
units, unlike seventeenth-century punctuation, which was dominated
by rhythmical concerns), since the punctuation is no more likely than
the spelling or capitalization to be Shakespeare's own. Thus, in the
Quarto the King promises that:

> No more the thirsty entrance of this soile
> Shal dawbe her lips with her own childrens bloud,
> No more shall trenching war channel her fields,
> Nor bruise her flourets with the armed hoofes
> Of hostile paces: those opposed eies,
> Which like the meteors of a troubled heauen,
> Al of one nature, of one substance bred,
> Did lately meete in the intestine shocke
> And furious close of ciuill butcherie,
> Shall now in mutuall welbeseeming rankes,
> March all one way, and be no more oppos'd
> Against acquaintance, kindred and allyes.

Modernized this reads:

> No more the thirsty entrance of this soil
> Shall daub her lips with her own children's blood.
> No more shall trenching war channel her fields,
> Nor bruise her flow'rets with the armèd hoofs
> Of hostile paces. Those opposed eyes,
> Which, like the meteors of a troubled Heaven,
> All of one nature, of one substance bred,
> Did lately meet in the intestine shock
> And furious close of civil butchery,

Shall now, in mutual well-beseeming ranks,
March all one way and be no more opposed
Against acquaintance, kindred, and allies. (1.1.5–16)

No doubt there is some loss in this modernization. Clarity
and consistency are gained at the expense of some loss of expressive
detail, but normalizing spelling and punctuation allows the text to be
read with far greater ease than the original, and essentially as it was
intended to be understood. Seventeenth-century readers would have
been unsurprised to find "u" for "v" in "heauen" in line 10 or "ciuill"
in line 13. Nor would they be confused by the spelling "Shal" in line 6
or "bloud" later in the line. The intrusive "e's" in a word like "hoofes"
in line 8 or "shocke" in line 12 would not have seemed odd, nor would
the absence of an apostrophe in "childrens" in line 6. Modernizing in
all these cases clarifies rather than alters Shakespeare's intentions, as
does the modernization of the punctuation, which clarifies the syntax and the logical relation between elements. If inevitably in such
modernization we lose the historical feel of the text Shakespeare's
contemporaries read, it is important to note that Shakespeare's contemporaries would not have thought the Quarto in any sense archaic
or quaint, as these details inevitably make it for a reader today. The
text would have seemed to them as modern as this one does to us.
Indeed many of the Quarto's typographical peculiarities are the
result of its effort to make the printed page look up-to-date for
potential buyers.

Modern readers, however, cannot help but be distracted by
the different conventions they encounter on the Quarto page. While
it is indeed of interest to see how orthography and typography have
changed over time, these changes are not primary concerns for most
readers of this edition. What little, then, is lost in a careful modernization of the text is more than made up for by the removal of the artificial
obstacle of unfamiliar letter forms, spellings, and punctuation habits,

which neither the playwright nor his publishers could have intended as interpretive difficulties for Shakespeare's readers.

Textual Notes

The list below records all substantive departures in this edition from the text of Q1 and Q0 (for 1.3.200–2.2.105). It does not record modernizations of spelling, corrections of obvious typographical errors, standardization of capitals, adjustments of lineation, rationalizations of speech prefixes, and minor repositioning or rewording of stage directions. The adopted reading in this edition is given first in boldface and followed by the original, rejected reading of the Quarto, or noted as being absent from the Quarto text. If the accepted reading appears in Q1 (for the section based on Q0), a later Quarto, or the Folio, that fact is indicated in the collation below in brackets (i.e., [Q1] or [F]). Editorial stage directions are not collated but are enclosed within brackets in the text. Latin stage directions are translated (e.g., *They exit* for *Exeunt*), and act and scene designations, absent from the Quarto, are supplied.

1.1.49 Lord L.; **1.1.62 a** [not in Q]; **1.2.16 art king** art a king; **1.2.75 similes [Q5]** smiles; **1.2.149 thou** the; **1.2.153 Peto, Bardolph** Haruey, Rossill; **1.3.9 ne'er** neare; **1.3.200SP [Q5–F]** [not in Q0]; **1.3.237 whipped [Q1]** whip; **1.3.289 Lord** Lo:; **1.3.292 our [Q1]** [not in Q0]

2.1.30SP First [not in Q0]; **2.1.51 Weald** wild; **2.1.61 Saint [Q1]** Saine; **2.2.0 Peto, [and Bardolph]** and Peto, &c; **2.2.11 square** squire; **2.2.50SP and 50** [part of Poins's speech in Q]; **2.2.51SP** [not in Q]; **2.2.105 fat [Q0]** [not in Q1]; **2.3.1SP** [not in Q]; **2.3.2 in respect [F]** in the respect; **2.3.48 thee murmur [Q2–F]** the murmur; **2.4.33 precedent [F, President]** present; **2.4.36SP Poins [Q4–F]** Prin.; **2.4.168SP Prince** Gad; **2.4.169 Gadshill** Ross.; **2.4.171, 175SPs Bardolph** Ross.;

2.4.237 eelskin elfskin; **2.4.275 lord** Lo.; **2.4.331 Owen** O; **2.4.383 tristful** trustfull; **2.4.461 lean [Q2–F]** lane; **2.4.526SP** [not in Q]

3.1.126 meter miter; **3.1.149 lion** Leon; **3.2.59 won** wan; **3.2.84 gorged** gordge; **3.2.115 Enlargèd** Enlargd; **3.3.33 that's** that; **3.3.54 tithe** tight; **3.3.85 How** Falst. How; **3.3.129 owed** ought; **3.3.166 guests** ghesse

4.1.20 lord mind; **4.1.54 is** tis; **4.1.107 dropped [Q2–F]** drop; **4.1.115 altar [Q4–F]** altars; **4.1.122 ne'er** neare; **4.1.125 cannot [Q5–F]** can; **4.1.126 yet [Q5–F]** it; **4.1.133 merrily** merely; **4.2.18 lief** lieue; **4.2.31 feazed** fazd; **4.2.34 tattered** tottered; **4.2.46 Saint** S.; **4.2.51 Lord** Lo.; **4.3.21 horse [Q5–F]** horses; **4.3.28 ours [F]** our; **4.3.82 country's** Countrey; **4.4.32 lord** Lo:

5.1.138 it [Q2–F] [not in Q]; **5.2.3 undone [Q5–F]** vnder one; **5.2.8 Suspicion** Supposition; **5.2.12 merrily** merely; **5.3.1 the** [not in Q]; **5.3.23 A** Ah; **5.4.57 Sir** S.; **5.4.67 Nor** Now; **5.4.91 thee** the; **5.4.157 The** *Prin.* The; **5.4.157 ours [Q2–F]** our

Henry IV, Part One on the Early Stage
by Matthew Dimmock

rom 1581 on, all plays were subject to scrutiny by the Master of the Revels before they could be published or performed. *Henry IV, Part One* was no exception. Perhaps the most intriguing aspect of the early history of the play lies in its encounter with some form of censorship, for the play as it has been subsequently printed, performed, and celebrated is different in some crucial respects from Shakespeare's initial version. Falstaff was originally named "Oldcastle," a name with its own controversial history, referring to an actual companion of Henry V, a soldier, who was also a Lollard leader martyred for his proto-Protestant beliefs. He appears to have divided opinion amongst Shakespeare's contemporaries much as he divides Shakespearean critics today, some arguing that he was a hero, some that he was a traitor. Similarly, Peto appears to have been originally named "Harvey," and Bardolph "Russell," both well-known aristocratic English families. Indeed, it is these historical references that seem to have prompted the revision, since in 1596–1597 the descendants of Oldcastle's widow, Sir William Brooke and his son Henry—the seventh and later eighth earls of Cobham, "objected to what they saw as a deformation of their ancestral name." As the Master of the Revels was executive officer of the Lord Chamberlain (the Privy Council officer ultimately responsible

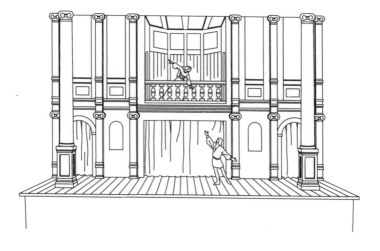

Fig 1. In the large London playhouses, the balcony above the stage could be used for staging, seating, or to house musicians.

Fig 2. English Renaissance drama made minimal use of sets or backdrops. In the absence of a set, the stage pillars could be incorporated into the action, standing in for trees and other architectural elements.

Fig 3. *The discovery space, located in the middle of the backstage wall, could be used as a third entrance as well as a location for scenes requiring special staging, such as in a tomb or bedchamber.*

Fig 4. *A trapdoor led to the area below the stage, known as "Hell" (as contrasted with the painted ceiling, known as "Heaven" or the "heavens"). Ghosts or other supernatural figures could descend through the trap, and it could also serve as a grave.*

for the playing companies), and the Lord Chamberlain at this point was Sir William Brooke, such objections had to be taken very seriously indeed.

Why is the story behind this revision important? Well, first it indicates the tricky politics involved in writing history plays. Second, it affords us fascinating insight into the processes through which Elizabethan state control of theatrical production worked in practice, and consequently it might also alter the way Falstaff was understood by a contemporary audience. Not only are references to Oldcastle preserved at various points in the text—see "my old lad of the castle" (1.2.41) for instance—but scholars have suggested that for much of the play's early history, Oldcastle may have continued to be used as the character's name on stage. This may also begin to explain why Falstaff's speech is packed with biblical allusions and phrases that appear to associate him with Puritanism. Perhaps, as some scholars have argued, Falstaff is a satirical jibe at the Puritans, those rigorous opponents of the theater with whom Oldcastle was often identified.

Regardless of their origins, such revisions do not appear in any way to have dampened the play's popularity (they may even have enhanced it). Indeed the play was popular both on stage and in the book stalls. Before the Folio (the collected works) of 1623, quarto editions of *Henry IV, Part One* emerged almost immediately upon its entry in the Stationer's Register in 1598. Two appeared in that year, and then one in 1599, 1604, 1608, 1613, and 1622. The play was and has remained among those most often performed of Shakespeare's plays and was one of the first to be played at the reopening of the theaters that followed the Restoration of King Charles II in 1660. This popularity no doubt had something to do with the extent to which the story was well known to theatergoers in the late sixteenth century. The transformation of Hal from madcap prince to the illustrious Christian warrior King Henry V was celebrated in numerous popular accounts and chronicle histories, and in at least one other contemporary play, *The Famous Victories of Henry the Fifth*, printed in 1598 but probably staged in the previous decade. As a result, a well-informed audience came to the play with certain expectations. The remarkable popularity of *Henry IV, Part One* on the early stage, and its enduring appeal since, lies in the way Shakespeare both manipulates such expectations and exceeds them. But it is not through theatrical spectacle that Shakespeare does this. As with any early modern play, the words are the primary source of the theatrical experience, for success in an open-air theater in the middle of the afternoon with no sets and minimal stage props required an imaginative leap that was facilitated by language.

The linguistic shifts in tone and rhythm between the different locations of the play are a crucial indicator of the kind of environment the characters are in, and this point is nowhere more apparent than in the movement from court to tavern. That Hal shows himself adept at the languages of both immediately indicates his verbal skill and psychological acuity, but also perhaps something troubling about his chameleon-like abilities (see "Introduction to *Henry IV, Part One*"). Language is in this way a powerful indicator of status and state of mind, and is, for example, particularly effective as a means of indicating Hotspur's impetuosity (his response to the King's demand for his prisoners vividly shows how language reveals character; see 1.3.124–125). This play was written for performance, however, not simply to be read aloud, and a range of other effects contribute to the impact of the drama.

The early modern stage offered an audience a complex system of signs and symbols that was informed by the careful arrangement of costume, music and sound, stage properties, and the organization of theatrical space. Not only are metaphors of clothing repeatedly used, but clothing itself plays a vital visual role in determining the status and allegiance of the central protagonists, as well as combining with the action of the play to pose more troubling questions, such as occurs when Douglas encounters other noblemen in the king's "coat" on the battlefield at Shrewsbury (see "Introduction to *Henry IV, Part One*). Hal argues that by their "habits" (1.2.165), or clothing, individuals are known—which is why he and Poins disguise themselves in "buckram" at Gadshill—and yet this too raises crucial points: How does Hal, the Prince of Wales, dress in the tavern scenes? Is his status immediately apparent from his clothing, or does what he wears correspond with the company he keeps? Does he change for the meeting with his father? Different directors have pursued different strategies, depending on their perception of Hal. It would seem that his entrance before the battle at Shrewsbury would have to mark a substantial change, however, since Vernon describes Hal and his brother, "All furnished, all in arms, / All plumed like estridges . . . Bated like eagles having lately bathed, / Glittering in golden coats like images" (4.1.96–99). The importance of heraldry in this and any history play—evident in the Welsh scenes and in "all the budding honors" on Hotspur's "crest" (5.4.71)—would have made the stage a riot of color and heraldic symbolism, serving to define adversaries on the battlefield. This again emphasizes the visual impact of the multiple wearing of the King's "coat," the power of which should lie in its exclusivity.

Sound also plays an important part in the drama. The disembodied music that Glendower summons at his castle in Wales, coming from musicians that he says "Hang in the air a thousand leagues from hence" (3.1.221), couple with the Welsh singing and sorcery to signify a strange and alien environment. The music would have been played from the upper stage (see Fig. 1 on p. 324), but—like the Welsh language in this scene—there remain no directions regarding exactly what was played. Battle was also accompanied by sound on the early stage: not simply the crash of swordplay (conducted by actors who were well-practiced swordsmen) but the military drum and trumpet, announcing advances and retreats.

Both the battle scenes and those set in the court required a stage that was simple and flexible, indicating a changed location by the introduction of simple props. The fluid staging still centralized the monarch (probably enthroned in the court), and, if the King might momentarily get swept up into the hurly-burly of battle, the entrances and exits from the field would have been conducted in a processional format that indicated status through position in relation to the crown.

One final effect is of interest because it involves one of the few occasions Shakespeare conspicuously uses the discovery space (see Fig. 3 on page 325) provided by the central doors in the early modern playhouse. When opened, these doors afforded a space, normally concealed with a curtain, that could be revealed to the audience when necessary. In *Henry IV, Part One* its use comes at the point when Hal discovers Falstaff asleep, "behind the arras, and snorting like a horse" (2.4.515–516), a moment of surprise and high comedy for the audience. This suggests that the play was written with a specific stage in mind, and it is likely that that stage was the Theatre playhouse in Shoreditch, a northern suburb of London, where Shakespeare's company, the Lord Chamberlain's Men, was based until the Globe Theatre was built in 1599. The part of Oldcastle/Falstaff was originally written for that company's famous clown, Will Kemp, an actor who could add physical comedy and satirical flair to the role. Soon after the play's debut, Kemp would leave the company, but the newly christened Falstaff would only gain in popularity above and beyond the original circumstances of his creation. As the actor Sir Ralph Richardson remarked, "Not until you play Falstaff do you realize how small the mere actor is."

Significant Performances
by Matthew Dimmock

1598 *Henry IV, Part One* is recorded in the Stationer's Register. The first two quarto editions of the play appear.

1660 *Henry the Fourth* is one on a list of twenty plays by Shakespeare acted at the Red Bull playhouse at the reopening of the theaters.

1700 A Quarto edition of *Henry IV, Part One* is produced, suggesting its continued popularity, and Thomas Betterton played Falstaff in an acclaimed production at Little Lincoln's Inn Field.

1706 Daniel Defoe (in his *A Review of the State of the English Nation*—August 10, 1706) remarked of a performance at Oxford, "Is not the Play as full of prophane, immoral, and some blasphemous Parts, as most now extant? Is not Religion banter'd in it, the *Church* ridicul'd, and your Maker dishonour'd?"

1709 Thomas Betterton, in the last year of his life, gave a benefit performance of *The Humours of Sir John Falstaff*, written by Matthew Prior.

1721–1751 James Quin famously took on the role of Falstaff, playing opposite David Garrick as Hotspur at Drury Lane in 1746.

1815   William Macready's performance as Hotspur, at the Theatre Royal in Bath refocused the play away from the dominance of Falstaff.

1824   Charles Kemble produced an excessively lavish *Henry IV, Part One* at London's Covent Garden in May.

1896   At the Haymarket Theatre, Herbert Beerbohm Tree performed a good-natured Falstaff of enormous size in a production that returned Falstaff to the dramatic center of the play.

1905   Frank Benson produced the "second tetralogy"—*Richard II; Henry IV, Parts One and Two*; and *Henry V* in sequence—emphasizing the thematic connections among the four plays.

1945   John Burrell directed Michael Warre as Hal, Nicholas Hannen as King Henry, Laurence Olivier as Hotspur, and Ralph Richardson as Falstaff in a taut, sober production at London's New Theatre.

1966   Orson Welles's film *Chimes at Midnight* (*Falstaff* in the United States) was released, a troubled Spanish/Swiss coproduction tracing Falstaff's life based on material from *Richard II*, the two parts of *Henry IV, Henry V*, and *The Merry Wives of Windsor*.

1975   Terry Hands directed the two *Henry IV* plays, *Henry V*, and *The Merry Wives of Windsor* for the Royal Shakespeare Company, bringing Falstaff again to the forefront.

1986   The newly formed English Shakespeare Company produced the play, directed by Michael Bogdanov, with a cold, Machiavellian Hal, brilliantly played by Michael Pennington.

1991 Gus Van Sant's film *My Own Private Idaho* was released, an exhilarating and idiosyncratic rewriting of the play as the story of street hustlers in Portland, Oregon.

2005 Nicholas Hytner's National Theatre production in London offered a somber version of the play, with Michael Gambon's Falstaff gregariously self serving, always aware of his vulnerable position.

Inspired by *Henry IV, Part One*

Throughout their performance history, the two parts of Shakespeare's *Henry IV* have had an uncertain relationship. Critics and directors are uncertain whether to take each play as an independent entity or to look at the two-part structure as a purely utilitarian strategy for breaking up the saga into manageable portions. The writers and artists who have appropriated *Henry IV* for their own works, however, tend to conflate the two parts into a single narrative. In addition, they often import details from other plays, particularly *Henry V* and *The Merry Wives of Windsor*. The vast majority of these adaptations focus not on the titular Henry IV nor on his son, Prince Hal, but on Falstaff. With more lines than the plays' ostensible main characters, and with more mentions in the critical literature than any character of Shakespeare's besides Hamlet, Falstaff—"the unimitated, unimitable Falstaff," as Samuel Johnson called him—may be *Henry IV*'s most important legacy.

Stage

The first person to recognize Falstaff's star power was Shakespeare himself. According to legend, Shakespeare revived his popular character at the request of no less than Queen Elizabeth I, who greatly enjoyed the roguish antihero in the *Henry IV* plays. Falstaff doesn't appear onstage in _Henry V_, although his death during that play is met with a simultaneously sad and comic tribute from his friends. He appears alive and well, however, in Shakespeare's farcical comedy _The Merry Wives of Windsor_, first published in 1602 and unique among Shakespeare's plays for taking place in the suburbs (as opposed to the court or the countryside) and focusing primarily on members of England's burgeoning middle class.

When _Merry Wives_ opens, Falstaff, who has left London and settled in Windsor with his entourage, has angered the locals by poaching his neighbor's deer and beating the man's servants. He gets himself into further trouble when—betting that the small-town ladies will be susceptible to his high rank and courtly flair—he hatches a plan to seduce and defraud two rich housewives. Mistress Ford and Mistress Page, however, are not easily fooled. After they compare the identical love letters Falstaff has sent them, the women decide to turn the tables, subjecting Falstaff to a series of humiliations that include being hidden in a laundry basket, dumped in a river, dressed up as a fat old lady, and harassed by a group of children dressed as elves and goblins. Readers of _Henry IV_ may be disappointed to see their beloved scoundrel, normally the ringmaster of all mischief, turned into the target of _Merry Wives'_ slapstick jokes. And yet, faced with utter shame and embarrassment at the hands of mistresses Ford and Page, Falstaff manages to maintain the most admirable aspects of his personality: his irrepressible good humor, his wit, and his optimism.

Adaptations focusing on Falstaff continued going strong through the 1700s. During the official closure of the theaters from 1642 to 1660, at least one short interlude starring the infamous Sir John was performed. _The Bouncing Knight, or the Robbers Robbed_ combined several of Falstaff's scenes from _Henry IV, Part One_ and was published in 1662 as part of an anthology entitled _The Wits, or Sport upon Sport_.

Some forty years later, Thomas Betterton continued this practice of maintaining Falstaff's scenes while streamlining other aspects of the plot. Betterton, one of the most famous actors of the Restoration period, originally performed the role of Hotspur but switched to playing the fat knight in 1700. His production of *Henry IV, Part One* got a simple title change—becoming *Henry IV with the Humours of Sir John Falstaff*—but he made extensive emendations to *Henry IV, Part Two*. Betterton removed sections of Shakespeare's text and rearranged others so that the play focused more firmly on Falstaff.

Falstaff's Wedding, William Kendrick's 1760 sequel to the *Henry IV* plays, follows the antics of the tavern gang after Henry V has rejected his former friend and mentor. Kendrick, who claimed that he wrote "in imitation of Shakespeare," combined elements hinted at in *Henry IV, Part Two* with others from *Henry V*. Falstaff becomes embroiled in financial troubles when Mistress Quickly and Justice Shallow both push him to repay old debts. To escape his financial woes, Falstaff agrees to wed Dame Ursula, a wealthy woman he had previously swindled out of money with empty promises of marriage. Meanwhile, he becomes mixed up with Cambridge, Scroop, and Grey, the conspirators from *Henry V*. The climax of the play occurs when the conspirators send Falstaff to kill King Henry V just prior to Henry's campaign against France. Falstaff cannot bring himself to kill his former friend and instead pleads for the King's pardon, which is eventually granted along with a return to Henry's good graces.

Film

Two modern film adaptations of *Henry IV* focus on Falstaff's relationship with Prince Hal. The script for Orson Welles's *Chimes at Midnight* (1966) is a patchwork of scenes from various Shakespeare plays—mostly the two parts of *Henry IV* but also *Richard II*, *Henry V*, and *The Merry Wives of Windsor*—and charts Falstaff's exploits as Hal's partner in crime. Welles had a lifelong dream to play Falstaff and considered *Chimes* one of his greatest films. The title comes from Falstaff's nostalgic comment in *Henry IV, Part Two* that he and his old friend Shallow have "heard the chimes at midnight," suggesting raucous nights spent carousing into the wee hours as well as the mournful tolling of funeral bells at the end of a long, full life. Welles's portrayal of Falstaff draws on both of these images, showing him to be a merry, boisterous figure but strongly emphasizing the tragedy and pathos of the character as well. Unlike most attempts to combine the two *Henry IV* plays, *Chimes* draws more heavily from the somber *Part Two* than the giddier *Part One*, which contributes to the film's somber mood. Even as they revel together at the beginning of the film, Prince Hal and Falstaff's relationship is slightly chilly. However, despite the way the film elevates Falstaff almost to a heroic stature, it closes with the narrator extolling King Henry V's virtues, as if to say that Falstaff's suffering was a necessary sacrifice for the good of the kingdom.

Gus Van Sant's *My Own Private Idaho* (1990) transposes the action of *Henry IV* from medieval England to modern-day Portland, Oregon. Prince Hal becomes Scott (played by Keanu Reaves), a rebellious mayor's son who defies his privileged upbringing and retreats into the city's urban subculture, becoming a prostitute and occasional thief. Bob (William Richert), an aging gay man who is also a gang leader and cocaine addict, takes up the Falstaff role as Scott's "street mentor." As Scott embraces Bob as a surrogate father, Bob openly proclaims his reliance on Scott, anticipating the day when the younger man's inheritance will enable them both to leave their lives of crime and degeneracy. The film's central relationship, however, is between Scott and fellow hustler Mike (River Phoenix). Mike is tormented by the scandal of his incestuous paternity (his father is also his brother) and haunted by idealized memories of his mother, with whom he hopes to reunite. At the same time, he struggles with his own gay identity and suffers from anxiety-induced narcoleptic episodes. Mike falls in love with Scott, who claims to be straight, and it is the poignancy of this unrequited affection that gives the film its emotional power. Their friendship, much like Falstaff and Hal's, is marked by an extreme imbalance of power. In both cases, the audience tends to empathize with the less powerful but more authentic character. Like Falstaff, Mike believes that his friend will remain loyal even after coming into his fortune, and, like Falstaff, he is crushed when Scott returns from a trip to Europe with a new bride, abandoning his street family to assume his role as the head of his biological one.

Literature

Literary adaptations of the *Henry IV* plays also tend to focus on the character of Falstaff. In 1796, an anonymous collection of letters was published under the title *Original Letters, &c., of Sir John Falstaff*. Later identified as the work of James White—a friend of Charles Lamb, author of the famous children's book *Tales from Shakespeare*—this fictional correspondence purports to be a series of letters between Falstaff and his associates. The collection includes letters from Prince Henry, Mistress Quickly, Pistol, Nym, Mistress Ford, and Master Slender, as well as Falstaff. A letter of condolence from Fluellen to Mistress Quickly upon the death of Falstaff also appears in the anthology. White successfully mimics Shakespeare's tone and style in the letters, expanding upon various events without significantly altering details from the original plots.

Jack Williamson's science fiction cult classic, *The Legion of Space*, stars the Falstaff-inspired hero Giles Habibula. Published in 1934, the novel is an early example of the genre that came to be known as "space opera." As the story begins, the human race has conquered and settled the solar system. The people have recently overthrown an oppressive regime called the Purple Hall and are preparing to make a first foray to a neighboring star populated by giant, jellyfish-like beasts called Medusae. Giles Habibula is a warrior with the Legion, the solar system's military and police force. Habibula is a semi-reformed criminal who retains a variety of skills from his former life, including the ability to crack any lock. Giles is somewhat more valiant and less corrupt than Falstaff, but, like his Shakespearean counterpart, Giles loves revelry and merriment and provides the perfect comic foil for his fellow warrior and friend, Hal Samdu. Williamson went on to write three more *Legion of Space* novels, concluding with 1982's *The Queen of the Legion*.

In 1976, after he'd already written two well-received novels about the life of William Shakespeare (*The Late Mr. Shakespeare* and *Mrs. Shakespeare: The Complete Works*), the British poet Robert Nye published the award-winning *Falstaff*, a fictional "memoir" by Sir John. In the novel, we learn that Falstaff didn't really die in Eastcheap, as described in *Henry V*—Mistress Quickly just staged the event so that Falstaff could escape his creditors. Now an octogenarian, Falstaff decides to set the record straight and rehabilitate his (undeserved, in his eyes) reputation as a coward while simultaneously reinforcing his reputation as an incorrigible, voracious old lech. Dictating to a troupe of secretaries, Falstaff tells a vulgar, erotically eloquent tale that not only illuminates his own history but the sweep of medieval Europe's as well. *Falstaff* offers alternate versions of many events in the *Henry* plays, as well as of some notable lines that Shakespeare seemingly raided for his own plays some hundred and fifty years later in the Elizabethan age—including one originally describing Falstaff's cook, Macbeth ("Macbeth has murdered sleep, and my digestion").

In Daniel Curzon's *The Bubble Reputation, or, Shakespeare Lives* (2006) Shakespeare awakens in his secret writing room in a Stratford inn only to discover that the inn has been purchased by a modern-day preservation society and moved to New Mexico. The apparent time travel is never really explained, though Shakespeare claims that he must have survived for all those years in a "crack in time." Prior to falling asleep in the 1600s, Shakespeare was composing the last act of *Henry IV, Part Three*. Convinced that his new play will still be a success, Shakespeare makes his way to New York City, where he must adjust to the hardships of modern American theater. Shakespeare shops his sequel to several theater groups, including a pretentious British company, a group of performance artists, and an all-female troupe. Curzon provides the full text of his *Henry IV, Part Three* at the end of the novel. In the play, the newly crowned Henry V feels guilt over having cast out Falstaff and attempts to make amends by secretly keeping Falstaff in the palace. Over the course of the play, Henry faces opposition from his brother John, but eventually John accepts Henry's rule, and Falstaff, realizing his negative influence on Henry, removes himself from the palace and retires to a monastery. In Curzon's novel, when Shakespeare finally finds an agent who is interested in the play, the agent encourages Shakespeare to change the ending so that Falstaff marries Doll Tearsheet rather than end up alone in a monastery.

Even a few poets have taken up themes and characters from the play. American author Herman Melville (1819–1891) wrote a poem called "Falstaff's Lament over Prince Hal Become Henry V." In a series of seventeen rhymed couplets, Falstaff mourns the loss of a friend that he "cherished; / Yea, loved as a son" before calling for more sack to drown his sorrows. The poem ends on a bittersweet note, as Falstaff decides to be "magnanimous" and dedicate his closing toast to Hal. In 1963's four-quatrain "Up, Jack," Richard Wilbur, another American poet, describes Prince Hal finding Falstaff's body on the battlefield of Shrewsbury. Fresh from killing Hotspur, Hal comes upon Falstaff and, thinking him dead, declares, "Poor pumpkin, I am cold since you are done, / For if you proved but yellow pulp within, / You were this nature's kindest earthly sun." Once the Prince exits, however, Falstaff rises triumphantly. This poem, too, ends on an ambiguous note, as Wilbur contrasts Falstaff's ascendance with Hotspur's "sink[ing]" and Falstaff's wine with Hotspur's "darker red" blood. The closing lines offer pleasure at Falstaff's resilience but also sorrow for the brave men who didn't survive.

Visual Art

During the eighteenth and nineteenth centuries, Shakespeare's plays became popular subjects among British painters and illustrators. The paintings and engravings based on the *Henry IV* plays—not surprisingly—tend to highlight Falstaff. Artists, including William Hogarth, Francis Hayman, Washington Allston, and Sir John Gilbert were drawn most often to the tavern scenes and were perhaps influenced by contemporary performances of the play.

Other artists chose to focus on the character of Hotspur. Henry Fuseli (1741–1825) and Richard Westall (1765–1836) both depict Act Three, scene one, of *Henry IV, Part One.* In *The Dispute between Hotspur, Glendower, Mortimer and Worcester* (1784), Fuseli paints the four conspirators seated around a map on a table. Glendower, Mortimer, and Worcester look anxiously at Hotspur while gesturing toward the map. Even the black dog in the lower right-hand corner of the portrait seems to be focusing his attention on Hotspur. In contrast, Hotspur is shown leaning back in his chair, his head resting lightly on his right hand, his gaze nonchalant. Westall also depicts this tense moment between the conspirators in *Hotspur, Worcester, Mortimer, and Owen Glendower* (1802). Westall's engraving echoes Fuseli's work in that the conversation is clearly centered on the map that rests on the table. However, in Westall's version, Hotspur and Glendower look directly at each other. Glendower's frustration is evident in his furrowed brow and his hand, which grips the hilt of his sword. Hotspur appears calmer in contrast, as he leans back in his chair, his legs spread, his arm barely grazing the handle of his sword as he gestures to the map.

The idiosyncratic English artist and poet William Blake took inspiration not from the plot of *Henry IV* but from its language and symbolism. 1809's *Fiery Pegasus,* or *As if an Angel Dropped Down from the Clouds,* derives from Richard Vernon's description of Prince Hal's surprising show of valor at Shrewsbury. Vernon describes Hal "vault[ing] with such ease into his seat / As if an angel dropped down from the clouds / To turn and wind a fiery Pegasus / And witch the world with noble horsemanship" (*Part One*, 4.1.106–109). Blake's watercolor shows a horse rearing up from the edge of a cliff, the sun blazing behind him. A nude man is splayed out in the air as if preparing to drop down on the animal; above the man, a benevolent-looking woman reclines on a cloud. Blake described his illustration as "the Horse of Intellect . . . leaping from the cliffs of Memory and Reasoning." As is typical of Blake, the painting may be less an enunciation of the themes of *Henry IV* than an appropriation of Shakespeare's poetry into the artist's own personal mythology.

Music

The most famous musical adaptation of *Henry IV* is Giuseppe Verdi's opera, *Falstaff*. Verdi composed the piece in 1892 at the age of seventy-nine, but his last opera is often called his greatest and most youthful work. It was only his second comedy, and completing it was a painstaking process full of stops and starts; in the end, however, it fulfilled his desire "to finish with a mighty burst of laughter." Although Arrigo Boito's libretto borrows its plot primarily from *The Merry Wives of Windsor*, a handful of scenes, as well as liberal references throughout, come directly from the two parts of *Henry IV*. The very first scene of the opera, for example, imports Falstaff's honor monologue from Act Five of *Part One*.

One could argue that in its complexity and subversiveness, the musical composition is also much more influenced by *Henry IV*'s Falstaff than by the character found in *Merry Wives*. *Falstaff* may be Verdi's most idiosyncratic work, one for which he abandoned many of his usual rhythms and formulas. The sonata that opens the opera and the fugue that closes it are the only convincing examples of closed musical forms in the whole composition. Instead, Verdi opted for more open-ended structures, which facilitate the story's many extreme and sudden shifts in tone. *Falstaff* switches seamlessly from jealous rage to pure farce in the space of a few measures, giving the opera a personality that is simultaneously flirtatious and edgy—much like its main character.

About twenty years later, Edward Elgar wrote *Falstaff—Symphonic Study in C minor, Opus 68*. Left cold by the frivolity of *Merry Wives*, Elgar drew his thematic material from the two *Henry IV* plays and *Henry V*. Elgar's *Falstaff* is divided into four sections with two complementary "interludes." Section I plays out the story of the friendship between the young Prince Hal and Falstaff, establishing the musical motifs that will, in different variations, represent the characters throughout the piece. This first part is playful and undisciplined, the soundtrack of inebriated adventure. Section II is a montage, starting with a vignette of Eastcheap hullabaloo, progressing to the Gadshill robbery, and closing with carousal at the Boar's Head tavern and a nostalgic dream sequence by Falstaff. Section III is full of galloping and stumbling cadences. It depicts the march into battle by Falstaff's ragtag regiment, the king's victory, and the news of Prince Hal's accession to the throne. In section IV, Prince Hal appears for the first time as King Henry V and publicly rejects his former friend. The music here resurrects motifs from the first section, but this time they are grand and imperious, dominated by horns and drums. The end of Elgar's work tells of Falstaff's retreat to an inn and his subsequent death. His death occupies about five minutes, alternating deep base and cello with long silences and lingering woodwind. A blast of horn and string intrudes with the final notes, a jagged shred of a musical phrase like the shock of grief, an excla-mation point at the end of a life.

In 1924, English composer Gustav Holst combined scenes from both parts of *Henry IV* to create his opera *At the Boar's Head*. Considered a chamber opera or musical interlude because of its ab-breviated length, Holst's opera centers on the tavern in Eastcheap and Falstaff's companions. Besides Falstaff, some of the characters who grace Holst's work include Hal, Poins, Bardolph, Dame Quickly, and Doll Tearsheet. Old English melodies and folk tunes make up much of the music, although Holst considers three of the songs to be of his own creation. Throughout *At the Boar's Head*, Holst successfully marries Shakespeare's text with traditional English music. The plot for the opera derives primarily from Act 2, scene 4, of *Part One* and Act 2, scene 2, of *Part Two*, but Holst also adds other sections and monologues from both texts to create a cohesive tale.

The American singer-songwriter Loudon Wainwright included a pop song called "Prince Hal's Dirge" on his 1976 album, *T Shirt*, and again on his live 2000 album, *The BBC Sessions*. The song, a drunken monologue from Prince Hal, begins with the Prince calling for a "a capon and some roguish companions," before instructing the listener, "If I vomit, keep me off of my back." The song describes how King Henry IV thinks his son is a "good-for-nothing," and how Hal plans to prove his father wrong. "Show me a breach, I'll once more unto it," he sings, alluding to the famous battle cry he will deliver as King Henry V before Agincourt, but the song ends celebrating the joys of the tavern.

For Further Reading
by Matthew Dimmock

Barber, C. L. *Shakespeare's Festive Comedy: A Study of Dramatic Form and Its Relation to Social Custom*. Princeton, NJ: Princeton University Press, 1959. An influential account of the festive and its transfer from popular culture to stage—useful on the origins of Falstaff.

Bullough, G. *Narrative and Dramatic Sources of Shakespeare Vol. 4: Later English History Plays*. London: Routledge, 1962. A compendious and essential reproduction of relevant source materials.

Greenblatt, Stephen. "Invisible Bullets: Renaissance Authority and Its Subversion, *Henry IV* and *Henry V*." Jonathan Dollimore and Alan Sinfield, eds. *Political Shakespeare*. Manchester, UK: Manchester University Press, 1986, pp. 18–47. A groundbreaking essay, reproduced in a number of early new historicist/cultural materialist collections, that explores the nature of power and potential for subversion in *Henry IV, Part One*.

Gurr, Andrew. *The Shakespearean Stage 1574–1642*. 3rd ed. Cambridge: Cambridge University Press, 1994. An indispensable introduction to the early modern stage.

Hadfield, Andrew. *Shakespeare and Renaissance Politics*. London: Arden Shakespeare, 2004. Wide-ranging yet usefully specific, an important consideration of Shakespeare in his political milieu.

Hodgdon, Barbara, ed. *The First Part of King Henry the Fourth: Texts and Contexts*. Boston: Bedford Books, 1997. Alongside the play, includes a wide range of texts that offer a sense of the play in its literary and historical context as well as perceptive analysis.

Howard, Jean E. *The Stage and Social Struggle in Early Modern England*. London: Routledge, 1994. An influential book that seeks to place the Elizabethan and Jacobean stage in its wider political context.

Joughin, John, ed. *Shakespeare and National Culture*. Manchester: Manchester University Press, 1997. A collection of essays that offers a range of responses to the issues surrounding Shakespeare and nationalism.

Kastan, David Scott. "'The King Hath Many Marching in His Coats'; or, What Did You Do During the War, Daddy?" Ivo Kamps, ed. *Shakespeare Right and Left*. New York: Routledge, 1991: 241–258. An important consideration of the troubling issue of royal authority in *Henry IV, Part One*.

Morris, Colin. *The Sepulchre of Christ and the Medieval West*. Oxford: Oxford University Press, 2005. A comprehensive study of the changing position of the sepulcher of Christ in the medieval and early modern Christian imagination.

Mullaney, Steven. *The Place of the Stage: License, Play, and Power in Renaissance England*. Chicago: University of Chicago Press, 1988. An influential investigation of the tension between the "liberty" of the playhouses and political control—contains a useful section on the tavern environment of Eastcheap.

Schwyzer, Philip. *Literature, Nationalism and Memory in Early Modern England and Wales*. Cambridge: Cambridge University Press, 2004. An important recent study that questions previous assumptions and nuances regarding national identity and early modern literature.

Taylor, Gary. *Reinventing Shakespeare: A Cultural History from the Restoration to the Present*. London: Hogarth Press, 1990. Taking 1660 as his starting point, Taylor explores the fortunes of the Shakespeare canon—contains a series of reflections on the popularity of *Henry IV, Part One*.

Taylor, Gary. "The Fortunes of Oldcastle." *Shakespeare Survey* 38 (1985): 85–100. Addresses the questions that surround the shift from "Oldcastle" to "Falstaff."

Tyerman, Christopher. *England and the Crusades, 1095–1588*. Chicago: University of Chicago Press, 1997. Groundbreaking investigation of how crusading affected medieval and early modern England, arguing that the idea and the impact of the crusade persisted long after many conventional accounts suggest.

Wiles, David. *Shakespeare's Clown: Actor and Text in the Elizabethan Playhouse*. Cambridge: Cambridge University Press, 1987. A detailed and illuminating discussion of Shakespeare's clowns and the actors for whom the rules were written.